DATE DUE

MAY 29 '86 NOV 14 1991		
SEP 0 4 1986		
SEP 13 1986 DEC 1 1986		
MAR 19 1987		
DEC 12 1987		
MAY 24 1988		
DEC 16 1989		
JUN 14 1991		

ALFRED ADLER

ALFRED ADLER

ALFRED ADLER

A Portrait from Life

by

PHYLLIS BOTTOME

New York

THE VANGUARD PRESS

TO
MY HUSBAND

'. . . since he is in contact not with images but realities, he will give birth not to images, but to very Truth itself; and being thus the parent and nurse of true virtue it will be his lot to become a friend of God, and so far as any man can be immortal and absolute.'

PLATO'S *Republic*

'. . . Blest are those
Whose blood and judgement are so well commingled
That they are not a pipe for Fortune's finger
To sound what stop she please. Give me that man
That is not passion's slave, and I will wear him
In my heart's core, ay, in my heart of heart. . . .'

SHAKESPEARE, *Hamlet*

Contents

CONTENTS

ALFRED ADLER

Preface to the First Edition: 1938

It was hoped that the preface to this life of Adler might have been written by one of his two most distinguished colleagues—Professor Birnbaum or Dr. Lydia Sicher—but unfortunately when this book was written both were living under enemy occupation in Vienna, and their names could not be mentioned.

The same political menace forced me to forgo thanking many other friends and associates of Adler's Viennese days for the generous help they placed at my disposal by sharing with me the garnered knowledge of a lifetime. This help they gave me unstintedly for the short ten months that elapsed between Adler's death and the German occupation of Austria. I would ask any interested reader of this book to turn to the appendix where they will find the deeply informed estimates of Adler's life and work, written by two of his most devoted and understanding colleagues.

I fully realize my lack of qualification in undertaking the great task of writing Adler's life; but it was a task laid upon me by Adler himself. He wished that I should write the story of his life in collaboration with himself; and when he died his family reinforced his intention and gave me their wholehearted co-operation and support.

I am neither a scientist, nor a teacher; nor even a fully trained lay psychiatrist; nor was I one of Adler's oldest friends. I came late to the feast of his life, and can only lay claim to being one of his students; a writer by profession; and the wife of perhaps his most intimate English friend. I was myself his friend, for Adler had a wise and wholesome custom of—whenever possible—taking families over as units into his friendship.

My husband first approached Adler for educational reasons and attended the summer school at Locarno at which Adler gave the opening address.

He became deeply interested in Adler's teaching and shared this

11

new interest with me. Neither of us came to Adler as patients, but as students who wished—for the sake of their independent professions —to deepen their knowledge of psychology.

Nevertheless, we soon realized that a purely intellectual knowledge of Individual Psychology was insufficient; and we both decided to undergo a complete Adlerian analysis.

My husband was first Adler's student, and then for geographical reasons transferred his analysis to Dr. Leonhard Seif of Munich, one of Adler's most prominent and understanding German colleagues. The process was reversed in my own case. I received my first analysis from Dr. Seif and worked later with Adler in New York.

After Adler's death in 1937, we went almost immediately to Vienna and remained there until the German occupation of March 11th, 1938. There we sought, and received, valuable information from Adler's old friends and associates of whom I was at liberty only to mention the few following who escaped from the Nazi occupation of Austria or who were not Austrian subjects.

Dr. Alexander Neuer gave us the fullest possible information upon Adler's later Freudian and pre-war period in Vienna. Neuer was one of the members of Freud's circle who left with Adler—a most brilliant younger colleague—whose knowledge of the forming and building up of Individual Psychology in its early days throws a light upon the whole subject of this biography.

Franz Plewa, who was Adler's former assistant in the Psychiatric section of the Franz-Josef Ambulatorium Hospital in Vienna, and the late President of the Viennese School of Individual Psychology.

Dr. Lydia Sicher, was also one of Adler's best-known Viennese colleagues of post-war days, to whom he transferred his appointment when he finally left Vienna. Both these colleagues gave me information covering their own exhaustive knowledge of Adler's post-war years in Vienna.

Dr. Greta Simpson, a well-known New York psychologist, worked with Adler for eight years in Vienna, and continued her friendship through the American period of Adler's life.

Dr. Babbott, the President of the Long Island College of Medicine, where Adler occupied the first Chair of Medical Psychology to be founded in the world—during the last five years of his life—put at my disposal a most interesting dossier of Adler's work while at the College.

Charles Davis, Adler's most devoted and intimate friend during the American period of his life, kept a valuable diary of all Adler's public engagements in America, which he kindly placed at the author's disposal.

Philip Mairet, the Editor of the *New English Weekly*, was one of the original members of the first London group of Individual Psychologists; and Dr. James Moore is also one of the most constant members of this original Gower Street society, as well as the first Vice-President of the Medical Society of Individual Psychology, which arose out of the earlier group.

Without the personal and professional help and counsel of Dr. Alexandra Adler, now accepted as one of the foremost of American psychiatrists, it would have been difficult if not impossible to write this family biography; Frau Alfred Adler also gave me her unflinching, truthful support, which deepened, if that were possible, the friendship and respect I already felt for her. This long and difficult task could never have been accomplished successfully or unsuccessfully had I not possessed the constant co-operation of my husband, whose faithful memory of Adler's sayings and intimate knowledge of his personality never failed me.

Alfred Adler loved paradox and his life was largely built up out of paradoxes.

He was a philosopher, who was known as the most brilliant practising psychiatrist of his day. He was a great psychiatrist distrusted by many of his colleagues because of the weight of his philosophy. He was a moralist without a dogmatic belief in any religion. He was a scientist who believed that man is a spirit and therefore responsible for his every act.

'*Tout comprendre c'est tout pardonner* is equally true,' Adler used to observe, 'if you put it the other way round: *Tout comprendre c'est rien pardonner.*'

Adler was at once the easiest of men to know, and the most difficult; the frankest and the most subtle; the most conciliatory—and the most ruthless. As a colleague he was a model of generosity, accuracy and wholehearted integrity, but woe betide that colleague who dared to presume upon his generosity; or who was himself guilty of inaccuracy; or who failed in common honesty!

Adler never again worked with a person whom he distrusted; except when that person was a patient.

He had a fiery temper, and the patience of an angel.

Adler was a most highly sensitive human being yet he could and did endure with unruffled equanimity 'the slings and arrows of outrageous fortune'. He was the most tolerant of men and the least

PREFACE TO THE FIRST EDITION: 1938

tolerant of intolerance. During the inflation, he lost all his savings, his country and his dearest friends.

In his early life he had a great love for Aristotle and founded his approach to life upon common sense. So deeply had Adler imbibed the spirit of Aristotle that it may even be said that he owed the first conception of his psychology to the timeless spirit of the Greek philosopher. Adler himself might have written the following paragraph:

'In order to judge whether what is said or done by any character be well or ill, we are not to consider that speech or action alone, whether in itself it be good or bad, but also by whom it is spoken and done, to whom, at what time, in what manner, or by what end. . . . To opinion or what is commonly said to be, may be referred even such things as are improbable and absurd; and it may also be said that events of that kind are sometimes not really improbable; since it is probable that many things should happen contrary to probability.'—Aristotle.

As a scientist Adler never allowed himself to stir beyond the zone of the concrete fact; yet he was the world's best guesser and took every advantage of this great human faculty.

Adler would have fully agreed with the Greek saying, 'It is a disease of the soul to be in love with impossible things,' but he would have thought it equally a disease to set any rigid boundaries to an idea.

'Everything may be different,' Adler was fond of saying. 'Even what I say to you now may be different!'

He was never understood by his eclectic colleagues since he refused to mix his Individual Psychology with other findings. This was not, as so many thought, because Adler took a narrow or egocentric view of his own contribution to the broad field of modern psychology, but because he believed Individual Psychology to be not only a theory but an attitude of mind, needed in order to accept safely any other theory.

He never underestimated the great work done by fellow-psychiatrists in other schools, but it would have been as useless to expect Adler to 'mix' his psychology with theirs as to ask St. Paul to share Christianity with the prophets of Baal. 'You cannot divide the Individual,' Adler would assert. 'Man is a whole human being.'

It would not be true to say that Adler did not believe in effects of heredity, environment, glands, nerves, drives, etc., upon the Individual, but his was not a 'possession' psychology, it was a psychology of use, nor could he take these influences from a casual point of

14

view. He judged each human being teleologically, and by his power
to meet the three main life tasks of man which Adler described as
'Work; sex; social contact'. The failure to adjust or refusal to accept
all these three life tasks was to Adler the sign of a potentially neurotic or potentially delinquent human being; the complete refusal to
accept all three pointed to a probable psychosis. Certain neurotics
having won for themselves what Adler termed a 'preferred position'
might, it is true—if fate allowed them to remain in cotton wool—
avoid a spectacular breakdown; but they remained failures as human
beings.

· It was this dynamic belief in human responsibility that brought
Adler into constant sympathy with educational and religious activities. He was satisfied that the goal of all great religions was the same
as that of science and founded upon the Law of Social Interest, a law
which the science of psychology could train the individual to understand and practise.

The rich stream of Adler's life ran through three main channels—
psychology; education; and ethics. The first period of his life laid
the foundations of his psychology; the second great period was its
flowering and fruition in the Viennese State Schools; and the third
was his final acceptance of 'love of thy neighbour' as a law, after the
war of 1914 had burned its agony of human suffering into his soul,
a law which to follow should be the goal of all mankind.

But this would be a false picture of Adler if it showed any real
division between these three great motives, since he never gave up
one for the sake of the other—he always used them firmly plaited
together like a strong cable to draw the human being towards one
common purpose—the brotherhood of man.

This life of Adler strives to show how he built up this 'wholeness'
in himself, and endeavoured to set all his friends and patients upon
the same self-freeing task. Adler might well have said of Individual
Psychology what Madame Curie once said to someone who wished
to purchase a piece of radium for a general purpose: 'Radium is not
to enrich any one. Radium is an element. It belongs to all people.'

When Adler was challenged, as he so often was, by his fellow-
psychiatrists for 'letting down science' by his complete naturalness,
and the ease with which he could be understood by lay audiences,
he would say, 'I have taken forty years to make my psychology
simple. I might make it still more simple by saying "all neurosis is
vanity"—but this also might not be understood.' Adler possessed the
genius of personality but it was a curiously unaggressive genius. In

a room full of people neither ear nor eye would have been drawn first to Adler.

He never made a gesture or a sound that would compel attention. You took what you wanted from him, and when you wanted you went away. He neither hurried you, nor held you. Nor was it ever easy to tell what his own wishes were. Nevertheless, he was most human and had decided likes and dislikes. He loved music; the drama; cinemas; cafés; country walks and swimming. He disliked social small talk; large entertainments; driving in motor-cars; long railway journeys or eating chicken—still I have known him do all these things with apparent contentment, because he always enjoyed sharing the tastes of his companions.

Some of his friends were what you would expect them to be— reliable, intelligent and satisfactory human beings; and some of them were the reverse; but Adler appeared to love them all equally. He would not, however, have relied upon them all equally. He was the most sceptical of men; but as he was equally sceptical of everybody— from the angel of the Passover in his childhood to the most rampant cheat of his later days, no one needed to feel discouraged by the benevolent but piercing speculation o· his hooded eyes; especially since Adler's scepticism did little or nothing to interfere with his affections.

Among the circle of his greatest intimates was one of the most unattractive human beings the author has ever met—repulsive to look at, and ferocious in his manners. Nevertheless Adler loved him, and companionated him whenever possible.

Adler had saved Sperber[1] when a boy from being 'put away' as a mental defective by rich relations, and had succeeded in training him towards a highly successful career. Sperber became a brilliant criminal lawyer, famous throughout Viennese Law Courts for his defence of the poorest type of prostitute. Adler had long ago discovered and released his humour; and freed a courage which Sperber used successfully against powerful, adverse interests, in order to defend the defenceless.

Sperber died in a German concentration camp, universally mourned in Vienna by the friendless and the needy.

If it was difficult to discover how Adler judged others, it was even more difficult to discover how he judged himself.

He spoke freely of his opinions; more rarely of his feelings; and never willingly of himself.

---

[1] This was not Manés Sperber. See chap. xix.

PREFACE TO THE FIRST EDITION: 1938

Perhaps what he most wished for was to be understood and known through his work.

'My difficulties belong to me!' he would say with a cheerful smile; and they were the only possession that Adler was never willing to share.

What he believed in—he was; and there are many of those who loved him, who believe that what he was will speak of him for ever.

Since writing this book, Adler's greatest friend—Professor Furt-müller—has escaped from Vienna and is now in England.[1] His name therefore I am now at liberty to mention. His friendship was in some ways the deepest and certainly the most lifelong friendship in Adler's life—the friendship of one great independent mind with another—two minds following one common aim: the educational betterment of mankind. Professor Furtmüller shared Adler's undergraduate days with him and also his entrance and exit from the Freudian circle. It was Professor Furtmüller who introduced Adler to the Minister of Education, Glöckel, who gave Adler the opportunity to prove his theories upon the child-life of Vienna. Until Adler's death this friendship remained, unbroken, equal, and serene.

PHYLLIS BOTTOME

London, 1938

[1] Professor Furtmüller has since died.

Preface to the Third Edition: 1957

When assigning their places in psychology to the three great giants of Vienna, in order of their seniority, Freud, Adler and Jung, Adler has always been the most difficult to define and the easiest to denigrate. The reasons for this are not hard to seek. Adler founded no school; he fought pedants and he disregarded potentates. He supported no political party and therefore received no public awards beyond, late in life, the Freedom of the City of Vienna.

Yet he was considered by the medical schools of his day to be the greatest of practising psychiatrists; while, in our own day, for one man or woman in a thousand who can quote Freud or Jung, all will have heard of the 'Inferiority Complex' and many will have some practical idea of its meaning; and 'After all,' Adler used to say with a twinkle, 'I *am* the legitimate father of the Inferiority Complex.'

In 1905 Adler published his first well-known book, *Studieren über Minderwertigkeit von Organen und ihre seelische Kompensation* (*Organic Inferiority and its Psychical Compensation*).

Adler was at this period of his life one of the most famous members of the Freudian circle before it had hardened, under its renowned leader, into a 'school' or dictatorship.

Adler was the circle's President, its champion speaker, and the brilliant editor of its *Psycho-Analytical Journal*. It is clear that he would not have been chosen by Freud for this post as editor, had not the group considered Adler, with Freud, as their most distinguished scientist.

Adler parted from Freud because he could no longer accept a causal rather than a teleological basis for his psychological discoveries; and because he had accepted Social Interest rather than man's freeing of his own libido, as the goal of the human race.

To Adler, man was an animal who chooses. While he never denied

19

the influence of physical heredity, environment, drives or defective glands, Adler looked on them merely as handicaps to be overcome; never as dead ends, destructive of man's personal responsibility for his thoughts and actions. Neurosis was not an entity in itself—the cause for a set of adverse symptoms—it was to Adler 'the exploitation of shock or strain' created by the patient in order to act as an alibi for the evasion of his life tasks—'I would do it, if—but . . .'

Sex difficulties were but one of these many evasions. Adler worked with Freud and his other associates only as long as they treated sex as of the same importance as the other senses—all alike subjects for the circle's 'unmasking'; but when sex became for Freud and his supporters a primary agent in all neurotic disturbances rather than a single factor, Adler felt that Freud had deliberately left the region of scientific fact and had created instead a 'sexual myth.'

Adler's Individual Psychology was founded on the 'wholeness' of man; and was a 'use' (*Gebrauch*) never a 'possession' (*Besitz*) psychology. Nor was the 'unconscious', for Adler, a convenient dark cupboard into which could be pitched the pampered child's responsibilities; it was the 'not yet understood' of a pioneering, unclosed science.

'To free the Libido' without breaking up the patient's egocentricity was to Adler a most dangerous and anti-social theory. The personality should be released but directed towards *Gemeinschaftgefühl* or, as Adler decided to translate it, 'Social Interest'. 'There is a law,' Adler always told his students, 'that man should love his neighbour.'

This teleological basis for Individual Psychology refused all fragmentation and led towards a universal, rather than a specialized, science. For this reason Adler lost much of the support of his own profession, since the cult of 'wholeness' seemed to many of them to undermine medical science.

There was to Adler always a patient behind the disease, an individual 'whole', of which the illness was but a symptom. 'Find out first how much health your patient has,' Adler advised his medical students, 'before you try to find out what is the matter with him.'

To many intellectuals outside the medical profession, there was, and still is, something suspicious in a psychology that can be understood and practised by the ordinary man or woman without the guidance of experts; even though Adler never denied that experts should be called in, under extraordinary circumstances, as in neurosis or psychosis.

Psychologists who pride themselves on their 'depth psychology' sometimes forget that Socrates was put to death for a simplicity that has survived the wisdom of his executioners.

James Hemming, one of our modern educational psychologists, writes: 'I suggest that those who have thus far taken Adler for granted will find a study of his writings most rewarding at the present stage of analytical theory. The value of his insight grows as our metaphors about the life of the psyche become more comprehensive. All that is superficial about Adler is that in the past most people read him superficially—or not at all. Adler was trying to formulate, as simply as possible, a set of principles of universal validity or, if you prefer it, "valid for all individuals". His academic "sin" was simplicity, not superficiality.'

Adler's *Der Sinn des Lebens* (*The Science of Living*) is well translated and easy for anyone to understand: so also is *Understanding Human Nature*. Both are published by Allen and Unwin, and can be found in most Public Libraries or else obtained in the usual way through a bookseller. The most comprehensive of Adler's work is probably *Social Interest: A Challenge to Mankind*, published by Faber and Faber. This was the last book that Adler wrote, and, owing to its concentration and the subtlety of its thoughts, perhaps it needs some previous knowledge of 'Individual Psychology' before it can be fully understood.

The real difficulty in Adler's psychology, and the reason for the sharp antagonism it often arouses, is that it involves a fundamental change in the human being who accepts it; and is something of a reproof to those who refuse it. A man can be a Freudian and yet remain very much what he was before he became one, plus some interesting intellectual discoveries. But if he becomes an Adlerian he must actually move towards a goal which destroys prestige-living; he must try to become a 'socially-interested' human being. 'I suppose psychology is where I go?' a boy of sixteen once intelligently remarked; and Adler would certainly have enjoyed this neat simplification.

It is strange as it is unfortunate that with a few exceptions—the late Archbishop Temple was one and the late Catholic Archbishop Downey of Liverpool was another—Anglo-Saxon religious teachers have taken very little interest in Individual Psychology. Many intelligent Christians will swallow eagerly the complicated mysteries of Jung, or even the anti-religious theories of Freud, rather than accept the one psychology that has a practical approach towards the goal of all religion—man's love of his neighbour. It is true that in their later works both Freud, and more markedly Jung, acknowledge social interest as playing a large part in the development of man. But Social Interest is not a 'part' but forms the 'goal' of Individual Psychology, while the treatment of all patients is founded upon a re-training towards 'Love of the neighbour'.

The break with Freud came from Freud's question, 'Why should I love my neighbour as myself?' (*Civilization and its Discontents.*)

Adler never claimed religion for his field; he left that to the theologians and, like most of his fellow-scientists at that time, he did not accept divine revelation. But although without dogma or any doctrinal faith, Adler always revered and supported religious values. 'Man,' he used to say, 'is incurably ethical.' He never failed to urge upon his students that they must never disregard the religious creeds of their patients but point out to them instead where their faulty life style interfered with the practice of their faith. To Adler, as to Berdyaev, 'Reality is the spiritual victory over egocentricity'.

It was not only in order to free *themselves* that Adler tried to show his patients the direction in which they were moving; it was for the sake of the world that they were living in. Yet he would never have claimed any final explanation of man's significance in the universe; this he left to religion. Adler's was the scientist's vision; and he stopped where the scientist's vision must always stop.

> *'Know then thyself: Presume not God to scan.*
> *The proper study of mankind is man.'*

Part of Individual Psychological treatment is to unmask the unreality of the neurotic life style for a patient, while helping him to replace it with a more courageous grasp of truth. Once a patient begins to free himself from the bondage of his own self-love, and the havoc of his tendentious wishes, he will find whatever religion he may possess become a far more living reality.

Just as Adler sought to release his neurotic or psychotic patients towards freedom of choice, so he deepened in them the sense of their cosmic responsibility. What he always wanted to know most about a new acquaintance was, 'Is he a contributor or an isolationist?'

I have called this sketch of Adler's life 'The Apostle of Freedom' because the essence of Individual Psychology is the release of a man from the compulsion of his own desires.

If love of our neighbour is a law as universal as the law of gravity and as catastrophic to disobey, then we must be free to love; and we are not free to love while we are slaves either to the tyranny of others or to the tyranny of our own wishes.

No man is happy as a slave. He is not even safe, for he is disobeying a natural law which is working against him. He will find himself accident or illness prone, a victim of tension and unnecessary fears; nor can he find a solution for his problems or be of much use helping other people to solve theirs.

There can be neither security nor gaiety in a man unless the law of social interest is working with him. No matter what austerity or self-discipline the saints practised, nor even what martyrdom they suffered, they were never gloomy human beings. The saints sparkle through the centuries, and leave a trail of light behind them.

'What can psychology then do for a man that Christianity cannot?' many Christians naturally demand. While our prisons are full, our mental hospitals crowded, while the shadows of universal self-murder haunts mankind, should we not rather ask ourselves, 'Is Christianity not badly in need of a fresh ally?'

A trained psychological priesthood might transform a dying Church into a living organism. A socially interested education for every child, founded upon co-operation rather than prestige, might teach whole nations, as well as individuals, to approach each other without greed or aggression.

It was to mankind as a whole that Adler's Individual Psychology was addressed; and before his death in 1937 he already knew that the time was short in which man could be saved from self-murder.

It will not be until we provide love and security for every child, with an education based upon Social Interest that:

> *'The beauty of the world, the paragon of animals'*

can play his rightful part upon 'this poor earth's crust'—or even be sure of his own continuity.

PHYLLIS BOTTOME

Red Willows
  St. Ives
    Cornwall
June 6, 1956

I

Birth and Early Memories

Alfred Adler was born at Penzing, a suburb of Vienna, in a house that was literally the last house of the city, facing the low sky that stretched away as if for ever, above the flat plain on which the city stands.

Alfred's parents, though they lived all their married lives in Vienna, both came from another land. His mother was a Hungarian and his father who was born in the Burgenland was also a Hungarian, since the Burgenland was part of Hungary before the War of 1914. He came from the same village as the violinist Joachim, with whom he always claimed relationship.

The whole Adler family was exceptionally musical; one of Adler's brothers played and taught the violin; his sister Hermine was an excellent pianist; and Adler himself had so beautiful a tenor voice that he was constantly urged in his youth to give up science for an operatic career.

Alfred had all the gifts needed for a great singer: an infallible memory; a perfect ear; and tremendous dramatic power; but he never for a moment considered giving up science for music. He merely spent every spare hour and penny that he possessed in walking, or if he were rich enough, taking the horse-tram, down the long road into Vienna in order to go to every opera and play that was running. Alfred's mind was a storehouse of wit and drama. He was unconsciously training himself in the study of character, and in understanding those situations which bring character out. Perhaps, too, it was in the theatre that he learned not to over-value displays of emotion on the part of his future patients.

One of Alfred's most useful qualities as a psychiatrist was the way in which he both cooled and lightened the weight of his patients' emotions. 'All that you feel', he would say, 'is very natural, but perhaps you need not feel it quite so much!' and then very often a happy story, or the sudden flash of an infectious joke would present his patient not only with a new light upon his personal problem, but also with a new courage with which to attack a mole-hill that had threatened all his life to be a mountain.

Curiously enough, whatever inner effect Alfred's early absorption in the theatre produced on his mind, he never exploited his dramatic powers while lecturing. On the contrary, Adler seldom raised his beautiful, cadenced voice. He spoke in an ordinary conversational tone, with the rarest possible use of emphasis. Perhaps he had no wish to exploit these special gifts, and wanted his words to be taken at their intrinsic value. He always chose the simplest words possible and the easiest for his hearers to understand; his power of forming an instantly friendly contact with his audience was so great that he had no need to fall back upon any oratorical effects, in order to win their attention. His success as a lecturer, and the large audiences that he drew, were a constant source of annoyance to some of his less gifted fellow scientists.

Adler sprang from Jewish people but early in life he became a Christian, as a protest against the isolation that he felt was a spiritual danger in the Orthodox Jewish faith. There were practically no other Jews in the village of Penzing, which was Adler's first home; Jews as a rule migrate to towns, and the Viennese Jews in particular inhabited a district of their own on the bank of the Danube. He chose to become a Protestant since, although Adler believed that 'God was the most enlightened idea that had occurred to man', he could not as a scientist accept revelation, and was against all forms of dogmatic rigidity. He thought, however, that there were many indications that progressive evolution was a scientific fact. To Adler a 'death-wish' was a neurotic retreat, and never any inherent part of a human destiny.

Adler's father was a corn merchant, and liked to be in touch with the country from which he obtained his supplies. It is perhaps owing to the fact that Alfred was never brought up in Jewish surroundings or with Jewish playmates that he became in many ways so unlike other members of his race. His accent was pure Viennese, and his whole outlook upon life, and his reactions to life were more typical of an Austrian peasant (a peasant with particularly keen wits) than of one of his own people.

Adler always escaped the isolating qualities thrust upon his race by persecution. He was at once more courageous and more modest than those who have had to face constant rebuffs and are sometimes forced to try to get the better of their opponents by flattery or through undue persistence.

At the time of Alfred's birth, his family were well-to-do, and Alfred always remembered the sharp and uncomfortable impression that it gave him when he visited the families of his street playmates, and found how much less prosperous their homes were, and how poor their food, compared to his own.

The village of Penzing is close to the Palace of Schönbrunn, and a long-standing feud soon arose between Adler and the custodians of the Palace garden. This feud began when Adler was first able to walk, and decided that he would share the flowers of the Schönbrunn garden with the Kaiser. He became a more bold and skilful marauder as the years passed, until the family moved to Währingerstrasse near Grinzing, which was practically part of the country and where they themselves had so large a garden that Alfred was able to satisfy his predilection for flowers without pillage.

At this period of Alfred's life the Adlers were a happy, independent and well-to-do family. They sprang from the tradesman-class, but from a highly civilized and intelligent trade; corn-merchants were a notoriously keen-witted community; and Adler's father was conspicuous both for his knowledge of human nature and the shrewdness with which he dealt with it.

When the Adlers settled in Währingerstrasse they were able to keep cows, horses, chickens, goats and rabbits; and Adler added country lore and open air habits to his village and town experiences; yet he was not, however congenial his surroundings, a wholly contented child. On the contrary Alfred spoke of his childhood as definitely unhappy—though made so chiefly by his own ambition. He felt himself put in the shade by a model eldest brother, a true 'first-born' who always seemed to Alfred to be soaring far beyond him in a sphere to which Alfred—for all his efforts—could never attain.

Even at the end of his life, Alfred had not wholly got over this, his feeling. 'My eldest brother', he once said to the writer with a sigh, 'is a good industrious fellow—he was always ahead of me—and for the matter of that, he is *still* ahead of me!' That this attitude to the eldest brother influenced Adler's whole life there can be little doubt. Freud was to him 'an eldest brother' with the threat that this involved to his own originality. The break with the Pedants, and Adler's persistent refusal to 'found' a school, or use any authoritative approach towards his patients, may well have been strengthened by his own revolt against his model 'eldest'.

However, in later life Alfred spoke of this eldest brother with great respect and even affection, as of one who did well at all his main life-tasks and always had a 'plus' with which to help the less successful members of his family.

There was a strong family likeness between the two brothers, in the tone of their voices and in their ways of moving, but the elder had a look of care and uneasiness in his eyes, whereas Adler, though his eyes were often sad, had always a look of inner strength and peace that seemed to belie—or to put aside—the ordinary cares of human life.

Adler's immediate family consisted of four brothers (including himself) and two sisters. The brother next in years to Alfred was highly envious and jealous of the popular Alfred, nor did he ever recover from this state of mind. Adler was fond of him but never succeeded in winning his affection. The youngest brother, Richard, adored Alfred, and clung to him throughout his life.

This youngest brother was born at a bad time in the family fortunes; the sudden poverty of his parents checked his education and darkened his prospects; while all his elder brothers and sisters had enjoyed a prosperous childhood and a good start in life, so that he had the bitterness of contrast to add to the difficulties of his fate. Alfred tried in every way to release and strengthen this favourite youngest, and helped him both materially and spiritually all his life.

The two sisters were vigorous healthy girls who soon married; and Hermine in particular was in early life a great favourite of Alfred's. She was two years younger than he, a brisk, useful, kindly girl with a great admiration for her next elder brother. She played Alfred's accompaniments on the piano; and he stole her skates to keep her from going out with other boys in his absence; but Hermine was left far behind Alfred in the race of life. Unfortunately she failed to get on with his wife, and Alfred saw very little of her in his home, though he managed to keep in touch with her and never forgot that in his bad days, after their parents became poor and before he was able to make his own way in the world, Hermine and her husband had given him all the help in their power.

Alfred looked like his mother and his mother's family. He was broad, short and very vigorous, with a massive thinker's brow and the most bright and lively eyes. Sometimes they became hooded with a veil of reflection and they seldom if ever betrayed what he himself was thinking. Kokoschka's portrait of Adler, made in early middle life, gives to perfection this strange brooding look. The face seems all eyes, but in their depths the life has withdrawn itself, as if to bring out more life. It is a great portrait, painted in Kokoschka's youth—perhaps one of the most interesting portraits in the world. The whole mystery of Adler's personality is in those hooded eyes—they look out from under the heavy brows as if he understood the soul of man but dared not tell all that he understood. It seems strange to think of the most genial of men as the most lonely—and yet it is Adler's loneliness that Kokoschka reached; and portrayed. Adler knew others; but did he know himself? or was he afraid of the self he knew—and so withheld it, even from his best and dearest friends? Perhaps this hint of fear of himself, in Adler, was what made him—for others—the safest person in the world.

Alfred inherited, or as he would himself have said, 'chose' his father's mental and spiritual qualities rather than those of his mother. His mother was nervous and gloomy. She worked from morning till night, giving herself no time even to attend to the wants of nature. One of her children declared that she had no humour, and that this was why she and Alfred failed to understand each other; but Richard, the youngest, who lived with her till her death, said that his mother had a great deal of very pleasant wit but that as their father was predominantly humorous, he rather overshadowed the drier and quieter quality of his wife's sense of humour.

Alfred's father was a very free and happy personality, tremendously proud, with the strength of will and aim to make his pride tell. He was a handsome man with a fine figure, and cared greatly for his personal appearance, brushed his clothes meticulously himself, and always cleaned his boots so that they shone like glass. He appeared invariably as if dressed for a party. Nothing ever prevented him from going his own way; if he were walking downstairs, he never moved aside for anyone walking up. When he saw people with their legs crossed in a tram, he would push one foot down with his walking stick, saying politely, with a charming smile: 'I do not like to clean my trousers on your shoes as I pass!'

He insisted on his children being allowed great personal freedom, and avoided either punishments or caresses, a most unusual parental trait in the '60's and '70's; and he had a horror of anyone talking about his health. He took it as an insult if asked how he was, and always ignored illness in his family; nevertheless if any of the children were really ill, he would tiptoe into their rooms in the course of the night, to see that they had all that they needed; and once when Alfred was very ill indeed with pneumonia, his father harnessed a

29

sleigh and drove across Vienna in the middle of the night to fetch the Kaiser's doctor to his little son's bedside. Alfred was, almost from the first, his father's favourite child. The elder Adler used to get up every day at five o'clock, take Alfred out for a walk and return to breakfast by himself at a café. He finished his day's work at about four in the afternoon, took his last meal at five, and went to bed at seven. He followed this routine all his life, and died a hale and hearty old man, at eighty-nine.

His wife had brought him a big dowry, but her husband gave large parts of it away to start his own brothers and sisters in careers in Vienna, where unfortunately none of them did well.

Had he possessed this extra capital, it would no doubt have carried him through the crisis that was too much for his limited resources. His career, however, flourished exceedingly until his two elder sons were started in the world, and when his own affairs began to go from bad to worse, his eldest son was able to look after his parents and even to assist his younger brothers and sisters. As soon as he could Alfred too took up his share of the family burden. His mother persisted in working herself to death to keep the business going, and died at sixty-one, worn out by her toil.

Alfred had always been much less attached to his mother than to his father. She was colder in her nature, and it is probable that she preferred her first-born to Alfred. Alfred did not understand, and never quite forgave her for smiling soon—he thought far too soon—after the sudden death of a little brother.

In later life, Alfred blamed himself for his attitude and said, 'I know *now* that my mother was an angel and loved us all alike, but as a child I had a wrong opinion about the matter.'

There is no doubt that his resentment coloured his earliest years with sadness, and made him forsake his home as much as possible, for the life of the streets. It is probable that there have never been any psychologists who were happy in their childhood.

The following are Alfred's earliest recollections told in his own words: they were written for the guidance of his future biographer; and also as an indication of why he chose his career as a doctor and psychologist.

'One of my earliest recollections is of sitting on a bench, bandaged up on account of rickets, with my healthy elder brother sitting opposite me. He could run, jump and move about quite effortlessly, while for me movement of any sort was a strain and an effort. Everyone went to great pains to help me and my mother and father did all that was in their power to do. At the time of this recollection I must have been about two years old.

'My next recollection is of an incident that took place when I was nearly four years old. My younger brother had been born. I remember him only very slightly, but his death remains firmly fixed in my mind. Before he was born, there can be no doubt but that I was reared and watched with the greatest solicitude on account of my sickliness. I am sure that I must have been forced to put up with a great deal less of this attention when my younger brother was born. I had a vague idea that I took this apparent loss of attention on the part of my mother very much to heart. But it did not affect me in regard to my father who was out all day working and to whom I became deeply attached. As I found out later, I wronged my mother in feeling that she deprived me of her affection. Throughout her life she loved all her children with the same degree of warmth and affection.

'I did not enjoy staying at home. Perhaps because my attitude towards my mother was at fault, but also without doubt because I did my utmost to excel at running, jumping and rushing around, activities of which my elder brother was constantly making me aware. I was always eager to get out of doors and was helped in doing this by the fact that almost next door to our home was an open, practically disused plot and a big field. There were almost no vehicles about and when there were they moved so slowly that there was scarcely any chance of our being run over or being involved in any accident. But despite this I was run over twice when I was four or five years old but without being hurt at all seriously.

'The field near our house was the meeting-place of all the local children. Most of the people in our district were quiet, humble and usually poor people who frequently asked me into their homes. Because of my friendliness and liveliness I was well received wherever I went.

'My elder brother was the only one with whom I did not get along well and he never took any part in our games. At an early age I became part of a wide social *milieu*, and in our games both the boys and the girls learned to look upon one another as communal equals.

'So, early organic inferiority, that I struggled hard to overcome, and an early connection with events beyond the family circle, definitely laid the foundations of my psychic structure and my attitude towards life. As an additional spur there was the urge never to lag behind my elder brother. Those who are familiar with my life-work

BIRTH AND EARLY MEMORIES

"Individual Psychology" will clearly see the accord existing between the facts of my childhood and the views I expressed in my studies of Organ Inferiority (see *Studies in O.I.*, 1907), and in my main work *The Nervous Character*, 1912 (4 Aufl. Bergmann, München). The similarity between my experiences and the basic views of I.P. is not without interest, when one considers the time I devoted in later years to: *Inferiority Feeling*, as the motivating power of the striving for achievement; *Social Feeling*, which aims at an ideal of perfection for mankind. We can also see quite clearly in these experiences of my childhood how they establish a certain characteristic tendency—more or less representative of my position in the family and my desire to *move* freely—*to see all psychic manifestations in terms of movements*. But it was not so much my childhood experiences in themselves that were important; rather the manner in which I judged and assimilated them.

'This applies to another incident that occurred when I was three years old. My parents left us two boys for a few days in the care of a governess. When they came back I met them, singing a street-song, the words of which are in my mind to-day, as is the melody to which I sang it. (It is possible that I sang or heard this same song at some later period so that my remembrance and understanding of its significance might spring from that later date). The song was about a woman who explained that she couldn't eat chicken because she was so hurt by the killing of her little hen. At this, the singer asks how she can have such a soft heart, when she thinks nothing of throwing a flower-pot at her husband's head. My father at once decided to dismiss the governess, concluding quite rightly that she had taken me to musical shows in the evenings. In spite of the fact that he was pleased at my singing he looked at what lay behind it, looked deeper, something I also learned to do. But I, too, saw deeper, in that I realized that I must in the future judge mankind *not by their spoken words and sentiments but by their actions*. Once the song had put this into my head the idea remained for ever and grew stronger and stronger.

'My early realization of the fact of death—a fact which I grasped sensibly and wholesomely, not morbidly; not regarding death as an insurmountable menace for a child—was increased when I had pneumonia at the age of five and the doctor, who had suddenly been called in, told my father that there was no point in going to the trouble of looking after me as there was no hope of my living. At once a frightful terror came over me and a few days later when I was well I decided definitely to become a doctor so that I should have a better defence against the danger of death and weapons to combat it superior to my doctor's.

'Shortly afterwards the father of one of my playmates, a lamp-maker, asked me what I was going to be in life. "A doctor," I said. He answered, "Then you should be strung up at once to the nearest lamp-post." This remark made no adverse impression upon my choice of a profession; I merely thought, "There's another who's had a bad time at the hands of a doctor. But *I* shall be a *real* doctor." Soon after it struck me that this man, a lamp-maker, had his trade, rather than me, uppermost in his mind. After that the determination to become a doctor never left me. I never could picture myself taking up any other profession. Even the fascinating lure of art, despite the fact that I had considerable abilities in various forms of music, was not enough to turn me from my chosen path, and I persisted although many complex difficulties lay between me and my goal.

'It is these physical trends, which even in my childhood have assumed form and style-of-life, to which I am indebted also for my insight into psychological manifestations.

'To this I must add what the friendly reader has guessed perhaps already from my account: *That I decided at an early age to come into close contact with all difficult problems, in order that I might be in a better position to solve them.*'

The author remembers two more characteristic memories of Alfred. At the age of five, bored by the long silent prayers in the synagogue, Alfred saw a piece of vestment sticking out of a cupboard drawer within reach of his hand. Very slowly and cautiously, he began to pull at this mysterious and intriguing piece of cloth, more and more came out, without anyone discovering what he was up to. Suddenly the whole cupboard lurched forward and fell with a crash on to the floor. Alfred leaped to his feet and ran for his life out of the synagogue, fully believing that he had brought down the pillars of the temple upon the congregation.

At the same age, or perhaps a trifle older, Alfred found that he could not quite believe in the Angel of the Passover visiting each Jewish home and being able to distinguish which was the leavened, and which the unleavened bread prepared for him.

Adler therefore, one Passover night after the rest of the family had gone to bed, crept downstairs in his night-shirt and substituted leavened for unleavened bread, sitting up for the rest of the night in a cupboard with the door ajar, to discover through the crack the

BIRTH AND EARLY MEMORIES

effect upon the Angel. 'Nor was I altogether surprised', he told the writer, 'when the Angel did not turn up.'

'Alfred,' his father often said to him, upon their early morning strolls, 'never believe what anyone tells you!' And this rooted scepticism was one of Adler's most marked characteristics.

When brother psychiatrists would unfold wonderful stories about their patients, remembering birth traumas and even the actual act of their coming into the world, Adler would murmur with his famous twinkle, 'And you *believed* what they told you?' Adler himself never accepted or made any statement without concrete proof. He was always interested in what reliable people told him, and even in some instances acted upon their advice, but he never accepted an opinion as a fact. His mind was ruthlessly critical; but his heart was cruelly vulnerable. From the day he first made up his mind about the sentimental lady in the song, who wept for the death of her chicken but threw flower-pots at her husband, to the day of his own death, Adler remained a compassionate cynic, suffering in the sufferings of all who really suffered, but never failing to see through the sham sufferings of those to whom in the long run come the worst sufferings of all.

II

Background of Adler's Boyhood, and its Influence upon his Development

A dler's boyhood and youth covered the span between 1880 and 1900, when Vienna stood at the peak of European civilization. Admittedly she was a luxury city ruled by the Hapsburgs and permeated by court influences; but she was also the worthy centre of a great empire.

Her university was the fountain-head of expert knowledge; her homes were circles of culture, musical talent and enlightened taste. There were no women better dressed or more beautiful than well-bred Austrian women. The banking system of Vienna was the best and most trusted in Europe.

The Austrians, though they had the most exclusive aristocracy in the world, had the smallest human gulf between the highest and the lowest classes. Emperor and cab-driver spoke the same broad Viennese dialect and enjoyed the same kind of joke. The Austrian proletariat was highly civilized and the aristocracy was not much, if at all, more highly civilized than the proletariat.

The forceful penetration of the best Jewish culture heightened rather than disturbed the lofty levels of Austrian society. The professional classes profited greatly by the interfusion of Jewish wit and learning, and the Austrian *laisser-faire* was solidified by the Jewish core of hard common sense. The names of famous Jewish scientists, doctors, lawyers, writers and musicians took root in the heart of a country that was wise enough to give them creative opportunities and adequate rewards.

Half the magic of Vienna lay in its unstinted ironic tolerance for all shades of opinion; and its warm-hearted international friendliness.

The boy Adler, with his big brain and his wild ambitions, felt everywhere at home in this catholic city of his birth. Nothing in it was too far beyond his efforts, or out of the reach of his dreams.

A genius, as Adler himself taught, is only a person who has a plus quality with the courage to use it. Every man is his own architect; but he cannot invent the materials which he finds to his hand.

The materials that surrounded Alfred Adler in his childhood were those of Viennese culture; Viennese tolerance; and Viennese kindliness.

In the circle in which Adler's family played their part, there was not much money, as money in these days is reckoned, but there was always enough for just those pleasures which all Viennese in common adored; and there was always music.

On summer evenings the Adler family, often accompanied by their special friends, would stroll towards their favourite vineyard, and there, under trellised vines, be served at long wooden tables with the special vintage of that particular vineyard. They brought their own food with them, and as soon as they had finished eating, the songs would begin. Sometimes there would be skilled part-singing in which the boy Alfred always took a leading part. Often a wandering musician with zither or guitar would stop on his way, and for a few groschen and a drink, play their accompaniments.

The shades of Schubert and Mozart haunted these orchards and hillsides of Grinzing and Cobenzl, and there is hardly a street in the nineteenth district of Vienna where the restless Beethoven did not shift his self-torture from one roof to another.

Adler said of his boyhood, 'I always had tunes running through my head. When I began to read as a student, they stopped, but while I was a young boy tunes came to me instead of thoughts.'

There was nothing in the least 'soft' about Adler in spite of his artistic tendencies. As a boy he was dangerously virile and adventurous, an outdoor boy with a fighting spirit which he always retained.

One of his brothers related that the family always knew when Alfred was home from school by the rustling of the pigeons wings. Alfred kept pigeons, and had a special whistle for them. However far down the road the whistling began, the whole flock flew to greet him. There was an element of disinterestedness in this act of welcome on the part of the pigeons, since they were not fed at this time. Alfred always retained this power over birds and animals; it was as if they sensed this 'plus' of protective friendliness in him. The writer once saw a highly nervous Alsatian, who barked himself hoarse at the approach of any stranger, welcome Adler's first visit without so much as a premonitory sniff, instantly laying his head upon the strange but friendly knee.

A doctor at a mental hospital where Adler acted as consultant said that dangerous and refractory patients evinced the same pleasure and lack of provocation in his presence.

The reason was probably that Adler had no desire to dominate; and no fear of being dominated by either animals or patients. He respected himself and treated every living thing with the same quality of respect that he himself exacted.

The only people Adler despised, though never when they came to him as patients, were shams. These he made dangerous by the cutting quality of his scorn and many of them did him a great deal of harm.

Most people have a very definite preference for city or country life. Adler loved both equally. He had the countryman's tastes and swift-reacting senses, and the townsman's ready wit and knowledge of human nature.

In half an hour from the Währingerstrasse garden, Alfred could climb through the sweet-smelling blossoming fields into pine forests, where he and his companions wandered for hours through sun-bathed woods, without meeting a soul or even catching a glimpse of the great city close to their feet. Yet Adler would often say, 'I love noise. There is no music I prefer to the traffic of a great road, full of human beings moving about their daily business!'

Mountain climbing and swimming were Alfred's favourite recreations all through his life. Währingerstrasse was in reach of the Danube, and though there were no swimming-pools in Alfred's youth, there were always the friendly banks of the Gänsehäufel, the open park, and the great shady trees.

'What do you first do when you are learning to swim?' Adler once asked a patient. 'You make mistakes, do you not? And then what happens? You make other mistakes, and when you have made *all* the mistakes you possibly can without drowning—and some of them many times over—what do you find? That you can swim? Well—life is just the same as learning to swim! Do not be afraid of making mistakes, for there is no other way of learning how to live!'

Adler himself did not come to his enormous ease and skill in living without bitter struggles and disastrous blunders. He was a passionate, wilful, ambitious boy, determined to get on, and yet with no great early success to reassure him. He did not do particularly well at school. He said that in most of his subjects he only achieved mediocrity and was without any outstanding success. Mathematics was an absolute and terrifying stumbling block to him, and appeared to be insoluble. He could not use his brilliant companionable brain upon anything so dull and lonely as figures.

One day, while Adler was gloomily watching the teacher of arithmetic demonstrating a sum on the blackboard, he suddenly felt sure that the master himself did not know what was the answer to the problem he was setting.

It flashed through Alfred's mind, he says, like an electric shock: 'This fellow doesn't know himself! There is a trick, too, about this business! Why cannot I guess the answer as well as he?' and even as Alfred felt this new sense of possibility, the answer sprang into his mind. For a time he could not summon the courage to raise his hand. He imagined how the whole room would laugh at his audacity in thinking he could solve a difficult problem where the others had failed, for it was well known that he was the dunce of the school at arithmetic, and it was unendurable to Alfred's proud spirit to be laughed at. Yet when a boy at the top of the class failed, Alfred found himself rising to his feet with his hand raised. His worst fears were realized when the master and the whole class roared with laughter at his presumption, but once up, the fighter in Alfred held him fast. He explained the solution that had flashed through his mind, and, to his triumphant relief, heard that it was the right one.

From that moment, Alfred had no further difficulties in mathematics; he even became a mathematical prodigy, solving problems as fast as they could be put to him.

His school life, however, was chiefly remarkable for the number and variety of his friendships; he made them with all sorts and conditions of persons in school and out of school.

It was not until his student days that books took full possession of his lively mind. His entire boyhood was spent in learning how to live as fully as possible, and how to respond and react to his fellows.

Alfred must have learned this hard lesson very early and very well, for even his envious elder brother confessed rather grudgingly after Alfred's death, 'When he was quite a little boy, Alfred was already terribly popular with everybody. It was always the same thing: everybody seemed to like him. But I never understood why, for I always found him quarrelsome and ambitious. *We* never got on together!'

His wit itself helped to feed Adler's omnivorous brain. He once told the writer that the gossip of Vienna was as vivid to him as the events of his own life.

What *had* really happened to the free-thinking arch-duke who fell out of the world on his travels? What *was* the secret of the tragedy of Mayerling? The romance of court life, overflowing from the central Palace through the cafés, and at street corners in gossip and good stories, helped to colour Alfred's vivid imagination.

The Kaiser's stables, the most beautiful buildings in Vienna, were of special interest to Alfred and his corn-dealing father; and the Spanish riding school, with the performances and records of its famous Pinzgauer horses, were as well known and nearly as exciting to Alfred as the life histories of his own goats and rabbits.

Arch-dukes in gorgeous uniforms, with shining swords, glittered through the streets, a fierce array of tall, strikingly handsome, self-indulgent, wild and pleasant people, who received far more education from their beautiful plebeian mistresses than they were in any position to return.

'Anna Sacher was one of my friends,' Adler told the writer proudly, 'though not until later in my life. She had a great deal of character and most of it was good.'

It was not for nothing Anna Sacher was the only woman who ever had a cake, a race-horse and a street named after her.

Anna ruled a choice circle of Vienna aristocracy with a well-garlanded rod of iron.

She was not only a first-class cook and the intelligent organizer of the best restaurant in Vienna; she was the counsellor, and the well-trusted counsellor, of kings.

Even after her great clientèle had fallen and were scattered to the four winds of Heaven, Anna remained what she had always been— the ruling woman of Vienna. She held together, through the War, through the Starvation, during the Breakdown, the threads of her regal entertainments. It was perhaps her fierce courage that most appealed to Adler.

No one knows with what bitterness or with what contempt Anna Sacher served the enemies of her fallen country; but even at the moment that seemed then the lowest ebb in the fortunes of Vienna, Anna never bowed her head to her country's enemies. Before Anna Sacher would serve a private dinner in her famous rooms, she insisted upon an introduction to the hostess; and if she disapproved of her, the entertainment, however profitable it might have been for Anna, did not take place at Sacher's.

Close to Adler's old home was Schöner's nearly as famous restaurant, with its far more beautiful mistress. At Schöner's were exquisitely furnished little rooms for private dinners. There was a garden under trees, and waiters of an infinite discretion, pouring wines from an arch-duke's cellar for the most favoured of the guests. Adler had no personal stake in all these discreet rococo gaieties, but they played a great part in his mind—brimming over to him at second-hand, through humble go-betweens. The great people of Vienna were to him like the actors in his favourite Mozart comedies.

Who can tell what is more real to the mind of a child—what happens or what he thinks could happen; what is, or what he fancies might exist? The writer remembers asking Adler once in a spirit of idle curiosity, 'Did you ever see the Empress Elizabeth, and was she really so beautiful?' For a moment he was silent, while his eyes seemed to re-create a picture of what they once had looked upon. 'Yes,' he said at last, gravely, 'I *did* once see her; and she was *really* beautiful.'

III

Youth and Romance

Adler, brought up as he was from the first in awareness of physical laws, had no great surprises to face in adolescence. Those daily walks and talks with an intelligent father, who made a friend of him; his own study and care of the family livestock, would perfectly have accustomed his mind to the way in which human beings are brought into the world, even if he had not played on the street as a child with every sort and condition of informed gamin.

His own experiences fell into line with his later study of all different types of mind in adolescence, and helped him to form his opinion that adolescence is *not* from physical causes a dangerous period and never the birth of a new personality, but merely the period when the child has for the first time to face up to his responsibilities as a human being. Adler held that until adolescence the human being has been a child with all a child's immunities; nobody has expected weighty decisions from him or made him responsible for the full consequences of his acts. Now he sees for the first time that the grown-up world is his to enter, and the price he pays for his usually longed-for entry is the weight of responsibility he must take upon himself for his own actions.

Whether the child fails or succeeds is largely dependent upon how much initiative and freedom from control he has already been accustomed to practise. A really well-trained child aware both of his responsibilities and of his power to face them, and not trained beyond his powers by over-ambitious parents, will pass harmlessly and almost unnoticeably through the period of adolescence into manhood.

It is not surprising therefore that Adler himself showed no particular disturbance at this time; the only change to be discovered in him was the very serious way in which his ambitions took shape.

He had always intended to be a doctor; he knew that he had his father's enthusiastic approval and support behind him; and he now took to his books with a steadily increasing purpose and absorption.

This is the time, Adler said, when he seriously and thoroughly read whatever he felt would be to his purpose.

It was astonishing in later life how much Adler had absorbed in these years, and how faithfully his mind had retained its knowledge.

Many of his friends were more learned than himself, and many more without full justification supposed that they were. It was often cast up at Adler as a taunt that as a philosopher he was very superficially grounded; nevertheless he found no difficulty in holding his own in the front rank of thinkers of his time, and he more than held his own in the Freudian group which numbered several serious scholars and writers: indeed, when the group broke up, it was with two notable exceptions—Jung and Stekel—the scholars and writers who left with Adler and who accepted his leadership. Jung and Stekel left not long after; Stekel because, like Adler, he could no longer stand the dictatorship atmosphere; and Jung to develop theories of his own which he felt incompatible with Freudian analysis.

During his university career, Adler mastered the history of psychology up to that date, and was thoroughly dissatisfied with its progress as a science. He began to form at this time the opinion upon which his whole after-studies and discoveries were based, that just as nature affords compensation to injured organs, so the spirit of man can also be trained to compensate him for all psychic disturbances produced by defective organs.

This discovery of the human being's power to turn a minus into a plus was the foundation of all Adler's work; and it came to him, as almost all great discoveries come to human beings, ground out from the mill of his own most deeply felt thoughts and experiences.

This theory of Adler's never changed; although in order to satisfy himself of its truth, he had to pass through many phases, to test many systems with which he hoped to combine and strengthen his own, but which he found could not stand the tests he applied to them, and which had therefore to be discarded. His active scepticism and hatred of all rigidity were a great strength to him as a thinker; for nothing but concrete proof ever interested him, and he never closed his mind to the possibility of a fresh contradiction. No biologist ever had a more open and adjustable mind than Adler; and no philosopher ever had a more rooted hold on biological fact.

So much has been said and imagined as to Adler's personal attitude towards sex and, as some think, under-estimation of its strength as an instinct, in contradistinction to Freud's over-estimation of sex as an instinct, that it is necessary for any biographer who is endeavouring to be truthful to give, as far as it is known, Adler's opinion and experience in this matter.

Because Adler believed in monogamy as a realizable and desirable aim for human beings, there is no more reason to suppose that he took—or practised—an under-sexed view of life than to suppose that Freud, because he advocated freedom from sex suppression, lived the life of a libertine.

Both these great men were scientific thinkers who had to a great extent freed themselves from tendentious thinking, and their theories should, therefore, be understood in this objective sense, and not looked upon as pegs upon which to hang their personal histories.

When we judge a human being by the deeds that he brings forth, we must always take into consideration both his race and the times in which he lives. This is specially true of sex morality, which is largely geographical, and much influenced by race traditions and practices. Adler was a Viennese by birth and training; and a Viennese of the pre-war world.

He was brought up in an atmosphere and tradition that took sex as an intense pleasure, even as the principal pleasure of a human being's life. Morality to the Viennese of those times was an elastic term, chiefly applied to married women and the protection of their progeny; while chastity was merely a short stage through which unmarried girls passed.

Women were not men's companions at this period of Austrian history, they were men's most prized possessions; and it was extremely rare that any Viennese confined himself to one of them.

Alfred Adler was an intensely virile active man, with an extremely tender heart and lively social manners.

He was never handsome, but his early photographs show a strong, attractive face with an open, engaging expression.

If one adds to the value of this physical appearance the fact that Alfred had a keen wit and was a good listener, it will be obvious that he could not fail to be a success with women.

His sister Hermine, who knew him both intimately and critically, nevertheless said that in his youth, mothers, who in those days made very strict rules for their daughters and seldom allowed them to go out with any young men unchaperoned, permitted them to go alone with Alfred, saying: 'I know that Alfred will take good care of you,' and it is certain that Adler could always have been trusted to take such a responsibility seriously.

This is, however, not contradicted by the fact that he was all his life long susceptible to women; and a lover of beauty in all its forms.

Adler was always a true friend to women, and deeply respected them as human beings. The author knew intimately a young and most attractive girl, who travelled alone with Adler to a foreign country, acting as his interpreter and secretary. This girl and her parents had an absolute confidence and security in his attitude, a confidence and a security which were fully justified. Another young girl, equally attractive, and more anxious to prove the powers of her attraction, was also at one time put in his charge, and was constantly with him over the space of months. She was an efficient shaker of masculine vulnerability, but she admitted that with Adler she had not succeeded.

It should never be forgotten that many of the women who sought Adler's company were neurotic and egocentric women, who had never known and never practised disinterested kindliness. To such women Adler's wide and open sympathies might well have appeared far more personal than they in fact were. Their passionate desire to exert their attraction over him and to increase this warmth was very often a source of great embarrassment both to themselves and to Adler. All practising psychiatrists have such experiences, Adler perhaps less than most, since except in his actual interviews with patients, he was rarely alone; and in later life so accessible to everyone that he was practically inaccessible to those poor vampires who wanted his life instead of their own.

The writer's own conviction is that Adler never loved any woman as he loved his wife; and that his most happy and successful friendships were with men. The fact that his marriage was in its early years almost fantastically happy is based on the well-considered evidence of his own and his wife's lifelong and most intimate friends; and there is the same evidence that it underwent a long period of partial estrangement which it not only survived but which ended in a happy and steady reunion. This is surely proof enough of what stout stuff this main sex relationship of Adler's life was made.

The man who believed that a human being is only normal when he fulfils every responsibility and obligation of human life, was certainly not the man to take the occupation of love and marriage lightly.

Adler was a man who rarely if ever spoke of his inner life and its events; but he more than once expressed the belief that love between man and woman is a single and instantaneous affair. He often quoted Shakespeare's 'He never loved who loved not at first sight.'

'Love', Adler used to say, 'is a task for two. A task in which two persons must be engaged has its own special form and cannot be successfully performed if it is treated as a task of one person alone. It is as though, for the right solution of the problem of love, each of these two persons has to forget his or her own self entirely and give complete devotion to the other; it is as though one life had to be formed from two human beings.'

Adler chose no easy mate for himself but a woman of unusual strength and independence, of a different country, with a different upbringing, and with an entirely different outlook on life.

Raissa Timofejewna was born in Moscow. Her parents were wealthy people in a good position; her uncle owned several of the largest railway lines in Russia.

She was brought up in a household or in a series of households where the question of money never came up, since it was always there to meet any desire or enterprise; so that Raissa never had Adler's early training, i.e. the school of poverty and equality. She had to train herself into a sense of responsibility towards money; and learn to take people as she found them.

She had a very strong, independent and upright personality; and she concentrated all her growing mind upon the hopelessly backward state of her great country; seeing that nothing whatever could come out of Czardom and its corrupt practices, she became an infatuated liberal.

It is easy to understand that to Raissa Timofejewna social betterment and political change became identical.

Women in her youth were allowed no education outside the home or an occasional royally endowed school or convent, where all they learned was taught them by ladies of high degree whose scholarship was—to say the most for it—uncertain. Raissa herself went to a *gymnasium* but she considered that what she learned there was very insufficient.

Girls of Raissa's stamp, if they were to have the education for which they thirsted, and the liberty denied them at home, had to go abroad for them.

Many Russian girls went to Switzerland, and some to Vienna, since it was nearer to them than Western Europe and a city where they were allowed to attend lectures at the University, though not to become members of it. These girl students must have made themselves very popular in Vienna, since at one time four Viennese University professors had Russian student wives. Raissa went first to Switzerland and then to Vienna.

Raissa's main interests were scientific and political. She was an expert translator, and had a talent for original writing as well. The German language soon became natural to her and she faced her student days in Vienna with an outlook full of courage, zeal and exhilaration.

To look at, she was small, sturdy, blue-eyed and fair, with a delicate colouring and good features. Raissa had singular eyes, full of a shining innocence. The whites were very clear, and she had a direct way of looking at you, as if her whole personality, fearless and friendly, were pausing behind her look, ready to spring out to meet half-way a new friend, or to deal, with trenchant simplicity, with an incipient enemy.

In later life Raissa's looks retained their charm, and her beauty may even have been increased by a greater gentleness.

In youth she must have been as provocative as she was fearless. She had already stepped out of the groove of her Russian life, to take the risks of loneliness and strangeness in a distant land. Her absorbing aim was to free herself mentally, so that she might help in the great struggle she saw ahead for her country. She must have been terribly attractive to a man like Adler, who was equally determined to break into the Kingdom of Knowledge and free its treasures for mankind.

Perhaps they both sought for different treasures, or for the same treasures in different places; and certainly they both felt that the world's sickness required different remedies; but in those early years their aims must have seemed one. Both were fearless; both were wildly generous; and both were out to save the world.

What more natural than that they should suppose they would save it better and quicker by tackling the job together? That Adler by degrees gave up entirely the hope of improvement through political changes, concentrating more and more upon his scientific and philosophical work, while Raissa still retained her old political fanaticism, naturally served to divide their interests. Perhaps nothing in married life is harder than for two people deeply in love to differ upon a fundamental aim. This difference did not play a great part in the Adlers' early married life, though it was always there—but it became stronger and more inimical to their relationship through the years; until in later life their wisdom and tolerance led them to accept each other's right to a different view; and while neither changed his individual point of view, both were content to allow the other the freedom that they claimed for themselves.

Alfred and Raissa Adler were two extremely sturdy and independent characters and a tremendous challenge—in the deepest sense of the word—to each other, and to the co-operation they tried, and in the end succeeded, in practising. That they both might have lived far easier and even happier lives with weaker and more amenable partners is quite possible; but it is doubtful if they would have been sufficiently attracted by any such human being as to wish for it; and it is certain that what they got from each other—and *in spite* of each other—deepened and enriched their contribution to life.

Both had superficial faults that must have been highly irritating to the other; but it is probable that it was the difference in their nationality, and in their virtues, that really caused the long and deep estrangement between them. It must never be forgotten that one was a Russian and the other a Viennese.

The end of Adler's university career was hampered by his straitened means and no doubt made harder to him by his falling in love with Raissa.

Although she had accepted the simple life of a Russian student and lived on a rigorously small allowance, Adler knew that she could have what she wanted at will, by applying to her parents; whereas he had to do without, and confine his activities to those that cost him nothing.

Raissa must have fired his whole romantic nature, for somehow or other by Herculean efforts and self-denials he twice managed to follow her back to her home in Russia, once with the excuse of attending a Russian doctors' congress. The first his family knew of his love affair was a telegram from Alfred in Russia: 'Am married, returning with bride, find home for me.'

The Adler family answered their son's telegram by giving up to him their own flat in Eisengasse, to which they had moved from their far larger house in Währingerstrasse, while they went to live elsewhere.

From the first, Raissa's family fell in love with Adler, and seem to have accepted without hesitation this penniless young doctor as the most desirable son-in-law in the world.

The young people could have had plenty of money to set up house with, but Raissa's independent views made her decide only to live on what they both earned, so that their financial life, in their early married years, was by no means easy, although they always had enough for their actual needs.

Adler's first married home was in the ninth district of Vienna, not far from the hospitals. It was one of a row of high, old-fashioned houses, built like French ones, with the same slightly pretentious shut-in look. It stood on the slope of a steep street leading down into the heart of Vienna. Raissa could have had nothing friendly or alive to look at in her new strange home. Nothing to remind her of the huge plains full of corn and sunshine, which must have haunted her mind in that dark narrow street, with its poor strip of sky.

Adler came out in every way more freely and with more effect after his marriage; his joy and pride in his beautiful young wife were visible to everyone who saw them together. 'If I had made her in my laboratory,' he told a friend, 'I could not have found her more to my taste!'

There was never from the first the slightest doubt as to Adler's success as a physician; but in those days many of his patients were too poor to pay him anything, and others could only pay him very little. Sophie, the family cook and mainstay for over twenty years, told the author, 'When I first came to the Adler family, the Herr Doktor was never without a book or a pen in his hand. When he came in from his rounds, he would sit up to all hours of the morning, writing and reading. It was not so later, for people came to the house all day long—and far into the night—but when he was a young man, he did not talk very much.'

Even without divergences of views and *milieu*, one can see that this must have been a very lonely life for Adler's young Russian bride, so full of energy and character; but the divergences were also there.

Adler was a Viennese, and the Viennese are by nature plastic and highly social people; they have a deep-rooted gentleness and fear of giving pain, or of receiving it. Their culture protects their sensitiveness.

Adler trained himself to use on his patients whatever firmness they needed, but in his personal life he disliked giving pain to the point of weakness, whereas Raissa was almost fanatic in her honesty and frankness of demeanour, and could never understand anything else.

She had a most generous and staunchly loving nature, but in contradistinction to a Viennese, she must often have seemed harsh and even cold. 'Those freezing Russians!' Viennese people often said of their student visitors; while to these visitors their hosts must often have seemed sentimental and unduly soft.

Raissa was not practical and she took no pleasure in the details of domesticity; nor was she vain, and at this period of her life she neglected all interest in dress. Such a standpoint in a woman must have seemed inconceivable to a Viennese.

Adler's own home had been particularly well run and physically comfortable, or he would not as a small boy have been so conscious of its superiority to those of his school friends; a mother, too, who worked herself to death at sixty-one, was probably almost too interested a housewife.

As to clothes, all Viennese women dress as well as they know how, and they usually know how very well indeed. Until the war forced them out of their homes to make careers of their own, they were the best exponents of their *métier de femme* in Europe. They could not have been very congenial company, or even very safe family friends, for the socially rebellious Raissa and her attractive young husband. Raissa was very far from being cold-hearted, whatever her more emotional Viennese sisters may have thought of her. Her real trouble was that she was honest to the core; and that practically all of her *was* core!

Honesty is a virtue that needs a good deal of tuning down in a family orchestra; and Raissa probably always kept hers at concert pitch.

Adler had a fundamental integrity but he knew how to hide it; and he both shared and enjoyed the Viennese manner. It is doubtful if Raissa as a young girl knew how to hide anything: her feelings, her likes or her dislikes. Later in life she trained herself into a greater discretion, but in her Russian student days and early married life, she was probably too bent upon what she thought constituted the character and duties of a human being, in a world that she intended to have a good try at changing, than in giving pleasure to an overworked husband, who spent almost no time at all in her company after having been madly in love with her.

Such transitions in married life are always difficult, and they are made none the easier by having to talk in a foreign language, living in comparative poverty after the unconscious smoothness of prosperity, and finding yourself playing second fiddle to a husband who is the brilliant centre of an alien circle, whereas you, yourself, were once the brilliant centre of a familiar one. Under such conditions it was appallingly difficult for Raissa to hold her own.

Nor could Adler ever have been an easy man to understand. He was a genius who had outgrown his own family, and families resent such growth. At the time of his marriage his powers were expanding at express speed but as yet they had only the most modest material to work on.

Alfred was happy, but what ambitious man is content with being happy? He was in love with his wife, and no doubt admired her for all the qualities that he nevertheless found inconvenient at close quarters.

He lived in a world, and he had been brought up in a circle, that did not believe in a woman's powers or rights to exceed domesticity, and who valued a wife far more for good cooking and careful housekeeping than if she had spoken with the tongue of an angel.

Theoretically Adler always believed in the equal status of women; he more than believed in it, he supported it; and thought that more than half the troubles of mankind came from the fact that women are not aware of possessing an equal value to men; and that—perhaps more serious still—men are not aware that women *do* possess this equal value. Nevertheless, fighting for the emancipation of women, and living with a woman who had emancipated herself, are two wholly different things; and it is probable that Adler found them difficult as well as different.

It is a great tribute to Raissa, that all through his life, whatever their difficulties may have been, Adler kept his high respect for women. Few men think better of women in the abstract than of the woman they love in particular; and Adler had no need to think less of the sex from which Raissa sprang.

There is an early photograph of Adler, standing by Raissa's side, holding his first-born child in his arms.

In spite of its old-fashioned stiffness, quaint clothes, and the inexpertness of photography at that stage of its existence, joy and beauty still radiate from this little group.

The father is looking down at the child, to see if the miracle in his arms is content, while Raissa looks into the distance, towards the world which was drawing them both away from her; yet she seems to be quite sure that they are wholly hers and will behave as she has a right to expect of them.

Life had many strange and cruel secrets in store for these three people, but for that brief moment they were in possession of a secret that held nothing else but joy.

IV

Adler's Early Life and Religious Opinions

No accurate details of Adler's career at the Vienna University could be given at the time of writing this book, since the German occupation prevented a promised access to the University archives. However, a fellow student of Adler's, Professor Furtmüller, contributed the following statement, which roughly covers the field: 'Adler did distinguished work both in biology and anatomy,' Professor Furtmüller stated, 'and took an excellent degree. There was never any question as to the greatness of his abilities, both as a scientist from the biological point of view, and as a thinker from the philosophical point of view. He had material obstacles to overcome and he had to work hard in order to overcome them; but from his university career onward, Adler moved steadily forward, and his success in any path he chose to follow was assured.'

Professor Furtmüller was his daily companion throughout their university careers and for many years afterwards. Both men married young and their wives and families carried on this closest of all Adler's friendships. Professor Furtmüller was probably the one friend of Adler's who really knew his mind. He by no means always agreed with Adler; indeed, as a scholar, he subsequently took the academic rather than Adler's 'simplifying' view of Individual Psychology, but disagreements in this case made no difference whatever to their fundamental accord. 'Our differences', Professor Furtmüller told the writer, 'were the superficial differences of men whose aim was the same. *I* believed Adler would have done better by sticking to science and working through and with scientists; *he* believed in making his science universal and imparting it directly to his fellow men. Who shall say which of us was right? Time alone can tell! I withdrew from any public participation in Individual Psychology purely for political reasons after the fall of the Social Democratic Government. I believed that my former views might be hurtful to the spread of

Individual Psychology; but I never disagreed with its fundamental concepts.

'Adler understood that my retirement was solely due to my desire not to embarrass his teaching, and he approved of my decision.'

Professor Furtmüller had joined the Freudian circle with Adler after they had read Freud's work on *Dream Analysis* and had thoroughly discussed Freud's methods; but Adler never gave up his own chief idea as to the advance of the human being from a minus to a plus.

'Adler read a great deal', Professor Furtmüller stated, 'on his own subjects, and had an impeccable memory. Whatever interested him stuck in his mind and became a part of it. It is a great mistake to suppose that Adler was not, in the truest sense of the word, a Scholar, in spite of the fact that he talked to his patients like an old grandmother.'

In the early days of Adler's marriage, the family lived in Czerningasse, their second Vienna home, and Adler practised as a General Practioner of Medicine. The Adler family lived very simply, but they always had enough for their needs. Adler only gave up his general practice after the break with Freud, when he went to live at No. 10 Dominikanerbastei and became exclusively a psychiatrist.

His first psychiatric case was that of a distant cousin who came to him explaining that she was suffering from an acute headache. 'But no one', Adler told her, 'has *only* a headache. Are you sure that your married life is a happy one?' The lady was very angry and left him in a temper; but within a month she had applied for a divorce.

Adler had been greatly respected as a general practitioner; he thoroughly enjoyed and believed in his profession, and was never known to act with anything short of the most scrupulous regard for all its rights and privileges. Long after he had given up general practice, Adler would be called in as a consultant in puzzling cases. He always showed the greatest interest and care for any physical symptoms in one of his own neurotic patients. Nevertheless he constantly lightened physical troubles by psychiatry. For instance, in the case of a patient who had a very definite mechanical bowel difficulty, Adler so completely made light of it that all the worst symptoms disappeared within a few months; nor did they ever return. The difficulty was still there, but unstressed by the psychic factor, it no longer interfered with his patient's life or work.

Another patient told him, 'I am distressed that in spite of my work in Individual Psychology, I have had three severe illnesses in the past year.' 'Tell me what they were,' Adler asked her. 'Diphtheria; pleurisy and bronchitis; and an increase in the organic weakness of which you already know,' the lady replied. 'The diphtheria and the pleurisy couldn't be helped,' Adler replied promptly. 'Bricks may drop on any head. But the organ infirmity—that you certainly need not suffer from, for if it were progressive, you would have died long ago: I should strongly advise you not to give it another thought.'

To a patient suffering from stage fright, Adler said, 'You should not try to chase two rabbits. If you do, you will not catch either. Now, you wish to give pleasure to your audience. This is quite a good rabbit. Follow it up. But you also wish to be an outstanding success while doing it. This rabbit you might very well leave to run off by itself.'

To another patient suffering from great timidity, Adler said, 'Once there was a rabbit who became very much attached to its owner. One day a stranger with a savage dog appeared at the door. The rabbit became furious and rushed at both of them, with its teeth showing and growling terribly. The dog ran away in a panic and the stranger quickly shut the door between himself and the rabbit. So you see what even a rabbit can do when it is roused!'

Adler not only treated every patient differently; but even everything liable to happen to each patient differently. On one occasion he was lunching with a lady who made light of the accidental death of her only son. It was obvious that she was showing off a particular trend of religious thought which she believed could turn her into a heroine. This, to Adler, was to 'bagatellize' a real grief, and quite as unhealthy a sign as to take the grief itself too much to heart. He, therefore, let the lady assure him at some length that she was perfectly happy, and, indeed, could by her new method of religion make herself even happier than when her son was alive; but when she paused for a moment, Adler said: 'Show me his photograph.' The lady got up and brought it to him. Adler looked at it a long time with intense pity in his eyes. 'What a dreadful thing!' he said at last, giving it back to her. The mother burst into tears; and it was obvious that having accepted the real truth, even for a moment, it had relieved the tension of the lie, under which she had been forcing her heart to live.

Adler's curious mixture of unmasking—but unmasking *with* love, and *into* love—was the secret of most of his cures. No one ever went to Adler with a need for help who did not get it; though they might not get help in the form in which they had expected, or had even desired, it. But the love was always there. A great friend of his said they were once discussing a man whom they both admired; each in turn praised him and went on praising him, until they came to a sudden stop. Adler leaned forward and touched her arm, saying very gravely, 'But he was not beloved!' This could never have been said of Adler, for practically everyone that came in contact with him loved him.

The author once had an important message to deliver and found that he was out. 'Are you sure', she asked the clerk at the desk, 'that Professor Adler will get this message directly he comes in?' 'Adler?' the clerk replied. 'If it's for him you needn't worry. He always gets all his messages. You can hardly keep the bell-boys or the porter out of his room. They'll take *any* excuse to talk to him, and as far as that goes, I'm not much better myself!'

A patient once went to Adler who was always supposed to take insufficient care of herself, and to do a great deal too much work. Perhaps she also supposed this to be the case. At any rate, after she had told Adler the extremely heavy programme that lay before her, he said: 'I see only one danger about all this—that you might be led to take too many precautions! To take precautions, that, I find, is really dangerous. Courage is the only precaution a human being needs!'

When Hitler took over the government of the German Reich, Adler said, 'I always foresaw that something of this kind would happen to Germany. It was in a dangerous condition with all those insurance societies. People should take care of *themselves*; but the German people always want it done for them!'

Nobody ever succeeded in deceiving Adler as to his character, but he always gave everyone the benefit of the doubt. Only where there was no doubt at all did he allow himself an occasional joke. When he was told that a malicious and egocentric acquaintance was engaged to be married, Adler exclaimed, 'What—that fellow—and is he really in love?' 'Oh, yes,' his interlocutor told him, 'this time he *really* seems to be!' 'Against whom?' Adler asked with a sly twinkle.

One thing that made Adler the best of good company was that he never attempted to raise the level of conversation. Whatever it was, he remained plainly and cheerfully a member of it, without forcing it into greater seriousness or breaking it up by any exhibition of his own wisdom. He might change a subject, if he thought anyone present was being put to a disadvantage, but seldom for any other reason.

On one occasion, a group of his friends were listening to an impassioned oration by a theosophist who believed in transmigration of souls. Adler never, by a sign, denied her theory, which was one in which he had no belief whatever. On the contrary, he entered into the subject urging every member of the group in turn to say what they would like to be in the next life. His special friend in the group said she would like to be an atom of energy, producing movement for ever. 'But this is lonely—to be an atom!' Adler objected. 'I—if I were to be brought back into this world again—why, I think I would like to be a rose—it is beautiful to look at, and it grows on a bush with many others.'

Adler would, however, if directly challenged, always answer with the truth. His hostess at lunch once said to him, 'Now, Professor Adler, I suppose you are one of the people who don't believe in ghosts. What would you say to me if I told you that I had repeatedly seen ghosts in this house?' 'I should say that you were mistaken,' Adler replied, with a charming smile. 'It is a thing I have been very often myself; but not about ghosts!'

Adler had very strong objections to any unprovable theories, but especially when they might disturb our personal control of our own destinies. He suspected such beliefs of an underlying desire to interfere with the responsibility of an individual, upon which he believed the progress of mankind to depend. Spiritualism, theosophy, astrology, even telepathy he greatly distrusted. 'I once suffered from a case of telepathy myself,' he explained. 'I woke up at the exact time of the sinking of the *Titanic*, and so vivid had been my dream that I seemed to see a ship foundering in mid-ocean, although I do not think that I invented the iceberg. It was a shock to discover next day that the ship had *really* sunk, but I was able to convince myself that it was not such a coincidence as it appeared, since I was in great anxiety at the time about the single copy of my book *The Nervous Character*, which was on its way to America. In this case, I had not taken a copy of it, which was my rule, and had the ship sunk, I should have lost the work of years. The book, however, was not on the *Titanic* and I soon received news that it had arrived safely. You will find, if you carefully investigate all such cases of telepathy, that they usually have some such underlying anxiety in the background. As for other rather far-fetched theories, you will notice that they all produce magnificent excuses for people who do not wish to control themselves.'

On the other hand, any form of real religion formed on obedience to approved moral precepts, Adler always acknowledged as of the greatest possible value to a human being; and, as he put it in *Social Interest: A Challenge to Mankind* , 'The best conception hitherto gained for the elevation of humanity is the idea of God. There can be no question that the idea of God really includes within it as a goal the movement towards perfection, and that, as a concrete goal, it best corresponds to the obscure yearnings of human beings to reach perfection. Certainly it seems to me that every one conceives of God in a different way. There are no doubt conceptions of God that fall far short of the principle of perfection; but of its purest form we can say—here—the presentation of the goal of perfection has been successful.' This spiritual conception of Adler's is in complete contradiction to Freud's materialistic statement that all religion is a form of obsessional neurosis.

Adler's beliefs, like his thoughts, always came from his actual experiences. He was a psychiatrist who possessed an absolute genius for discovering the workings of the human mind, but it is a curious fact that throughout the period of his association with the psychoanalysts, Adler was never himself analysed, and, as he afterwards jokingly remarked, neither had he received the benefit of an Individual Psychological training. Adler was, therefore, in the truest sense of the word, a self-made man. No one at any step of his career could fail to realize that the self he was making was a most enriching and reliable human being, and a great advance towards that 'wholeness' which was the core of Adler's belief in man; but this does not imply that Adler was himself a perfect human being or even that he ever expected to be one. 'When I hear the word "ethics",' he once remarked, 'I always look to see where the fingers of the speaker have gone. Are they not, I ask myself, perhaps in my pocket?'

On one occasion, the author brought Adler an expostulation from an outraged friend who had just been badly cheated by a young man Adler had recommended to him. Adler was very angry at this friend's rebuke, and also at the author for having brought it to him. He was perhaps even more angry with himself for having caused the trouble. 'Have I no right to make mistakes?' he demanded passionately. 'I tell you that I have the same right anyone else has! I *have* made mistakes and I *will* make them, and that is what you will please tell X!'

Nevertheless, the author eventually discovered that Adler *had* warned X, when leaving his young friend behind with him—a warning that X did not know Adler well enough to understand. 'I tapped the boy's shoulder,' Adler afterwards explained, 'and said to X:

"Do not forget that this friend of ours has been gifted with a great deal of imagination!" '

It is quite probable that Adler did not know himself as well as he knew others; but when one remembers how deeply and accurately he knew others, one realizes that he must have known himself far better than most of us ever attempt to know ourselves. For every blunder that Adler committed he paid, as perhaps no one outside the circle of the greatest saints has ever paid. 'What are our hearts given us for but to consume?' he once said gravely to a friend burdened by remorse.

Those who have read Adler's *Understanding Human Nature* will remember what he writes in its pages about a broken and a contrite heart, and will realize that no one could have written it who had not a reason for knowing the price man pays for his 'pleasant vices' and who had not paid that price, as few of us ever pay it, to the uttermost farthing.

'What are the best of us—in the end—' Adler once demanded, 'but repentant sinners?'

V

Adler's Café Life and Political Opinions

The intellectual life of Vienna up to the time of the German occupation ran swiftest in its cafés. To a Viennese—and Adler was a Viennese to the last drop of his blood—his café was a place where he felt most alive.

If an Englishman's home is his castle, to a Viennese his café was both his home—and his escape from home. Here whatever dull care he had, he cast behind him; here he read the world's news hot from the printing press hour by hour. Here he met his friends and took care to avoid, by a swift glance round before entering, too close a proximity to his enemies.

Here he could be warm and comfortable, concentrated or relaxed; silent or garrulous at will. Here he could look through his business correspondence in peace; read or write letters in private; sustain himself, and pay for his right of entry, by drinking the best coffee in the world, or the lightest beer. Here he could make love; carry it on, or break it off, within the bounds of a discretion which may also sometimes have served as a protection.

Each Viennese café had its own specialty, its own faint or distinct flavour of something, in the enchanting word of the Viennese, 'apart'.

What wonder in those unforgettable days when Vienna was itself, that there was a café at almost every corner of every street, and that no café was ever altogether empty?

Still there were café rush hours, when life was at its fullest, from five to seven in the afternoons, and between nine o'clock and midnight. At these time whole groups met for animated discussions; tables were linked together, each member of a group ordering what he chose and paying for it himself. Here Adler would come after a long exhausting day's work, with his easy effortless smile; or fresh (and he was always fresh after a lecture) from an admiring audience whom he had skilfully evaded. He was now prepared to settle down

58

for a happy evening. Free to come and go as he liked; surrounded by the friends he was entertaining, and by whom he was himself entertained, and for whom at the moment he had no responsibility whatever. What other form of social intercourse could have pleased Adler as much, or could he have found less rigid and more fruitful, had he himself invented it?

Above all in the Viennese cafés jokes were born, they flew from lip to lip, from eye to eye. No one was an outsider. The humblest of men had his tastes studied; the most unpopular of men knew that at least he could make, by an unpretentious tip, the waiter his friend; although behind his back the waiter could no doubt give a very accurate estimate of his character. Adler's life in Vienna could very well be followed by careful attention to his successive cafés.

As an undergraduate, he attended the nearest and cheapest café, Grinsteidl, where his fellows were of his own age and standing. But as soon as he had left the University, he was oftenest to be found at the Café Dom near the great church of Stephansdom that rules the heart of the city. The Café Dom was at this time the haunt of struggling intellectuals, and their free speech and easy give and take were best suited to Adler's enterprising spirit. Later the pick of the artists, scientists and writers migrated with Adler to the Café Central, a still more popular stronghold, where political thinkers and journalists joined forces with poets and scientists. The old world was beginning to break up round them, and they were the stormy petrels of the new world's thought—flying ahead of the violence to come.

During the war of 1914 itself, when Adler returned from his two years' medical service at the Front, it was to find the Café Central almost emptied of its former circle. Some of its brightest wits were dead, and others dulled by respectability or the more solid obligations that the years had brought them. The Café had a different public and its prices were too high. Adler therefore vanished from the Café Central, and was for a while to be found, to the scandal of his more prosperous and less 'advanced' colleagues, at 'The Whiff of Tobacco', a comparatively low haunt in close proximity to a 'middle-class kitchen' where very cheap and reasonably good meals were to be found. Here Adler established himself with his group of friends during the starved and shaking years that followed the war. But Adler's group of followers soon grew too large, and his own reputation too considerable for this cheap haunt; and he was driven to leave it—though with obvious reluctance—for the commodious and far more pretentious Café Siller.

Here, until his life in Vienna ended, and later on throughout his subsequent yearly visits to Vienna, a big upper room was placed at his disposal by his staunch friend the café owner, where Adler could hold his meetings and give informal lectures to small and friendly audiences, though they always tended to grow, as all Adler's audiences grew, out of the space provided for them. When the evening's work was over, stretching away across the pavement towards the broad Danube Canal, gay little flowered tables awaited the lecturer and his audience.

It is difficult to say whether the café habit of Vienna was caused by, or resulted in, the extreme openness and friendliness of the Viennese mind. But it is a fact that up to the time of the German occupation, the city of Vienna was the most cultured, the most tolerant, witty and internationally minded capital in Europe. Nor is it surprising to any observant mind that a type of psychology founded upon social interest should have sprung from its soil.

Adler's mind was wholly suited to the café habit. He hated all limitations or social rigidities; and here he could enjoy complete freedom of speech and action. No time limits beyond those of his natural habits; no company from which he could not withdraw at will; in a word, no form of dictatorship, social or otherwise. Here men, as Samuel Johnson said of his club contemporaries in the eighteenth century when England too had her wits and their cafés, 'must stand upon their own bottoms'.

Adler was the most highly socialized human being who ever lived. 'Conduct springs from contact,' he said (and practised it); 'there are no virtues on a desert island'; but for that very reason he loathed any sort of empty or rigid society.

What he prized in social intercourse was a free interchange of opinion, and the most direct relation possible between human beings. What he most enjoyed was a good joke flavoured by a universal truth.

A whole volume *could* and *should* be filled with Adler's jokes. They were never personal—except that what is true universally must to a certain extent be true individually; they lit up the subject of conversation without detracting from its weight or ruthlessly bringing it to a sudden end; and when the conversation had no weight, or was seen to be tending towards any social rock, one of Adler's timely jokes often served to direct the flow of conversation into both a safer and a deeper channel. One café friend of Adler's, a famous Viennese dentist, said, 'I do not know much about Adler's psychology—but I do know no one ever made better jokes!'

ADLER'S CAFE LIFE AND POLITICAL OPINIONS

Even Adler's politics could be traced and punctuated through his successive cafés. They were at their reddest while Adler attended The Whiff of Tobacco during the starvation years.

From his student days, even before he met Raissa, Adler was linked to the cause of social betterment.

At this period in the Hapsburg dynasty if you wanted any form of improvement at all for any of 'the lower classes' you were branded as a 'Socialist' of the deepest dye.

The court and its circle naturally felt that things were best exactly as they were; and Adler, while fresh from the University, had dared to write a pamphlet on *The Health of Tailors*. This had occasioned a good deal of comment, partly because Adler himself was a highly popular young man, and partly because it was considered a scandalous thing for a young doctor to concern himself at all with the health of cruelly sweated tailors, other than to prod or poultice them, according to their momentary requirements.

Adler's personality had an unhappy knack of spreading his words far beyond the circle in which they were spoken. Even though he was poor and insignificant socially, this pamphlet exposing the frightful conditions under which a whole section of Viennese workers lived, stirred public opinion and went on stirring it until something was actually done for the tailors, and some of the most atrocious of their wrongs were gradually righted. After all, people have to have their clothes made by tailors, and it is inconvenient and even risky if the diseases thrust upon the tailors by their circumstances can infect the materials out of which the clothes of the more fortunate are made. During the years that preceded the war, Adler was, however, so preoccupied with his professional duties, and the long Laocoön struggle with Freud, that the question of his politics became less pressing.

No doubt both in the Dom and in the Café Central, 'the fundamentals', to use Rossetti's historic phrase, 'were rattled' whenever the young wits of Vienna came together to discuss the state of the world; but at any rate Adler did nothing further to upset the conscience of his city, or to expose his political sympathies.

He was always more interested in the concrete fact than in any theory. There was for this biologist intent on the laws of life itself, a dubious flavour of personality about a 'theory' divorced from instant practice. Not '*what*' do people think but '*why*' do they think it; and if they think it—why do they not practise it—were the questions oftenest on the tip of Adler's tongue.

But during the war and in the disastrous years that followed, once more the concrete fact was at his heels, forcing him to take a stand with the working classes.

For a time Adler actually joined (under the Social Democratic Government) the councils of soldiers and workers, although his one contribution to their meeting was a lecture upon Individual Psychology with a determined swing towards *Gemeinschaftsgefühl*; and he withdrew from them, much to the dismay of his wife and some of his most devoted friends, soon afterwards.

Adler was never an advocate of revolution in any violent form, since he never accepted politics as a substitute for spiritual growth. His fundamental belief was that only a better individual can make a better system; and his contribution to psychology stands alone in this —that he believed the human being capable of, and responsible for, his whole spiritual growth including better politics.

This difference of cart and horse (for Raissa also believed and faithfully and courageously practised her responsibility for spiritual growth and differed only from Adler in thinking that a change in the political system would automatically improve human nature) did not smooth the domestic path. Raissa would not budge from her Russian revolutionary tendencies, nor was the War, and the subsequent history of her country, likely to decrease her vehemence. Adler too, had a section of devoted Communist followers, who made every effort to identify Adler's views with their own, and were furious when he refused to support them.

Finally, Adler with increasing emphasis insisted that Individual Psychology had nothing whatever to do with *any* form of politics; and could be accepted and practised whatever political or religious views were held by anybody. 'Individual Psychology', he was fond of saying, 'is like a basket of fruit, out of which any passer-by can take whatever agrees with him!'

After the War, the two chief conflicting parties in Austria were the Christian Socialists, who were in league with the Catholics and represented a definite swing towards the right; and the Social Democrats who took over the Government after Karl's abdication, and who were representative of all branches of the Left. Even the Communists preferred them to the Christian Socialists, though their affection was tepid and could at times be dangerously diverted.

That Adler, after his one short excursion, never definitely identified himself with either party, is proved by the fact that neither party ever rewarded him for his services when it came to power.

ADLER'S CAFE LIFE AND POLITICAL OPINIONS

Glöckel, the Minister of Education in the Social Democratic period, urged by Professor Fortmüller, did indeed give Adler the opportunity to link his child guidance centres with the State schools, the first time that this experiment had ever been tried; but Adler received no State appointment or any financial support, in spite of the fact that this great experiment in education was a triumphant success and brought teachers from all over the world to study it. Rival psychologists have tried to minimize, and outside his own country have had some success in minimizing, the greatness and originality of this undertaking, but there was never any minimizing of it in his own country. Between the years 1921 and 1934 Adler revolutionized the education of the *Gemeinde Wien*; every child between the years of six and fourteen in the Viennese State schools could, if he showed any signs of potential delinquency or neurosis, be treated either by Adler himself or by specially trained psychologists—with a few exceptions, by those of Adler's own School of Psychology; and the miraculous decrease in delinquency and neurosis in Viennese Adolescents' Courts during these years silenced the bitterest of his critics.

Adler's politics were like everything else about him, a disinterested expression of his personality. They followed the lines of his unruffleable common sense. He always stood for what was fair, open-minded and easily adjustable to human needs; and he supported whatever country or party most fulfilled or most struggled towards sane and practicable ideals.

'Don't join things,' Adler once said earnestly to a friend seeking advice upon a political issue; and when a Leftist attitude was thrust upon him by a follower, 'No! I have had enough of these Nazi-minded Communists!'

When asked what he thought of the Totalitarian State in Germany he replied, 'Sixty-five million people in search of an author!'

When Kunkel, one of his German disciples in Berlin, urged Adler to visit Berlin (and, as he had himself become a Nazi, offered Adler his protection), Adler said to the friend who brought him the invitation, 'Tell him, I laughed.'

Since Adler believed in every individual's right to a creative life, he viewed with deep apprehension any attempt to standardize or force the minds of human beings into a mould, or to take away from them their personal responsibility for every act.

'After all,' he said once with a sly twinkle, 'a lunatic is a being who is *not* responsible for his acts!'

His refusal to pin himself down to either party in power cost him his one great personal ambition. There seems no doubt that the University of Vienna would have conferred the professorship that was Adler's due, had his politics not seemed to the authorities too strongly socialist.

Extremists sacrifice what they hate for what they love; but moderates often find themselves sacrificed alike by both parties. Nor do they receive any other reward than the freedom of their own minds.

Adler suffered and suffered deeply from his refusal to support his own politically minded adherents. He lost a string of powerful friends in high places on the Right; and he lost some of his dearest friends and shook the confidence of his wife by his refusal to identify himself with the politics of the Left.

While he lived, and with increasing conviction, Adler kept—and urged upon all his followers to keep—Individual Psychology free from either party. He wanted his 'science,' as he loved to call it, to be open to all the changes and chances of man's development, but closed against the short interests of political creeds and their empty slogans.

'It is always easier to fight for one's principles than to live up to them,' Adler once murmured to an over-emphatic friend.

Out of his café life Adler formed many lasting friendships.

One of these was with the owner of his favourite café, with whom he used to play chess nightly, in the early days of his professional life. Adler had saved Siller's life, when he had been given up by two famous Viennese specialists and thought himself face to face with death. 'Why, you are bursting with health!' Adler exclaimed when called in by the despairing wife, 'I never saw anyone more naturally vigorous!' The next day, although telephoned for, Adler did not come. When he appeared upon the following day and his patient demanded a reason, Adler replied: 'Well, why should I make you pay me for nothing? I knew that you would be much better, and you *are* already much better!' Adler was soon able to convince this patient that his diagnosis, though perhaps a little exaggeratedly optimistic at the moment, was fundamentally right.

Another café friend, of an even more intimate kind, a man in whose company Adler was always glad to spend every spare hour of his Viennese life, was also a chess crony; but Frankel was a great deal more than a mere game comrade, and Adler had one of the happiest friendships of his life with his engineer friend.

Frankel was a typical Viennese of the best type, an easy-natured, witty fellow, honest minded, and always open to new ideas; a man who combined a kind and sensitive heart with a penetrating judgment.

For four years these two friends met daily, and when Adler left Vienna to live in New York, returning only for long summer visits to his beloved city, their reunions took up instantly their jokes and the intimacy behind the jokes—as if no interruption from time or space had ever taken place.

Those who speak of the friends Adler lost, forget or perhaps have never met those he retained. A comparison between the two categories would be interesting.

The friends he lost were often very dear to Adler, and deeply prized for their intellectual resources. Some of them were specialists who tried to hem Adler into their own narrow pathways; others were careerists who wanted the feather from Adler's genius to wear in their own caps. Sometimes his lost followers were political fanatics who repudiated Adler for his tolerance; and sometimes Nicodemuses who visited him only by night, so that they should not be seen with so venturesome and unconventional a person; oftenest of all they were men and women who found the relentless sincerity of Adler's words and thoughts 'a hard saying, and walked no more with him'; but though the friends he lost were many different types of people, the friends he retained had a strong family likeness: whatever other courses they might pursue or whatever differing qualities they possessed, the friends Adler kept had this in common—they loved him for 'himself', as we say, and never found sufficient reason for giving up their great discovery.

It was not an easy matter to be Adler's friend, because it involved to some extent knowing oneself. He did not force this knowledge upon his friends, but it took place in them often without their being fully aware of the process.

No one was ever a better listener than Adler; but he never talked for talking's sake; nor even when he had something to say did he talk at any length. 'We have nothing more to say about this subject,' he once said to a friend and patient, 'when we have once discovered what can be done about it. This we *have* discovered, so we will say no more!'

Often he would sit for two or three hours at a café surrounded by his friends and hardly uttering a word. He was, however, perfectly happy, silently absorbing all that went on about him, and feeling himself part of the movement of his friends' lives.

With complete economy of word or action Adler seemed at one with every member of the group about him, and brought out each man's best, to meet his own.

The aggressively vain held their vanity at bay in these café discussions; the nervous and impulsive calmed down; those who believed themselves incapable of argument suddenly found the right word with which to express their opinions; and those who wished to browbeat or dictate to their audience were checked by a mere glance of those strangely hooded penetrating eyes. Adler had a look that seemed to pierce through layer after layer of outward defences until it reached the very core of the heart, but he very rarely used this glance for an attacking purpose; it was much more often used to fortify or relieve discouraged or anxious persons. Not that there was much pity in Adler's glance, but there was expectation in it; an expectation that you would do your best, and that your best would be quite good enough if you *did* do it.

Still Adler did on occasion check a friend's faults in company; but when he did, it was with a swift decisiveness—like that of a friendly hand dragging a man back from a traffic danger. Very often the only person who knew that this rebuke had taken place was the person who had felt that momentary grip upon his spirit. The author remembers being once astonished at the lack of rancour or even annoyance shown by an intensely vain man at some very plain words of Adler. 'Dear So-and-So,' Adler had written, 'I cannot publish your article in my journal, it would do a great deal of harm—' the recipient actually read the letter aloud without showing a shadow of discomfiture. 'I wonder what harm Adler thought my article would do?' he observed quite calmly. 'I wish you'd ask him next time you see him, and let me know.' Yet this was a man whose sensitiveness to any criticism or the slightest reproof could hardly be exaggerated.

A very discouraged girl once said to the author about a social occasion where a large number of people were present, 'Did you notice that Adler seemed to be thinking of me all the time? He kept bringing me forward into the conversation, but quite comfortably, and I really felt for the first time as if I could say *exactly* what I wanted to say!'

Beyond the fact that Adler always met sincerity with sincerity, it was quite impossible to calculate what effect his company would have upon him. Some of his dearest friends seemed a surprising choice, and he occasionally appeared hostile towards, or even made an opponent of, someone that there seemed no reason to attack. Nevertheless Adler was an almost omniscient detective of the motive that lies beneath the surface in human beings, so that it was never safe to assume that he had made a mistake about anyone.

He told one of his most intimate friends that in general company he never concerned himself with people's motives or idiosyncrasies, and carefully avoided using his own particular knowledge outside the field of his consulting room; but it can be doubted whether anyone can succeed in *not* practising an understanding of other human beings, while in their company.

Pain in others Adler instantly detected. Once after an enormously successful lecture on an important occasion, Adler hastened to a side door where a friend was standing, and said with an urgency that showed he had nothing else on his mind, 'I think you had better go straight home and take an aspirin!' Yet the friend had omitted to tell him of his toothache, and indeed, enchanted by the great success of Adler's lecture, had almost forgotten the jumping of an exposed nerve.

Adler was equally sensitive to a friend's pleasure or success; and he always remembered and if possible gratified their tastes. 'I should like', he said to a very fastidious dresser to whom he was greatly attached, 'you to choose three really suitable ties for a friend of mine who has great taste. I have not time to do it myself; besides I can rely more upon *your* judgment—do not be hampered by the price!'

The friend spent a whole morning carrying out this commission to his satisfaction, only to discover that the really beautiful ties he had procured were a present to himself.

VI

Adler and the Freudian Circle

I n entering on the period of Adler's life which deals with the ten-
year struggle between him and his lifelong antagonist, Sigmund
Freud, the author has tried to keep as far as possible an unbiased
standpoint in order to show, without exaggeration, the part which
each played in the other's life and work.

This has not been an easy task, since even apart from a deep personal resentment felt by these two great men for each other, there has
been the bitter back-wash of unreasoned jealousy and hate felt by
the more ignorant of their disciples.

There remain certain facts which, robbed of distortion, stand out
sufficiently objectively to be accepted as such by disinterested ob-
servers. The Ansbachers' compilation of Adler's writings between
1904 and 1937, chronologically correct, and documented, entitled
'The Individual Psychology of Alfred Adler', published by Basic
Books Inc., is the most valuable of these sources. It is brought
up to date by Dr. Ansbacher of Vermont University and his wife,
by their comments, and comparisons with modern American psychology.

It is astonishing that Ernest Jones in his life of Freud contradicts
Freud's own words as to the depth of this intimacy. For Freud
writes in a letter to one of his friends, quoted in Jones' life, that
the three most heart-breaking losses in his personal relationships
were the breaks with Breuer, Flies and Adler.

There would probably have been far less resentment, and far less
acrid controversy, between these two great men had it not been for
the intellectual sympathy and genuine admiration each felt for the
other's gifts, an admiration and sympathy that forced them to remain
together long after the divergence of their opinions indicated that
they would do better work apart.

There is no doubt, from their earlier correspondence, that they

68

were at one time intimate friends, and that their work as scientists was enriched by the dynamic force and difference of their minds, until their difference became inflamed by a habit of personal resentment.

Probably they both felt that they should gloss over, or when possible, sink the points at issue between them, in order to strengthen their contribution to mankind.

Each had gifts that the other lacked, and each must have depended consciously or unconsciously upon the other's equipment. 'Freud', a neutral observer told the author, 'never treated his other antagonists with the bitterness he reserved for Adler, because he well knew that Adler was the only one of them he had to fear as a rival in the eyes of posterity.'

Professor Furtmüller entered Freud's circle at the same time as Adler, and much of this chapter is taken from his account of their mutual experiences.

Furtmüller was a well-known Viennese scholar, a Professor of the Viennese University, a man of great courage and high moral reputation. Furtmüller remembers Adler first speaking to him of Freud in 1899-1900, when the famous book *Dream Analysis* was published.

'This man has something to say to us!' Adler exclaimed with great earnestness.

It was the fashion at that time, in Viennese medical circles, to mock at Freud; and when an article appeared in the *Neue Freie Presse* holding his new book up to ridicule, Adler answered it by a strongly written defence. Adler was personally unknown to Freud at the time, but was himself already accepted by his medical colleagues in Vienna as a sound and rising physician, so that his defence had a definite weight, as well as being, on the part of so young a man, against the whole feeling of his profession, a courageous deed.

Freud was much touched by it, and sent Adler a postcard thanking him for his defence and asking Adler to join the discussion circle of psycho-analysis. This postcard has a certain importance since it shows quite clearly that Adler was never a 'pupil' of Freud's, as his opponents always claim, and never had a didactic Freudian analysis; but was invited to enter the circle as an equal, and indeed as an asset to its respectability and strength. Adler had a reputation to give, as well as to receive, by this act, and he was at first against accepting Freud's offer.

Adler expressed to Freud his doubt if they *were* in fundamental agreement in spite of his strong sympathy with Freud's new manner

69

of tackling the science of psychology; but Freud persuaded him at least to join the discussion circle in which Adler's own new theory—the basis of Individual Psychology—might also have a hearing.

Adler was already working upon his idea of a psychical compensation for organic imperfection, and although Freud took little or no interest in this theory, Adler hoped to win him over to it, as no doubt Freud also hoped to make a more thorough-going advocate for his own ideas out of Adler. Both men were—in the nature of things—doomed to disappointment.

One natural obstacle to their work together was their position in their own families, for—according to Adler's theory of Family Constellation—Freud was the eldest, liable to be an authoritative type; while Adler, a second child, was equally liable to be a rebel. But even without this separating influence, few geniuses have ever been known to work successfully together.

Freud was a small town German Jew of peasant extraction; to-day we should probably call him a *petit bourgeois,* for his immediate family were cultured people, and he was brought up in a circle of cultured people; and he was never in touch, as Adler always was, with the actual proletariat.

Freud was from all accounts a grossly spoilt and pampered child, a beloved Jewish 'first born'.

From the first he accepted his father's patriarchal ideas and sternly authoritarian attitude. He also accepted the sacrifices of his family to enable him to carry on his own career.

Incalculable and continuous help was forthcoming from Freud's renowned older colleague Breuer, and stimulation and support came to him from his early engagement to an ideal wife.

Yet Freud, as well as Adler, had hard financial struggles before he attained his comparatively early success in life.

Freud's dictator pattern of life may well have accounted for his dangerous and irresponsible attitude to the cocaine discoveries in which he had shared. It was indeed fortunate for Freud that he was born in an unscientific period when such blunders were more readily overlooked; nor was there enough psychological knowledge during this period to warn his contemporaries that here was a man whose autocratic impatience made him often turn a blind eye towards any contradiction of his theories, while it led him to over-emphasize and isolate his triumphs.

Freud always escaped his fellows whenever possible, except for his few intense intimacies, and did not willingly risk placing himself at a disadvantage. He did not let himself appear where he could be publicly questioned, and only spoke in small intimate circles, always preferring writing to speaking.

Adler, on the contrary, was full of a sort of open genius and ready to attack or defend a subject at a moment's notice, never at a loss to grasp his opponent's meaning, even when questioned in a foreign tongue.

Adler was instantly at home in any personal contact, and leapt to meet a challenge; but writing bored him, and he often deliberately fogged his meaning (for no one could be clearer when he wished to be) in order not to be pinned down to a slogan or to limit the future growth of a subject.

Freud was a great systematizer, a most lucid thinker and writer, developing a style that is a pleasure for even a non-scientist to read—so clear and forceful are his thoughts, and so suitable their framework.

Adler treated his patients on a footing of absolute equality; they might have been fellow gamins, setting out to play a trick upon their elders. There they sat, Adler and his patient, hob-nobbing knee to knee, and often smoking like chimneys while they talked; each trying to outwit the other and both agreeing to outwit anything or anyone else who came up against them. 'Of course he wants to spit in your soup,' Adler would say reassuringly to a patient complaining of a near relation. 'Let us see how we can prevent him!'

Freud did not unbend with his patients. His method was to master the patient, who was in the position of being his subject. No doubt he was a wise and patient master, and when unprovoked a benevolent dictator. Freud's patients had to assume a passive position, lying down on a couch, with the psychiatrist sitting behind them, listening, but invisible to his patients.

Adler, Furtmüller related, read a great deal upon his own subjects, especially before his marriage; he knew far more than anyone (from his inherent modesty) could have guessed; and as his memory was wide and retentive, he often surprised his friends by the depth and accuracy of his knowledge. It was always factual rather than theoretical since his innate scepticism made him shy off from anything that could not be proved.

The mind with which Adler was most in sympathy from a psychological point of view was that of William Stern of Hamburg. This writer agreed with some of Adler's leading conceptions in Individual Psychology, but he approached his subjects quite differently from Adler.

Stern liked to tabulate his psychology and to express all his thoughts in diagrams. He worked from the periphery to the centre of his cases, whereas Adler's mind always worked from the centre outwards towards the periphery.

Adler disliked precise definitions or 'prescriptions' as he used to call them; when he was asked to explain his exact meaning, he would say, 'But now you want to milk the life out of the cow!'

This was partly because Adler thought people who asked for precise directions were lazy people trying to evade the responsibility of working things out for themselves; and partly, as we have already pointed out, because he did not want to limit the growth of the subject itself.

Among his contemporary philosophers Vaihinger was his special favourite; and he particularly valued Vaihinger's most important work, *Philosophy of As If*.

Freud was Adler's exact opposite in behaviour. Freud's manner was restrained; he always stood on his dignity, and laid great stress upon ceremoniousness. Adler went to the other extreme (though he corrected this tendency later in life); he spent no superfluous time or money upon his personal appearance, and avoided any conventional approach.

Even intellectually he would not take pains to construct his sentences carefully, and when Furtmüller complained of his lack of style, Adler replied: 'If the truth is there, bad writing won't hurt it!'

Freud erred in the opposite direction; he was so systematic and meticulous that he sometimes stifled the sense of what he was expressing. He was a born 'eldest' and often forced his own theories into the symptoms he was studying.

Freud was interested in 'picking out parts' and stressing divisions. Whereas Adler always insisted on the patient's 'wholeness' being the key to his symptoms and would indeed attach no value to symptoms apart from the individual personality. 'You must not only ask yourself', he would say, 'what effect a bacillus has on a body—it is also important to know what is the effect of the body on the bacillus!'

Once an American lady asked Adler suddenly in public if he could tell her why in a time of strict Prohibition there were so few fish on the market? Adler thought for a moment and then said, 'Might it not be possible, since fishermen are good smugglers, that their interest in boot-legging takes off from their time to go fishing?'

This *was* the actual fact; and it is interesting to see that here again

Adler went to the character of the fisherman as a 'whole', in order to deduce his performance or lack of performance with the fish. 'The main difference between Freud and Adler,' Professor Furtmüller concluded, 'was that Freud wanted knowledge; and that Adler looked for truth.'

His fellow scientists often criticized Adler adversely for going off as they said into *Weltanschauung* instead of keeping to his particular field of biology in which he was able to play so brilliant a part. But Freud too was equally open to this criticism, as is proved by his book *Zukunft einer Illusion*. In fact, no great thinker exists who is not speculative upon world subjects. Freud and Adler, probably *because* of the speculative reach of their minds, were able to give most practical contributions to medicine and surgery. It was Freud who first discovered the value of cocaine for eye-operations; and Adler who, long before the actual treatment of diabetes by insulin was discovered, always stressed the desirability of treating diabetes by extracts of the pancreas.

Adler's books after he left Freud's circle continued to make an immense impression upon his former colleagues, who greatly modified their own practice and teaching by them, although extremely loath to acknowledge the fact.

Adler's books, however, did not until later, when his personality as a lecturer had already won him a great reputation in Germany, attract German thinkers. Adler was too simple and forthright a thinker to be accepted with tolerance by the academic German mind. However, once he was heard in Germany as a lecturer, his work soon became widely known and the knowledge of it spread all over Central Europe. Adler had the same contact-making powers with an audience as with a neurotic or a child, or indeed with any other human being. Good fellowship shot from his heart into the audience. There was no tension in Adler and no striving either to please or to shine; and the sense that here was a person without fear and equally without a desire to display superior powers, drew off all antagonism from his audience.

A highly important member of the circle that surrounded Freud —one who from the first became specially attached to Adler and his theories—was the brilliant philosopher, Dr. Alexander Neuer.

Neuer came to Vienna to study philosophy from 1905 to 1909. He was bent on making a complete comparative study of psychology from William Wundt's *Synthetic Principle* to the newest theory in psycho-analysis.

73

Finding that the cafés were the centre of cultural life in Vienna, Neuer soon joined up with the Café Central circle. These debate and discussion circles were open to all outside influences and escaped the domination of schools. They were full of active intellectual life and the constant interchange of creative ideas.

The psycho-analytical movement, in which Neuer from 1905 took a prominent part, was not in spite of the greatness of Freud's creative powers and natural leadership by any means a one-man movement.

Freud, Adler and Stekel developed in the *Café-haus*, and each contributed his special discoveries to the common pool.

Adler's special contribution—Individual Psychology—was a 'social training' and at the same time a literary movement.

Men of all schools and parties were drawn to it for different reasons. The Socialists were attracted by a science that they could connect with Marxist theories. Adler's phrase: 'Out of organic weakness of constitution springs the truth' they took as direct support for Karl Marx's: 'The truth is an economic factor.'

Hofmannsthal, Wassermann, Schnitzler, Auerheimer, Karl Kraus, and Peter Altenburg, the poet (one of Adler's most intimate friends), the leaders of Viennese intellectual thought at this period, all joined the psycho-analytic circle, and made their different contributions towards its theories.

Freud and Adler both took detection and unmasking as their main scientific method; and it was their use of this method that drew the literary group with enthusiasm to their ideas.

Thinkers who accepted this detective psychology worked as psycho-analysts. One can find the underlying theories both of Adler and Freud in many contemporary Viennese writers' novels and poems; and it is to their discoveries, perhaps, that the modern movement in thought is largely due. Artists are often the birds who help to carry the seed of new thoughts over the cultural world.

There was no direct clash between Adler and Freud until Adler wanted to use the detective and unmasking process upon psycho-analysis itself.

Adler was fourteen years younger than Freud, and apparently thought that this fact should not óbstruct the freedom of their arguments.

Stekel, usually Adler's sharpest opponent, agreed with him on the unmasking of psycho-analysis. They both rebelled against Freud's suggested safeguard—that their future articles should be censored for the *Psycho-Analytical Journal* by the new and more orthodox recruit, Jung, who had not yet himself broken with Freud, and who was then not yet even editor.

Freud was forced to give way, after some heated discussions, upon the point of the censorship; but his opposition and that of his more compliant followers stiffened against any of his special beliefs—such as the universality of the phallic symbol—being put to the question by these irreverent unmaskers.

Both Adler and Neuer accepted the inherent truth of *Dream Analysis*, while using a different principle from Freud's to analyse by. Both accepted the value of 'free association' but neither could tolerate the Œdipus Complex and still less the sacrosanct attitude of Freud and his disciples towards what Adler always referred to as the 'mythology of sex'.

It was a difficult situation, since Adler had been made, largely by Freud's influence, the leader of the Viennese section of the psychoanalysts and their constant spokesman, as well as being editor of the *Psycho-Analytical Journal*. He, therefore, had everything to lose and nothing to gain by leaving Freud. On the contrary, as Freud became more and more famous, owing to his increased renown and financial security, Adler and the younger men working with him had at their disposal the means of carrying on their psychiatric experiments under the most favourable auspices; and also owing to the fact that Freud had no time to handle all his patients, Adler in particular (who was acknowledged as the ablest physician of the group) took over more and more of Freud's cases.

Such opportunities as these, to a young man with his way to make in the world, were not to be lightly set aside, nor can the only bond between Adler and Freud have been an interested one. Both men had genius; both also had magnificent human qualities, a kindred ardour, a courage and fineness of perception hard for either to forgo in the companionship of the other. It is perhaps not so surprising that they held together for so long as that they ever made up their minds to part with each other. The struggle when it came was cruel and prolonged; and without doubt needlessly embittered by third parties.

Curiously enough their chief bone of contention, the Œdipus Complex, was—as Adler was fond of relating—Jung's contribution, and received by Freud at first with marked distaste, until he saw what support it gave to his central idea of the domination of the sexual instinct. 'I enriched psycho-analysis', Adler told his friends, with a grim smile, 'by the aggressive drive. I gladly make them a present of it—and Jung is responsible for the Œdipus Complex!' but it is

probable that the particular point of difference was by now im-
material—the gulf between the two personalities of Freud and Adler
could no longer be crossed either by interest or affection.

There is no doubt that Freud had gradually become increasingly
jealous of his brilliant younger colleague, and allowed, if he did not
instigate, the 'heresy hunt' that followed. The constant bickering and
persecution became exceedingly painful not only to Adler, but to
other members of the group. Dr. Hilferding, told the writer that not
being able to stand the perpetual harrying of Adler whenever he
opened his mouth, she withdrew from the group altogether, though
still firmly convinced of the truth of the Freudian theories. 'It was
impossible not to believe,' Dr. Hilferding told the writer, 'that these
constant attacks upon Adler were a determined and envious intention
to get rid of him altogether, or else to completely suppress his original
genius. I left, not because I agreed with Adler's theories, but because
I disapproved of Freud's and his followers' behaviour. It was un-
worthy of scientists and truth lovers.'

On Freud's behalf it must be admitted that to find first a diver-
sionist, and then an antagonist, when he had looked for a powerful
advocate, must have been a galling disappointment.

The extent to which Freud had leaned upon Adler for support and
sympathy will never be known; but it can be suspected from the fact
of his subsequent bitterness, and from the efforts he made, too late,
to retain his injured colleague.

While Adler was away on a summer holiday, the proprietors of the
Psycho-Analytical Journal received a letter from Freud saying that he
must withdraw his name from the Journal unless Adler's was taken
from the title-page. Adler relieved the proprietor from this dilemma
by immediately resigning his editorship; and wrote to Freud his
reasons for having done so, and for now withdrawing altogether
from the psycho-analytic group.

Freud begged Adler to reconsider this last decision and asked him
to a private dinner so that they might try to find a common field to
remain together. Their search was a failure. Once more Freud begged
Adler to reconsider their parting: 'Why should I always do my work
under your shadow?' Adler demanded. Those who reproach Adler, as
if this were the petulant cry of an ambitious student, should remember that Adler was now in his late thirties, a man of approved
genius whose book, on *Organic Inferiority and Its Psychical Compensation*, ranked with Freud's *Dream Analysis*.

Adler frequently explained in after life that these words: 'Why should I always do my work under your shadow?' were greatly misinterpreted by the psycho-analysts.

What Adler really meant was that he feared to be made responsible for the Freudian theories in which he more and more disbelieved, while his own work was either misinterpreted by Freud and his followers or pushed to one side. With every year that Adler worked with Freud, his doubts grew stronger, until he came to believe that the whole process of psycho-analysis was inimical to the welfare of mankind. This was the 'shadow' under which he would not work because he dared not be made responsible for what he feared might be the results of Freud's thoughts upon mankind. Who shall say that he was mistaken while we are watching to-day the effects of a freed *libido* upon the civilized world?

It was Freud who pleaded for Adler's continuing with him, but it was Adler who had to make the greater sacrifice in order to leave him. There were three meetings of the group for a full discussion of their differences, and then the question was put to the vote: were Adler's views compatible with his remaining in the psycho-analyst group—or not? Adler was out-voted, the majority of fourteen remained with Freud and flourished under his increasing discipline; but Adler, the heretic, left—taking nine like-minded heretics with him.

Adler had to begin his life work over again on a much slenderer financial basis, with a growing family.

One more effort was made to heal the breach. Freud went to meet Adler and those who had followed him, to discuss if they could not at least agree that members of each group should be free to attend the other. But this too was found to be impossible; and the two men, who between them have done most to influence the thought-life of their time, parted to meet no more.

Adler showed at first the most forbearance. It was not until the publication of *The History of Psycho-Analysis*, in which Freud wrote his almost scurrilous attack upon his former colleague, that Adler allowed himself to speak in public against Freud. Even then, Adler never failed to do justice to Freud's contributions to thought; he encouraged his followers to read Freud's books and to attend his lectures, whereas Freud, true to his authoritarian nature, issued a fiat forbidding his pupils to attend the lectures of Adler. Neurosis was to Freud the starting point, the 'mother' and the aim of his psychology. The 'whole' man, and his development towards social interest, was the goal of Adler's psychology; and all his discoveries supported it.

ADLER AND THE FREUDIAN CIRCLE

It would perhaps have been better if Adler could have restricted himself to scientific criticism of Freud's theories; but it was impossible for Adler, with his belief in the 'wholeness' of man, to divorce Freud's ideas from his personality. Freud's famous question, 'Why should I love my neighbour?' (see *Civilization and Its Discontents*), seemed to Adler to be the cry of a pampered child, a true wrecker's remark, impervious to our individual responsibility for the moral development of mankind. Adler did not hesitate to combat this tendency of Freud's which he believed would set back moral evolution; and his sharp criticisms drew down upon his own head vials of wrath from all Freud's disciples.

These attacks followed Adler to his grave, and after. Perhaps even more after, since while he lived Adler's powers of retaliation were such that few chose to challenge him in public, whatever they felt free to say of him when they were safely beyond his reach. This malicious back-chat of followers and disciples, even the smarting unwisdom of the two great antagonists themselves, must eventually die down and leave serene the memory of these two great men— alike high-minded, courageous and benevolent—working together with a common aim—to bring the light of knowledge to mankind.

VII

Development of Individual Psychology

The year 1910 was Adler's launch into freedom. The work of his mind was his own and could freely bear his name.

He now gave up his general practice to devote himself entirely to psychiatry; and the whole household moved from Czerningasse to a roomy flat in the heart of the city close to the old University, No. 10 Dominikanerbastei.

Adler loved this spot best in Vienna. The Dominikanerbastei was once manned against the Turks, and had held the city—with its freedom and its learning—safe from barbaric hordes.

No one who before the 11th March 1938, strolled through those courtyards and sheltered alleys, under trellis-covered cafés, will ever forget its freedom and light-heartedness. Here on long summer evenings, hatless, coatless people sat in old doorways, or in the open-air cafés, greeting each other with kindly eyes. Tourists passed through these alleys sometimes but did not linger. There was no traffic and the rich never entered them.

The very houses leaned forward as if to greet each other; the wind of time had shifted the crooked roofs; forgotten trees bloomed in the corners of cobble-stoned courtyards. Here and there through a break in the houses flashed the shining roof of the Stephansdom.

Medieval signs still swung in front of tradesmen's shops, an Eye of God above a chemist's, or a cheerful reminder of the Holy Ghost. Many of these old doorways were graced by a statue of Saint Florian flaunting his rickety watering-can in one hand, apparently sure that its playful trickle was enough to deal with the sheeted flame attacking his toy church in the other. Lamps still burned before age-old madonnas in dark stone niches.

The old University, opposite the post-office, had long been out of use, but its ghosts still seemed a part of the moonlight lingering upon its cobbled square and in the shelter of its ancient walls.

Close by the University, Adler's new school of psychology was founded, calling itself, in token of its new liberty, 'The Free Psychoanalysts'.

The next three years were years of great liveliness and expansion. The rooms in No. 10 Dominikanerbastei that had seemed so opulently spacious at first, became more and more crowded out by the rapidly expanding circle.

Adler had, since 1907, arrived at the opinion that the process of human thought was not basically causal, but teleological. Laws governing the inanimate did not exclusively control what has in itself the power of movement. The belief that behind the regular laws of causality lurked the greater influence of an aim or goal now took final possession of Adler.

As Einstein had discovered the element of uncertainty in the courses of the stars, so Adler too in his studies upon the mind of man came upon this variable element in human beings, an element that defied any materialistic conception.

Adler and Neuer used to argue these questions, in the Café Central, from eight o'clock in the evening until four in the morning, when, still arguing, they would walk back together through the silent alleys, to the perhaps legitimately exasperated Raissa.

Adler was never satisfied with the limits of his profession as a doctor. 'Sickness and health in the body are natural processes,' Adler explained, 'but sickness in the soul is cowardice—courage is the health of the soul.'

When a patient came to see him, Adler did not ask himself 'How ill is he?' but always 'How much in him is still healthy?' since he believed that the basis of the cure would be the man's power of resistance rather than the power of the illness itself. 'There is a logic from the head,' Adler told Neuer; 'there is also a logic from the heart; and there is an even deeper logic from the whole.'

Adler's theory against the decisive power of heredity has always been the cause of much misconception, some of it wilful, so that Neuer's evidence upon this point is particularly valuable.

'Adler', Neuer says, 'always believed in physical heredity; but not in the heredity of the psychic factor.'

Adler admitted that a child born with the same organic defect as a parent might even use it psychologically in the same manner, but only by observing and adopting for purposes of its own the parent's aim; the child was not in any way *forced* to adopt this particular aim, *because* of the inherited organic defect.

This could be proved by observation upon children whose organic defects were inherited from the parent, but who developed psychic aims of quite a different kind. Some children with a similar but even more pronounced organic defect than the parent might altogether ignore or overcome it psychologically, while others reacted to it in quite different ways; only a few, and those most attached and consequently most able to observe and copy the parent in question, developed the same psychological handling of the situation, and then they usually exaggerated the symptoms, so as to go one better than the parent.

A girl came once to consult Adler, with a rash all over her arms and shoulders, which she explained was caused by her eating certain vegetables. Her mother, she added, always suffered from the same rash whenever she touched these particular vegetables. Adler saw the mother alone, after seeing the child, and asked if this were a fact. The mother agreed that the daughter had told the exact truth. 'But,' she said, 'the queer thing is that she isn't my child at all! I don't want her ever to know it—but she is the illegitimate daughter of my greatest friend. I adopted her from her birth, because I was married and my friend was not, and my husband and I agreed to bring her up as our own. We have never had any other children, and she has no idea that we are not her actual parents!'

Adler, who loved Shakespeare more than any other writer, was fond of quoting in support of his theory Richard the Third's speech: 'And therefore, since I cannot prove a lover, to entertain these fair well-spoken days, I am determined to prove a villain.' 'Yet,' Adler would conclude with a twinkle, 'I have known very good hunchbacks.'

Adler's new circle devoted themselves to studying and discussing the teleological principle, as well as the free unmasking of psychoanalysis itself, which Freud had denied them. Many of them still held with, and needed time to reconsider, Freud's earlier discoveries.

Adler, who had joined the psycho-analysts in 1900, when they were still working upon Freud's shock-effects theory, never wholly repudiated their earlier conclusions, although he had not agreed at any time to an invariable sexual cause for these shocks.

Freud's *Mechanismus Hysterischer Phänomene*, written with Breuer, had come out in 1894, and with much of it Adler remained in agreement; but his experience with children who had been subjected to sexual shocks had led Adler to believe that whether they had permanent shock effects or not depended entirely upon the individual courage and common sense of the child itself. A courageous, well-balanced child did not suffer at all in after-life from such an experience.

Frank of Zurich built a whole school upon Freud's shock theories, or rather upon Freud's development of Breuer's theory. This school taught that a neurosis is caused by a shock received in youth, which can be brought to the surface under hypnosis. It was not until 1910 that Freud attributed such shocks invariably to sexual causes.

Adler, Stekel and Jung all reacted against this development of the original theory, although they reacted against it upon different grounds. Adler's objection was upon teleological grounds. 'Neurosis', he said, 'is the exploitation of shock,' i.e. the alibi, as it were, of the human being who uses this shock as an excuse for evading one or other, or in extreme cases *all*, of a normal person's responsibilities.

'Anyone', Adler was fond of telling his patients, 'can have the difficulties you mention—in fact we all have them, or other kinds of difficulties just as hampering—but we need not attach such a serious meaning to them.'

'What would drive one man to suicide,' he often said, 'could be taken in the light of a joke by another man. You see, you have a large field of choice!'

Alexander Neuer, who from the point of view of a philosopher as well as of a physician watched these two Viennese schools of thought in their separation from each other with great interest and acumen, used an interesting historic parallel to explain their differences.

'Freud and Adler', Neuer said, 'in their histories were very like Stalin and Trotsky. Adler like Trotsky broke away from the parent stem, ruled over by Freud, who attacked him as promptly as Stalin attacked Trotsky; after attacking Trotsky, Stalin took his theory of world conversion—which was the very core of their difference—away from him; and then produced it as his own doctrine. Freud did substantially the same thing with Adler. He first demanded that Adler should give up his "aggressive drive" theory, and then incorporated it, as part of his "free association" theory. When Adler developed his "masculine protest" theory of 1910, Freud promptly countered it with a "castration complex". When Adler in 1916 asserted that the "hidden law" behind the human mind was *Gemeinschaftsgefühl* (Social Interest)—which man must learn to obey or perish—Freud first scoffed at it with his famous "Why should I love my neighbour?" and later developed something suspiciously like it in the *Ego and the Id*. It was no wonder that Adler used to quote Nestroy with a sly twinkle: "I have taken a prisoner—and he will not let me go!" '

In 1911 the group of Free Analysts accepted as proved to their satisfaction Adler's theory of teleological control and decided to call themselves by the name of his science, 'Individual Psychology'; only the Grüner brothers and Geiringer dissented and withdrew from the group. Neuer's brilliant but devastating lecture on 'The Eggshell' was probably responsible for this withdrawal.

This lecture was a sharp attack upon the materialism and positivism founded by Locke and spread by Voltaire over all Europe; indeed it was a revolt against any materialistic or mechanistic interpretation of psychology, and had the strong support from Adler and the rest of the circle. 'Mysticism is any science,' Adler used to say, 'that scientists do not understand.'

In 1894, the same year as Freud's *Mechanismus Hysterischer Phänomene*, Dilthey wrote a pamphlet, *Ideen über eine beschreibende und zergliedernde Psychologie*, an interesting contribution to psychology which had something in common with Adler's ideas. Dilthey believed that there were two kinds of psychology: the psychology of description and the psychology of understanding. Dilthey's pamphlet was not for a long time recognized outside Germany or even outside his own province, and he and Adler never came into contact with each other's work. However, at a much later date, after Individual Psychology had already defined itself, Spranger wrote a book largely founded upon Dilthey's pamphlet, *Lebensformen*, with which Adler found himself very much in sympathy. Both Dilthey and Spranger gave some support to Adler's theory of *Ganzheit* or 'wholeness', but theirs was a psychology of work, not as Adler's was, a psychology of personality.

In reality, Smuts of South Africa almost simultaneously with Adler worked out a far more similar theory to Adler's Individual Psychology in his book *Holism and Evolution*.

J. C. Smuts has very kindly sent me copies of the full correspondence between his father and Adler, which is now kept in charge of the Librarian in the Cape Town University archives dealing with General the Right Hon. J. C. Smuts's correspondence.

I do not publish the letters in full, since they largely deal with Adler's offers to make arrangements for translating *Holism and Evolution* into German, and finding a suitable publisher; but perhaps the following extracts have interest, since they show the similarity of their philosophies, arrived at independently of each other's knowledge.

DEVELOPMENT OF INDIVIDUAL PSYCHOLOGY

From Adler to Smuts. Vienna, January 31st 1931:

'Dear Sir;

Reading your book *Holism and Evolution*, I felt very much moved by all your explanations. I could see very clearly what had been the key of our science. Besides the great value of your contributions in many other directions, I recognized the view in regard to what we have called "unity" and "coherence". I feel very *glad* to recommend your book to all my students and followers as the best preparation for Individual Psychology.'

Adler then offered to have Smuts's book translated by either of his friends, Professor D. Oppenheim or Professor G. E. Kransz, and to seek a suitable German publisher after the book had been translated.

Adler then sent Smuts an article on the basis of Individual Psychology, to which Smuts replied: 'Your paper has reached me, and I have found it most valuable and interesting. I can quite well see how our two points of view are connected and mutually support each other.'

Since then, Lincoln Barnett's brilliant book *The Universe and Dr. Einstein* , explaining Einstein's 'Unified Field' theory, could well be used in support of the theories of these two philosophers. Freud belonged to the materialistic school of causal absolutism, while Adler moved forward into the open and changing universe of Einstein and the Twentieth Century physicists.

A friendly correspondence took place between Smuts and Adler upon their kindred theories, which is quoted in Sarah Millin's *Life of General Smuts*.

It was from his belief in the indivisibility of personality that Adler came upon the title 'Individual Psychology' for his science.

'You must not divide the individual,' he was fond of saying.

Often the mothers of his child patients would say to him, when he asked about the child's dreams: 'But what he dreams—that's just nonsense, isn't it, Herr Doktor?' 'But is it not your child that dreams,' Adler would reply, 'and are not his dreams a part of him?'

Pavloff in Russia and Watson in America both accepted the idea of 'wholeness' but theirs was the more materialistic 'wholeness of the situation' whereas Adler's belief was in the 'wholeness of the personality', as it were, the inner spirit in man, animating alike and necessarily alike, body, mind and soul.

That this spirit in man could be in touch and be reinforced by being in touch, with the spirit of Life itself, was an active belief of

Adler's. 'I am in a world full of difficulties,' he used to say, 'and my difficulties belong to me. Why should I quarrel with them?'

This belief in Life as a beneficent colleague was no doubt the ground of Adler's heroic optimism, and gave him the extraordinary ease and strength which characterized him.

One of the most convinced and sincere of Adler's disciples also showed a perfect example of this inner law. When smitten with a most cruel form of cancer, she worked up to the last possible moment with an undimmed courage and serenity. 'I believe that pain belongs to this illness,' she said to a friend who was distressed by her suffering, and in overcoming all resistance to her pain, she seemed as it were to surmount the illness itself; and died undemoralized, after the shortest possible period of inaction, her spirit exquisitely cheerful to the last.

Adler used to tell a story that showed the opposite side of this picture—the punishment given by Life itself to those who sin against the law of social interest.

There was a foreman in a factory who persecuted a beautiful young girl engaged to a fellow-worker. Both of them were under his control, and he threatened to dismiss them if the girl would not yield to his passion. It was a time of great depression and other work was unobtainable. The girl was in despair; and she told her comrades in the workshop of her dilemma. None of them dared attack the foreman, but the girl was deservedly popular and the anger of her comrades was intense; when the foreman entered the room, all turned their eyes away from him, and answered him only in monosyllables. He went out to get his dinner, and in crossing the street was run over and killed.

'He had sinned against the spirit of his community,' Adler explained, 'and this confused him so, that he could not take common-sense precautions—people with a bad conscience often have accidents happen to them. Life itself is against them.'

VIII

Adler's Children and their Training

T he family of a psychologist, as well as the family of a clergyman, is always looked on with suspicion. If the proof of the
pudding is in the eating, as Adler would be the first to admit,
so the proof of the value of a great educationalist is what he has been
able to do with his own children.

It should be remembered, however, that psychologists do not
spring fully fledged from the moment of paternity. Adler learned
much from his own children; and until he had learned it, they were
without the benefit of his knowledge.

There are besides at least two other concessions which ferocious
critics of psychologists' families should allow their victims: one is that
a father must always take second place in the education of his children,
since the first co-operation that takes place must be between mother
and child; consequently the mother's influence for the character-form-
ing years is usually predominant; and second that a doctor such as
Adler, who often worked sixteen hours a day, has not much time to
spare, whatever part his feelings may play, in helping to form the
habits of his children. In spite of these handicaps, it was astonishing
how greatly Adler managed to enrich and assist his children's lives.

At the time when the Adlers changed their home to the Dominikanerbastei, the family was already complete. Nelly, the youngest
member, was two years old, and had no supplanter; Valentine and
Alexandra (known as Vali and Ali), the two eldest, were their father's
constant companions whenever possible; they accompanied him on
his holidays and excursions from their earliest years, with only this
condition, that they must be prepared to dress and undress themselves.

As they grew older they both became good musicians, and Adler
sang to their accompaniments and took great delight and pride in
the family musical performances. Kurt, the only boy, was adored and

86

perhaps spoiled by both father and mother alike; but Adler had a special confidence and comradeship with his son, who lived to justify the faith his father had in him, and has become a distinguished and loved psychiatrist.

Each of the four children had his or her special relationship with their father. He was not only their unwavering rock of defence, he was their best and most enriching playfellow. One of Adler's severest critics, who was in touch with the ménage from its earliest days, said: 'I can only say that as a father—whatever his faults may have been in other directions, and you know that I believe that he *had* these faults—Adler was nothing short of *perfect*. I had reason to know, for I saw the children almost daily over a space of years, and taught the youngest.'

But it was upon Raissa that the full burden of bringing up four extremely healthy and lively children, without punishment or spoiling, chiefly fell. Fortunately Raissa was also a rock—what she thought right to do, she did, cost her what it might. She gave her children, especially the two elder, that complete freedom from interference and that training in self-reliance in which both parents equally believed.

Vali and Ali had as much to thank Raissa for, in her stoic withdrawals, as they had to thank their father for in his wisdom and invisible guidance.

The two younger children, Kurt, the only boy, and Nelly, a most attractive and beguiling 'youngest', suffered from their position in the family, as well no doubt as from the fact that their father had not the time to put at their disposal that he had had for the two elder.

Kurt must have suffered severely from his two elder sisters, both highly developed and courageous girls, as well as from Nelly the youngest, who had all the importance of being the wind-up of the family.

Nelly too was the cook Sophie's favourite; and this can have been of no great advantage to her, since Sophie was the type of woman out of whom spoiling comes as inevitably as milk from a cow. Her description of the four children and their father is as follows: 'Each of the Herr Doktor's children thought he belonged to them most! It was hard to say which of the children I myself liked best, for I too loved them all and each differently. But the eldest everybody loved; the second girl Ali was the kind of friend—once she *was* your friend— you could always rely on. That one never forgot! The boy Kurt sometimes gave us sorrow, he worked badly at school—and this specially hurt his father—but we loved him—his father could not pass him in the room without stroking his head. They were all of them the sort of children you couldn't put out of your heart, and they too had hearts—that one could say for them. But perhaps I loved Nelly—the little naughty one—the best of the lot. She had such pretty ways!'

One day Kurt and Nelly had a fight. Nelly was sure that on this occasion at least she was wholly in the right, but wanted her father's immediate ratification of her virtue. Although she knew that he was seeing a patient and must never at these times be disturbed, she rushed to his door and knocked. Receiving no answer, she threw herself on the floor and kicked at the door with both feet. Adler appeared, looked down at her without speaking; then picked her up and solemnly carried her to the furthest room of the big flat, put her down on the floor, and said: 'Stay there until my patient has gone. I will then come back and hear what you have to say.'

Nelly says that before he came back, she had realized that her anger with Kurt was perhaps exaggerated, and an insufficient excuse for interrupting her father's work. When her father returned, he asked: 'Have you anything to say to me that matters?' and she found herself saying, 'No, I don't think I have!'

It is probable that Raissa's stoicism and patience may have broken down a little over the upbringing of her two youngest. She was more unhappy at this period of her life than perhaps she had ever been, or would ever be again. For she knew now that she must face essential loneliness. Her husband was swallowed up in his work, nor was she able to follow him as she had once hoped to follow him, through all his developments. Other people were the material of his work. Doctors' wives have always a difficult part to play, and the wives of psychiatrists an even more difficult part. It is not necessary that psychiatrists should have love-affairs with their patients; it would often be astonishing if they should wish to, since neurotic types are not attractive except to themselves and, for short periods, to each other; but there is an intimacy that involves time and attention, between such patients and a healer of souls who is bound to do his work in privacy, and must use more wisdom and discretion than perhaps he would be called upon to use in any other profession.

Raissa had no real sphere to take the place of the one she had meant to fill. She had practically given up her two elder children to their father, and it is not surprising if she failed to instil as much strength and independence into the two younger. It was in the first instance Adler's psychology that took him away from Raissa; she probably never said to herself that if their two children were spoiled a little, psychology would suffer; nevertheless psychology was one of her enemies, although her dauntless courage and stubborn truthfulness made her, in the end, its friend. Certainly Kurt and Nelly both had difficulties, and both continued to have them through childhood and adolescence.

Their two elder sisters perhaps seemed to them to block the path to all mental or moral advancement. How could they compete with such energetically successful Family Flowers?

Vali, the eldest sister, was almost extravagantly good, while Ali the second was extravagantly naughty; but no one could doubt the efficiency of her wits. Ali, fortunately, had more strength than envy in her, and used her striving against her elder sister in a most useful manner as part of her education. She was a brilliant scholar, and Professor Pötzl of the Viennese University told the writer, 'I have had many talented pupils in my classes and still more pupils who excelled through hard work; but only one genius—Alexandra Adler. There is no doubt whatever in my mind that Ali Adler is a creative genius of the first order!' As Professor Pötzl was, to say the least of it, a not unhostile critic of Alfred Adler's, his recognition of Alexandra's abilities suggests that they were of a most exceptional kind. She too, like Adler himself, had had an early difficulty with mathematics, and once returned from school greatly distressed, saying to her father: 'My teacher says that I am a fool about mathematics and that I shall never be able to understand them.' 'And do you believe everything your teacher tells you?' Adler demanded. 'What makes you suppose that she is right?' This question completely altered Ali's attitude, she says that she never again accepted anyone's opinion as to her own or other people's limitations; and from that time forward became a highly successful mathematician.

She also tells another story of herself and her relation to her father. Once on a holiday, the two little girls and their father arrived in a hotel where they were given one big room with three beds in it, a high one in the middle, and two low ones on each side of it. Ali had a sudden overwhelming longing to sleep in the high bed, and see the other two reduced to low ones. 'Father,' she asked anxiously, 'may I sleep in the middle bed?'

'Certainly,' Adler told her, 'choose which you like!'

Ali's ecstasy was complete, but after they were all three in bed, she had an uncomfortable feeling that perhaps, after all, her big father would have been more comfortable in the higher bed.

Alexandra was a perfect example of what right education can do for a child in a difficult situation, in order to produce courage and social interest.

Alexandra's elder sister was so much and so deservedly loved and admired that her advancing second must have felt she had no worlds left to conquer, and had better press all her activities upon the anti-social side of life; but as against this very natural idea, Ali found so much love, freedom and understanding at her disposal that she was enabled to turn all her strength and energy into useful channels. Instead of becoming the really difficult being her early childhood promised, she took the exactly opposite creative path and became an asset of the highest value, a help and inspiration to all those privileged to know her.

That Kurt should have been a little daunted by all these mental and moral fireworks in his elder sisters was, according to his father's theories on 'family constellation', only to be expected. He had a hard row to hoe, even without the spoilt baby, Nelly, snatching at his laurels by the mere act of birth, and retaining them for purposes of her own well on into later life.

There were psychological rocks all round these two youngest, and they both at times came sharply into contact with them. Their adolescence was stormy, and there must have been moments when both their parents actually wondered what it was they had done, to present themselves with such insoluble problems.

Adler's theory of the inequalities, dangers, and trials of the 'family constellation' were proved to him over and over again in his own heart, and through his own children. He may indeed have been said to have beaten out this important theory upon the anvil of his own family life. Subject to the same heredity, and brought up in the same environment, each of his four children took their own tempestuous, creative way. Two things only bound them together, and two things were common to them all alike: they had the same material to build from—the strength and alas! the disunity of their parents.

Each child used this material to suit his or her own creative purposes; but while the two elder were born at a time of serenity and joy, having the easy atmosphere of happy love for their soul's climate, the two younger had to meet the stormy blasts of conflict and weather them as best they might. No one has yet been able to fathom how deep is the influence upon a child's heart between the happy or the unhappy marriage of its parents; but no one can deny that the effect *is* deep, and fraught with all manner of consequences to the child's development.

Kurt, after a prolonged and troubled adolescence, continued into early manhood, matured favourably and developed great balance and geniality, with a deep understanding of human nature. He took his medical degree at the Long Island University of Medicine, after his father's death, and after serving as psychiatrist in the American forces, became a well-known and highly popular practitioner.

Nelly made a conspicuously successful start as an actress upon the Viennese stage, some of the best critics of drama declaring that she was as fine an actress as her contemporary, Paula Wesseli. Unfortunately Nelly broke off her profession for an early marriage, and her life was further uprooted and disintegrated by the German occupation of Vienna. She is, however, still young, and may take fresh root in America, with a greater freedom to develop her undoubted powers. She has since made a second, and successful marriage.

Vali, the eldest, became a doctor in economics and a social scientist; but after her marriage, to the lasting sorrow of her family, she was imprisoned as a hostage for her Russian husband for ten years, dying subsequently, still in prison, long after her release was announced by the Russian Government. Everything possible was done by the American authorities to free Adler's daughter and to effect her return to her family, who had all become American citizens —but without success. Adler used to call Vali 'the most intimate of his children'; the sense of her suffering and privations no doubt hastened her father's death. The following letters will give an idea of the relationship between them.

Birthday letter to a daughter.

No date.

My sweet good little Vali [Walerl]

You know already that you are a big girl and have a pretty good idea of what life is like. Perhaps, however, there is one thing that you don't know yet—or, to put it more clearly, that you do not think about—as many others do not think about what they already know! Once it was the same with me, and perhaps I came to this knowledge a little too late.

It is really a very simple thing to understand. Life is full of difficulties that keep turning up, so that, looking at existence from one of its many aspects, it looks as if we were fighting continually against

91

difficulties and obstacles. Seen from another aspect, life appears differently again—as if one person were always lucky and another person always unlucky. However, this luck depends chiefly upon the view that we ourselves adopt; and always depends upon the goal which we have set before us. If this goal is too high, perhaps even unobtainable, then naturally there are constant setbacks and disappointments. It is the misfortune of such people that very often they don't know even of the existence of this over-strained goal. If you watch them, however, you can guess it very easily from their always being discontented and ill-humoured.

Things *can*, however, become easier for them if they understand the connection; and when they are able to recognize that there is only one thing lacking in order to be happy and cheerful, and that is to stop taking their former goal too seriously. The difficulties of life which still remain have a definite value and serve to prove our mettle by the way in which we overcome them; or, if they cannot *be* overcome—learn how to put up with them.

I once knew a boy belonging to a very rich family, who wanted to live the life of a lotus-eater, in this busy world. He did what he could to accomplish this aim—by doing nothing; and the members of his family came to his assistance by eagerly sparing him every difficulty that came his way. The results were lamentable. His powers remained unused, he was extremely backward for his age, he did not feel at home anywhere, and everybody laughed at him.

Instead of looking for the cause of his failure in his own conduct and trying to alter it, he looked for it in other people, so that he grew suspicious, envious, timid and unsociable—all in order to prove to himself that he was in the right (as he had always been) and would not, therefore, have to give up his mistaken attitude.

In some ways all of us are like this boy. All of us—men as well as women—like putting the blame for our mistakes on others or upon adverse circumstances—i.e. facts which cannot be changed—and we only remember with reluctance that worries and difficulties exist for everyone, and that they only allow of one solution—that we strengthen ourselves by overcoming them—and by not being afraid of them, even if they *are* unalterable.

I have learned to look at life like this; perhaps you also have reached the same standpoint! If you have not, try just for once to look at your life from this vantage point. It is, I think, the best thing that I possess, and, therefore, the best present that I can give to you for your birthday, my dear little Vali.

I wrote to you once years ago (unfortunately, I am so seldom with you on your birthday!) that you had only brought me joy; that you have always been with me in spirit; and have never caused me one moment's anxiety. If it gives you pleasure to know this, let me tell you that I can repeat it to-day—as always in the past. This day, too, I am with you in spirit, and live in your happiness.

Your loving old father greets and kisses you.

The first letter was written to Vali on her eleventh birthday, the second on her successful graduation from the University.

Krakau, d 6. VII, 1917.

Your telegram reached me at the hotel yesterday evening. How I wish I could have been with you, laughed and sung with you, and helped you make jolly plans for the summer and for the more distant future.

But we'll make up for it—sometime—somehow!

Now you are entirely free and you must build up your own life in your own way.

There are no more special rules and regulations to restrict you, and there are many paths that are worth while for you to follow.

It is not, you know, ever a question of what you choose to do, but how you do what you have chosen, and the level that you have set yourself to reach. Up to now you have only had to deal with the everyday difficulties and demands of life, such as would scarcely bother you unless you allowed yourself to be frightened by prejudice or superstition. Now you have to deal with the demands of your own ideals, which you must not misuse by turning them into excuses and pretexts in order to evade realities.

If you want to know upon what you can pride yourself as really a part of you, setting to one side your knowledge and ability, you can say, looking back upon your life until now, that you have never done anyone any harm.

Try also to acquire a really good relationship with our dear Ali and with our boy, for you *can* do this.

Your very happy Papa sends you thousands of greetings and kisses.

Alexandra Adler followed her father to America, after taking a high medical degree as a neurologist in the Viennese University; only political pressure prevented her from greater honours, and a position of importance in her own city.

She practised successfully in Boston and was a Research Fellow of Harvard University for which she did some valuable work in the neurological department. For a year she became Professor of Neuropsychiatry at Duke University of Medicine in Durham, North Carolina; and is now practising as one of the leading psychiatrists of New York City.

It may well be said of the Adler family that their particular pudding *has* proved itself in the eating; and that the world has need of what Adler's children still have to contribute towards its knowledge and variety.

IX

Adler with his Patients

There were many famous names among Adler's patients, but as psychiatry is still so little understood as to be in the eyes of the general public an uncomfortable alternative to going mad, instead of the releasing and development of a human soul, few people would wish it to be known that they had ever resorted to Adler. Nor did Adler himself ever mention his patients' names, or any fact concerning them. The most famous and the humblest of his patients were equally sure of his discretion. It was a joke in the Adler family that if ever a 'friend' became a patient no fact even of the most innocuous nature concerning them could thereafter be extracted from Adler. When a member of his family once asked him about two people who had recently become his intimate friends, Adler replied: 'They have been my patients; I can therefore tell you no more about them than that I love them both.'

This was no peculiarity in Adler since all discreet psychiatrists act in the same way, but what was perhaps a peculiarity was the completeness with which this secrecy was maintained.

Nevertheless, it was of course impossible to deny the presence of famous film stars or other public characters in his consulting room; and in some cases these patients or their confidential friends gave a certain amount of information to the public.

Noel Coward, who never was a 'case' of Adler's, but who declared himself cured of a severe breakdown by reading one of Adler's books, writes of it with refreshing frankness in his autobiography.

A charming incident took place between Coward and Adler. When Adler came to England on a lecture tour, Coward put a box at the theatre at his disposal so that Adler could see the play *The Astonished Heart*, which Coward had written after his own clarification had taken place.

There was a moment in the play when the chief actor (Coward himself) looks into the glass at his changed face.

One of Adler's friends, who shared his box and was herself an actress, felt that Coward for a moment forgot his part and let slip the veil of anonymity that hid him from the audience. It was as if he remembered in that instant his own soul, and that its healer sat watching him. This revelation, if it ever took place, passed in an instant, but Adler too had suspected it. 'I think', he said, 'that he *may* have felt, for this one moment, "an old man sits there who knows what I am up to—" but he soon forgot, since he is a real artist!' Adler's psychological friends who were with him criticized the play adversely. One said, 'No man who had such a success in his profession and had a wife he loved, who was not only willing to forgive, but actually understood his infidelity, would have committed suicide because he didn't know whether his mistress were faithful to him or not! The hero, himself a psychiatrist, would have known that his mistress was a worthless type, and either put up with it, or given her up.'

'You are wrong,' Adler said. 'For one thing there are no "worthless" types; and for another, why he committed suicide was not because his mistress was unfaithful, but because he could not make up his mind whether she were faithful or not! It is an unsolved conflict that drives a man to suicide. The man's whole being was absorbed in this conflict—there was not enough of him outside it—for him even to remember that he had a wife or a work that he loved. Coward decided justly.'

One of Adler's most earnest and successful patients was a very famous actress and film star of our day. She declared that Adler had set her free from a difficulty that threatened her whole career. A male film star of equal renown could for a time neither speak nor write, till Adler restored his powers. Many writers, musicians and artists profited in varying degrees by Adler's training.

'Artists,' Adler once said, 'if they are genuine, make good patients since there is in all of them an objective point—their art! They cannot be wholly egocentric, but many of them are very much spoilt or discouraged, so that they badly need re-training.' Adler believed that the three main tasks in life are: social contact, work, love or marriage. 'The fourth life task', he once added, 'is art.'

Adler once visited Nijinsky by request, after his mental illness had lasted many years. Adler made such an instant impression upon Nijinsky that his caretakers begged Adler to take over his case. For the first time in many years, Adler succeeded in getting into real contact with Nijinsky and even made him laugh; but Adler could not follow up the treatment, since he foresaw then it would take at least two years' constant work, and that he must have Nijinsky under his own roof. 'Still,' Adler added regretfully, 'if I had had time enough, I think I could have helped him.'

Adler once explained to a questioner that the chief difference between a psychotic and a neurotic is that while a neurotic builds up an unreal world to live in, he can live in it or not as he chooses, and he more than suspects its unreality; whereas a psychotic is *compelled* to live in his unreal world, while he has ceased to doubt that it is unreal.

'I always feel a cold sensation at the base of my spine,' Adler used to say, 'when I find myself in the same room as a psychotic. He is a man who has cut himself off from the rest of mankind.'

Adler did not believe that the psycho-therapy in treating a psychotic was different in kind—but merely in degree—from that of the treatment of a neurotic; but in his opinion the treatment of a psychotic is always a far longer and slower business, with far more likelihood of serious relapses. He thought that a neurotic patient, once he had made a step forward, usually improved upon it, since he was returning to a freer life, which he had never wholly given up; but that a psychotic if he again found life too hard for him would find his way back into complete irresponsibility much more quickly, and with less resistance from his self-respect, since he had already gone the whole way into this escape from reality.

'Still,' Adler concluded, 'there can be a complete cure of any case that is not inaccessible. Paranoiacs in their later stages, especially if their breakdown comes at an advanced age, cannot be approached successfully by psycho-therapy, but with young paranoiacs in early stages of the disease, I have known lasting cures. But paranoiacs are very deceptive patients; for they go on very well for a while, until they have succeeded in binding their healer himself into the iron web of their suspicion; and then he can do no more for them.'

Adler once had a very interesting artist patient, a young man who was determined to use a fear of syphilis as an obstacle to a normal married life. He was engaged to be married and declared that the fear of this disease was driving him to suicide. He went from doctor to doctor, through the great city in which he lived, trying to find one that would admit his symptoms to be those of syphilis. Each doctor in turn made a thorough examination of him and came to the conclusion that he did not have the disease. But the young man argued that some early cases cannot be easily 'spotted' and that his belonged to this evasive category. He had made a study of all the possible symptoms of any case that had defied investigation in its earlier stages, and triumphantly produced them. Finally he came to Adler, who also went through the usual tests, and satisfied himself that the young man had not got the disease. When the examination was over, the patient demanded: 'Well, Dr. Adler, what is your opinion?'

'I think', said Adler, 'that you are wholly right! You have got syphilis, and should on no account marry. I should advise you to break off your engagement—at least for the present.' The young man was horrified and instantly began to challenge Adler's verdict, quoting all the denials of the other famous doctors. Adler countered him with his own evidence of doubtful cases in their earlier stages. The young man went away much shocked and chagrined at this actual justification of his wildest imaginings.

He was, however, as Adler well knew, an extremely intelligent young man, and after a few hours of cogitation he realized that Adler had seen through him; and he, in turn, saw through himself. He never again made a claim upon this disease; but returning to Adler, worked with him satisfactorily until his fear of women and marriage had been overcome. 'It would not have been enough', Adler said, 'to cure his symptom and release him of that particular alibi, since he would only have produced another, but by waking up his courage and by giving him faith in his own manhood, a cure was not difficult with so intelligent a fellow!'

Adler never denied his patients' difficulties, he merely showed them where their exaggeration of their difficulties lay, and how to tackle whatever was the real obstacle in a sensible manner. 'You cannot alter facts,' he said to one of his patients, 'but you can alter your way of looking at them. I have found that there is always a less bitter way, if you look hard enough.'

'If I believed in a "possessive" psychology,' Adler often said, 'and that man is controlled by drives—glands, hereditary factors, etc.—I would give up psychology altogether, but I do not believe that these factors are in control. I believe that by changing our opinions of ourselves we can also change ourselves; so that I see no reason for giving up the struggle!'

To a patient who made excuses for not carrying out his treatment, Adler said: 'We are not curious as to your motives—a man can always find grounds for refusing to do his duty. I could probably find for you even better grounds than you have discovered for yourself. But what really interests us—and *is* our business to find out—is whether there has been a contribution or not!'

Adler always answered the questioner as well as the question. A patient of Adler's who suffered from nervous outbursts of temper once asked him, 'What is the real cause of ill-temper?' 'It may spring from many causes,' Adler answered him. 'It is, however, often a desire to be right too quickly, rising from an over-sensitive conscience.' On another occasion and in respect to another person's outbreaks of ill-temper, Adler said, 'You do not have to explode if you are not vain.'

Adler looked upon hate with all its forms of cruelty and persecution as a turning back into the isolation of a Death Wish. 'Cruelty', he once said, 'is the bridge to death.' Whereas human love in its widest sense has a creative force and actually helps to produce life.

He believed that dictators dig their own graves and carry the seeds of death about with them. 'I can be king of the world', Adler explained, 'only in a strait-jacket.'

It was perhaps not surprising that Adler had an almost incredible success with mental depressives, and saved many unhappy souls from misery and suicide. He was always careful to point out, however, that you could not be in any way sure of such successes, and that he himself had had two failures with this class of patient. In one case, the patient after Adler's treatment lived to do many useful years of work, but on a fresh difficulty arising in an unexpected quarter fell back into his former defeated state and committed suicide.

The other case came to Adler as a last resort, and only presented himself once, committing suicide the next day. 'I always know', Adler said, 'that if a case comes twice, there is a reasonable hope of cure, however advanced the symptoms—but if a patient comes only once, he does not intend to be cured, but merely to show me that he is stronger than I am. I am always very willing to grant this, since I believe that no one can save a person who is determined not to be saved!'

To another patient who, Adler knew, had sufficient courage to come out of his depression, Adler said, 'You must either take life and its consequences, or shoot yourself. There is no other way.' This patient promptly recovered. Adler was once sent for to see a depressive patient at Brno who was in a bad melancholic condition, after prolonged treatment by a psychiatrist who had finally thrown up the case. Adler found her in tears, and asked her the reason. She told him of her desertion by the psychiatrist to whom she was deeply attached. 'Tell me how he was trying to cure you,' Adler asked her.

'First of all,' she said, 'we were in the stage of exposition, and I industriously exposed my life story to him. Then he said we had reached the stage of opposition and I made a faithful opposition to him. Then he said we were in the stage of transference—and I made a faithful transference; and then we reached the stage of enlightenment, and I became faithfully enlightened. Then he said we were in the stage of friendship—and left me—and now he refuses to see me any more!'

'Don't *let* him see you any more!' Adler suggested; the lady promptly recovered.

If a patient could be induced to take a humorous view of his difficulties, Adler always took advantage of it; but he only used this method with people who were accessible to a humorous interpretation, and understood the underlying seriousness of their situation. Adler himself was never more serious than when his eyes began to twinkle. With highly sensitive and easily offended patients, Adler could be exquisitely gentle and tender. 'They are probably missing the warmth of their mother's love,' he would say, 'and I must for a while be a mother to them,' but with those who he felt needed a sharper treatment he could speak with a ruthless bluntness.

He was specially apt to do this with any class of patient who had great responsibilities, or power over others. He never, however, quenched the smoking flax. One highly sensitive and suffering patient came to him with a long history of failure. Whatever he had attempted, in his own eyes, had come to grief. 'Well,' Adler said, 'I can see how you feel about all these matters, but since these failures of yours are so invariable, could you not make a success out of them? A success is very important for you, I admit; then why not try to fail, since according to your own evidence, you would be almost certain to succeed in bringing it off?'

This patient, a man of great ability who had not sufficient confidence in himself, was much helped by this advice, and had sufficient humour to repeat it with relish. On another occasion a depressed patient complained to Adler of all the things that, owing to a defective education, he was unable to know—while others, with perhaps fewer natural abilities, could pose successfully as authorities upon these subjects. 'Do you notice that greengrocer's shop across the road?' Adler asked him. 'I believe that the greengrocer knows more about brussels sprouts than I do—yet you see that I remain perfectly calm!'

Another depressed type of patient who hid beneath apparent humility an exceedingly stubborn spirit, reacted on her second interview with Adler by a refusal to speak at all. Adler too remained perfectly silent. At the end of their agreed time, the patient suggested, half insolently and half apologetically, to pay for Adler's loss of time. 'On the contrary,' Adler replied, 'for the interview you will pay nothing at all. You have done nothing and neither have I—nothing therefore in the shape of money shall pass between us!' The patient returned the next day, having got rid of her resistance.

An extremely irritating and selfish patient had a habit of ringing Adler up at all hours of the night to ask him unimportant questions. On one occasion she rang him up at three o'clock in the morning to ask if oranges would be good for her, adding, 'I see it's very late, I'm afraid I must have disturbed you!' Adler, who well knew that her chief aim was to disturb others, instantly replied, 'Oh no! why should you think that? I was even expecting you to ring up, and had been sitting for the last half-hour close to the telephone!'

This was the last time the lady resorted to this trick.

Adler's treatment of children and their instant understanding of him were spectacular.

All Vienna loved to go to his open child clinics, and the Volksheim, where he held them, would be crowded out.

Once Adler was brought a child who he immediately saw was in a very low, discouraged state, and feeling almost overwhelmed by a passionate desire to shine. Adler promptly sat down on a step below the child so that he should feel himself to be the bigger and the more important person.

Adler once asked a very solitary, egocentric child, unable to make contacts with his fellows, what he liked to do best. 'Football!' the boy replied. 'Yes,' Adler said, 'I can understand that very well—there you are all alone in the goal—and that is what you always like best, isn't it?' The boy *was* a goal-keeper, although Adler had not been told this fact. He was followed by a boy who was a very passionate, irascible child, a torment to his family on account of his outbursts of fury. 'What is it that you like to do best?' Adler asked this child as well. Again 'Football' was the reply. Adler nodded. 'It's fine barging into other boys, isn't it?' he suggested.

Another boy was brought to him who was the despair of his teacher, as he was always drawing attention to himself by naughtiness and buffoonery, and upsetting the whole class.

Adler, after shaking hands cordially with this child, did not say anything to him, but when he saw that the child's eyes were fixed upon him, Adler rose very slowly on tiptoe as high as he could draw

101

himself up, and then sank slowly back. 'I am making myself bigger than I really am,' Adler explained. '*You* want to make yourself a little bit bigger than all the others, too, don't you? But there are other ways of doing it than by upsetting your class.'

Nothing more was said; the boy only *once* afterwards started to act like a clown and it was then only necessary for the teacher to stand on tiptoe for him to blush with shame, and the class was never again disturbed by his exhibitionism.

Adler always used to advise his doctors to use cautious terms in talking with their patients. 'Perhaps,' he said, he had always found a most useful and unprovocative word; and he often referred doctors and other psychiatrists to Benjamin Franklin's autobiography, where he explains his success in life to be due to his lack of expressed convictions.

One of Adler's most obstinate asthma cases once told him that he realized that his asthma was definitely better, but that he could not get over the insomnia that followed his last attack.

Adler said, 'I find that insomnia often takes place in asthma just before a final cure.' The patient, who was not anxious to be completely cured, promptly discovered that he could sleep perfectly.

Adler was always very particular never to disturb a patient's religion, or his philosophical creed, and most careful to tell his disciples never in any way to let their treatment interfere with a patient's beliefs. 'Instead,' he told them, 'you should show him where his personal life-style is obstructing or distorting his beliefs.'

A priest of the Catholic Church once came to Adler as a patient. 'Before I decide to have your treatment,' he told Adler, 'I must be assured that you will say nothing against my religion.' 'I think that I may safely assure you of that,' Adler replied quietly, and when the priest—after a successful cure—paid him a good-bye visit, he said, 'I want to tell you, Dr. Adler, that you have *more* than kept your promise about respecting my religion; in fact I have found you to be the most really religious person that I have ever met!'

Adler always tried to make his disciples and helpers act and think in a creative rather than in a formal or fixed way with their patients. 'Experience has an actual value,' he told them, 'but art penetrates further than experience.'

X

'Organ Jargon'

I n an article of Adler's called 'Physical Manifestations of Psychic
Disturbances' he gives a short account of what he used more
often to term 'Organ Jargon'.

'Some day,' he wrote, 'it will probably be proved that there is no
organ inferiority which does not respond to psychic influences and
does not speak the organ's language, a language conditioned by the
problems confronting the individual.

'This is important in regard to symptom selection and particularly in regard to what we still call hysteria, or functional neurosis.
It also justifies one of the basic tenets of Individual Psychology.

'When a transitory or permanent defect becomes apparent in an
organ, this organ should be scrupulously examined, so that it may be
determined in what way it is characteristic of the individual himself.

'It must always be remembered that the organic structure is a
unity; and that a shock in one sphere throws the whole body into
vibration.'

Dr. Arthur Holub of Vienna was a sincere and highly skilled Individual Psychologist, and particularly noted for his successful treatment of asthma.

He told the writer that except for short and single attacks of
asthma after some severe long illness, when the lung is in a leathery
and unreactive condition, he believed the basis of all asthma cases to
be psychological, and that therefore all chronic asthma cases could
only be cured permanently by psychiatric treatment.

He gave as illustration of his theory two severe and typical asthma
cases which he had permanently cured through Adlerian analysis.

One of these patients was a man of thirty, who was in a serious
condition from perpetual attacks. He had suffered increasingly from
these asthmatic attacks since he was two years old. He was a younger
brother employed by his elder brother in a furrier's business. It was

naturally supposed that the fur used was in itself bad for him, though it could *not* have been the cause of his trouble since the illness had started at two years of age. Every possible treatment had been tried on him, including that of injections made from the hair used in the fur itself. Holub soon found that it was not the fur but the elder brother who was the cause of the asthma. The man is now working for another furrier with no further asthmatic trouble. Nor had he any further attacks for over three years since Holub had last heard from him.

The second case was that of a young married woman, living with her mother-in-law, who had been taken alternately a thousand feet higher than her home; and then sent down a thousand feet lower, and had tried every known asthma cure in vain. Holub found that her mother-in-law lived under her roof and invariably accompanied her upon her useless excursions.

He ordered her to take a holiday without her mother-in-law, and no attacks took place; he was then able to prove to her and to her husband that it was the presence of the mother-in-law and not the altitude that affected her condition adversely. He set to work to cure both wife and mother-in-law of their psychological difficulties, and he was sufficiently successful to enable them to live under one roof without the wife's suffering from any further asthmatic attacks. Holub said, 'When a person is ill, the soul always needs curing as well as the body.'

It would not be true to say, as Groddeck did, that a sore throat is always caused by the desire of a person to hide, or to suppress any particular secret; yet it could quite often be found that a person suffering from chronic sore throats had a disposition to over-control his temper, or to secrete more of his personality than was good for him.

This 'Organ Jargon' is of course a pointer rather than a proof of the psychic factor in illness, but its practical use is far too often disregarded by able doctors who have had themselves no psychological training.

'Structural changes,' Adler writes, 'resulting from psychic irritation are seen particularly clearly in cases of scoliosis and flat-foot. Such cases as I have seen were predisposed to these troubles; they had not always had them, but began to be troubled at some definite time—usually when the patient lost his poise and self-confidence on being confronted by a difficult or painful situation. We have known now for twenty-five years that pains in the spine are more significant than appears at first glance. There are pains which become localized on the anterior wall of the chest and begin when the patient is in a depressed state. This symptom we find, for instance, among melancholics; but also among individuals who do not feel melancholy in spite of being set back by similar physical difficulties in their situation.

'Many glands can be affected by the psychic factor, including the liver, which responds differently in each individual case. There are some persons who, while one might expect the psychic irritation to induce anger, respond with attacks of pain in the liver area. It has been demonstrated that such irritation also causes a change in the bile outflow, and that it can affect the pancreas and the Islands of Langerhans.'

For instance, jaundice or other septic conditions may very well be caused by jealousy, envy or, as in the case of flyers, extreme physical fear; all these threats directly attack the security—psychic or physical —of the human being. 'Patients', Adler used to say, 'sometimes know more about their illness than doctors; for instance when they speak of certain trials as "making them sick" or say "I cannot stomach it", you will often find that they actually suffer from acute indigestion.'

Giddiness may no doubt arise from serious organic trouble, but it may also be caused by an inability to come to a decision upon some important subject. Constipation is often caused by tension and can frequently be found in over-controlled persons. Functional heart trouble is very often caused by disappointed love; lung illnesses by deep inner discouragement and a desire to escape the challenge of life. This may be the reason why so many lung cases are chiefly dangerous during the period immediately after or during adolescence when it becomes necessary for the individual to tackle the more serious problems of life for the first time. Sex troubles may be due to the organs themselves, but much more often from a failure to co-operate with the opposite sex on a friendly basis.

Adler says, 'The basis of all proper functions is a state of being properly integrated within the current of human evolution. Integrated society is a goal, something to which we must aspire.'

Dr. Alexandra Adler once made a highly interesting analysis of group accidents taken from a factory near Vienna, and it was difficult to resist the conclusion, after following this analysis, that the psychic factor was the cause of all these accidents. Later on she made, at the request of the Boston City Hospital's and Harvard Medical School's neurological departments (of both of which she was a member), an equally interesting analysis on the shock effects of patients badly burned in the disaster of the Cocoanut Grove fire; and again she proved conclusively from the analysis of forty-six of these patients how greatly the psychic factor in each case had influenced recovery.

As Adler used to say, 'There are few illnesses that do not have unnecessary symptoms.'

The writer once had to study the life of Olive Schreiner, who suffered increasingly from asthma. It was most interesting to observe that while the earlier attacks were inconsiderable and always cured by change of work or even by change of scene, the later much more serious attacks were never curable without prolonged absences from her husband, to whom she was ostensibly deeply attached. Neither climate nor change of occupation influenced these later illnesses, but a flight from an association in which she felt herself hampered or worsted was invariably beneficial.

Dr. Lomax, the American specialist on epilepsy, told the writer that his own theories upon the cause and cure of this most mysterious illness had been logically justified, and complete light thrown upon them, by the findings of Individual Psychology.

'I had come independently to the same conclusions as Dr. Adler,' he told me, 'but it was not until I came to know him personally that I was able to clarify my findings. The point that fully convinced me of the psychic origin of epilepsy,' he went on, 'is that while all the usual factors in epilepsy and even the typical nerve reactions are found in certain cases, it does not necessarily follow that such a person has fits! For instance, I knew an old gentleman of eighty who had the correct head formation and every single confirmatory symptom of epilepsy; but he died without ever having had an attack.'

My husband and I once had a young boy under our roof for over a year suffering from very frequent and alarming attacks of epilepsy. Two European and two London specialists had diagnosed true epilepsy in this case; but we observed for ourselves that these attacks always followed any crossing of his very strong will, or any reflection upon his high self-valuation. If he considered that his personal prestige was at stake and might be worsted, an attack invariably supervened. He was later on cured by Adler, who, without I believe ever mentioning his attacks to him, retrained him in social interest and greatly modified his egocentricity, so that his aim became a desire to use his many fine talents towards the good of his community rather than towards enhancing his own personal prestige. Two years after his last attack he was able to marry, and has had perfectly healthy children. All psychiatrists have noticed the very strong anti-social lives of epileptics and other mental patients but they generally put the cart before the horse, and imagine that the disease causes the anti-social behaviour rather than that the anti-social life-style has been the cause of the disease.

In all such cases moral retraining is the essential factor of cure, although it would never be possible to expect moral retraining to have any positive result without the full co-operation of the patient, or to deal with the physical illness that often arises in such cases and is as real as the psychic factor without the usual medical supervision.

Adler always pointed out that no patient could be psychologically cured unless he *wanted* to be cured. Many patients have got into the position they prefer by their neurotic symptoms, and will not, unless these become too painful for them to endure, make the required effort necessary in order to give them up.

The chief criticisms brought against Individual Psychology have always been that Adler ignored the hereditary factor, or that his moral retraining was too 'simple'—'too obvious'—'too short' to be a permanent cure.

Adler never denied the hereditary factor in illness. He made an extensive study of inherited organ inferiority in his book, *Studien über Minderwertigkeit von Organen und Ihre seelische Kompensation*. What he asserted was that the psychic factor in each individual after birth can be decisive in the use made of this organ inferiority. Dr. Lomax's old gentleman with every mark of typical epilepsy no doubt could have produced true epileptic seizures in a way quite beyond the powers of a man with an organ inferiority of the stomach, but without the epileptic predispositions. But neither—unless he had had a weak stomach—could the old gentleman have produced chronic indigestion.

All doctors know of congenital heart diseases, with the most alarming sounds; and no symptoms. A patient, retrained by Individual Psychology from a highly discouraged to a slightly more courageous attitude, may even swap a severe organ inferiority for a much less serious one.

I myself knew very well a former patient of Dr. Adler's who had suffered from active T.B. and had nearly died from the results. This patient had no further lung breakdowns after the Adlerian analysis, but he had a lifelong inferiority of the larynx; and subsequently when he was exposed to strain or shock beyond what he thought his released powers could stand, he would have an attack of laryngitis.

On one occasion he had a very severe attack, caused by prolonged strain, followed by a somewhat severe shock, and his doctor thought that there were indications of fresh T.B. activity and sent him to a lung specialist. This specialist after taking X-rays of his lungs told him that he was after all only suffering from the remains of a severe attack of laryngitis, not yet wholly cured. 'But considering the lung damage that I see from the X-rays you have already sustained,' he told this patient, 'I should strongly advise you to go on suffering from laryngitis!' He was speaking more wisely than perhaps he knew; for in this blow to his courage, the psychologically cured patient realized that he had cared too much for life to have wanted the more severe threat to it, and had therefore fallen back on the slighter one nature had also provided for him.

Dr. Nowotny, who took his 'Dozent' on Individual Psychology and subsequently received the position Adler should have been offered at the Vienna University, was both a follower and an opponent of Adler's. He spoke to the writer with all the authority of a fellow expert upon Adler's great scientific abilities, but deplored his refusal to confine himself to science and scientists. 'Had he done so,' he told my husband and myself, 'it would surely have resulted in Individual Psychology becoming the corner-stone of medicine. Through his refusal to accept his colleagues' suggestions or to modify his own to meet their objections, Adler lost the support of his own profession in Vienna.' 'Nevertheless,' Nowotny added, 'I am wholly convinced after a long and successful practice that Adler's Individual Psychology is not only the best method, but the *only* method of curing neurosis, and therefore scientifically right.'

It is necessary to realize that this 'Organ Jargon' requires the detection of a skilled psychiatrist and cannot be applied to epidemics, or to those illnesses which obviously arise from natural causes, or to progressive organic diseases. Such illnesses are usually decisive—and the patient within a reasonable term gets well or dies. But in long chronic illnesses or in those which return at times of special strain, or in illnesses that seem specially convenient to the patient's hidden wills, a psychic origin is always indicated. A skilled physician, not a psychiatrist, once remarked to the writer, 'When one of my patients says to me "Ah, doctor, I have one of *my* sore throats" or "One of *my* sick headaches", I always suspect a psychological cause for it. The sense of ownership sounds too affectionate to be quite natural!'

XI

The Nervous Character and Understanding Human Nature

T he first book Adler wrote after leaving Freud's circle was *The Nervous Character*, which he then offered to Vienna University as a thesis for his Professorship or *Dozentur*.

For such a purpose, *The Nervous Character* was a disastrous choice. Although a book of the highest importance and originality, it was written with an attempt to break down the archaic solemnity of scientific phraseology and not at all in the manner that appeals to the academic mind.

Professor Pötzl, who was at least partially responsible for this refusal, explained his reasons to the writer in the following terms. 'Had Freud brought us his *Dream Analysis* as a thesis,' he said, 'I am quite sure we should have refused him his Professorship upon it, in precisely the same manner that we refused Adler his, for *The Nervous Character*. Psychology was, and still is in our academic circles, not considered to be a science in itself, nor should it be given a philosophical handling, such as Adler's *Nervous Character* presented. Freud received his Professorship from a specialized thesis upon *Aphasia* in pamphlet form. Adler, had he chosen to deal with any neurological or biological subject (upon which he was an undoubted expert), would have been granted his Professorship in the same way. It was Adler's refusal to take a specialized basis that made it impossible for us to bestow this honour upon him. No one regretted it more than Wagner Jauregg, who had to make the final decision.' Wagner Jauregg was a distinguished neurologist and a Nobel prize winner; and even to this day neurology is considered the more orthodox field for psychological research in academic circles.

Freud and Adler were equally disliked by this school, since there is no doubt that between them they revolutionized psychology, and raised it at least as high in the scale of scientific importance as its

109

more orthodox brother, the kindred science of neurology. Neurologists have naturally never played a very welcoming part towards this dramatic Joseph in his coat of many colours, but have always murmured together in the manner of their Biblical prototype, 'Behold, this Dreamer cometh—let us cast him into the Pit!'

There is, however, a final factor to be remembered in fairness to Jauregg and to his assistant judges. *The Nervous Character*, although a valuable book full of first-hand thought, is by no means clear to read. Like a diamond mine before the pickers have been at work, a mass of blue clay obscures the jewels.

The Nervous Character is packed from end to end with first-hand creative thought. What Adler did not know about the 'nervous character' is still to be sought. Perhaps it is the greatest book ever written upon the dual struggle of human beings in a love relation. Adler believed that during a child's first five years, he was apt to take a member of his family as a sort of *Gegenspieler*, a person to compete with at all costs in an endless neurotic duel. This person 'played against' is occasionally a parent, when one may see what is termed 'a mother fixation' such as D. H. Lawrence suffered under all his life, or what the Freudians describe as the 'Œdipus Complex' situation of a son fighting continually against his father; but in Adler's belief, more often this *Gegenspieler* is a contemporary brother or sister, by whom the child has felt dethroned or otherwise out-distanced. The danger of this situation lies in its unconsciousness, as well as in the fact that in almost any intimate relationship that follows, the child as he develops into the man will build up the same perpetual antagonism between himself and *any* loved person.

One often notices, after the break-up of a marriage, that the partners again choose mates of a similar type or disposition to the first, and with the same disastrous result. Willa Cather has written a wonderful study in which Adler was much interested, called *My Mortal Enemy*, of a devoted married pair who worked torturingly upon each other till their deaths.

It would be difficult for anyone who had once grasped the truth of Individual Psychology and who then read *The Nervous Character* not to be made aware of what part he or she was playing in a love relationship, and, if aware of it, be urged by his conscience to avoid occasions for this cruel wrestling match. One is constantly reminded in it of Wilde's cry in *The Ballad of Reading Gaol*, 'Each man kills the thing he loves'; but that it is not *necessary* for a lover to be a murderer is the aim and goal of Adler's whole psychology, and was never so clearly brought to the surface as in the packed pages of this astonishing book which seems to contain the collected wisdom of saints, poets and scientists throughout the ages. Nevertheless, without the key to it—i.e. the understanding of Individual Psychology—it is not easy to grasp the full meaning of *The Nervous Character*. Adler's friend, Professor Furtmüller, says of it, 'It is probably the most creative work on psychiatry in existence; but until it is rewritten, perhaps in the form of a novel, very few people will understand it.' In view of the part co-operation played in Adler's sex theories the following letter to a daughter upon her marriage is of interest.

Letter to a Daughter on her marriage.

Dear Vali and dear Georgey [George],

I send you my fondest greetings and take you in my arms and congratulate you with all my heart!

My thoughts are always with you. Do not forget that married life is a task at which both of you must work, with joy.

Remember that the monogamous form of life means the finest flower of sex culture.

I ask you to fill yourselves with the brave resolve to think more about each other than about yourself, and always try to live in such a way that you make the other's life easier and more beautiful.

Don't allow either of you to become subordinate to the other. No one can stand this attitude. Don't allow anyone else to gain influence over the shaping of your marriage relation. Only make friends with people who have a sincere affection for you both.

Now a few words about the practical demands of the moment.

The money that you need for Georgey has been lying ready for some time. You can have it whenever you like.

You, Vali, will require more money. Write at once and say how much and where you want it sent. Try to get your citizenship where there are no passport difficulties.

If you still have my signature for the Bank of Commerce and Industry [formerly 'Känderbank', Prague], utilize it and have the money sent direct to you. If not, write to me at once.

I gather from your last letter that you are not coming to Gmunden. We shall see each other in Berlin, then. Perhaps you will invite Mama and Nelly to the Baltic [Ost See].

Many kisses and greetings,
PAPA.

111

When Adler wrote *The Nervous Character* he was labouring under two great disabilities. He was too poor to give himself the needed time to get his thoughts clear and in the right sequence (his servant, Sophie, describes how he often wrote far on into the night after a long day's practice); and he was himself living from day to day this Laocoön struggle with his own wife. The wisdom in this book is the wisdom that has entered every beat of a man's heart. Like Beethoven, Adler might well have said: 'My passions are the grapes that I tread out for mankind.'

Writing was a medium that irritated Adler. It seemed to him like an attempt to corner an organic truth, and stifle it under a flood of manipulative words. Books of his taken from his lectures, such as *Understanding Human Nature* or *What Life Should Mean to You*, do not suffer from any obscurity. They are far plainer and easier to read, for the ordinary layman, than the books of any other psychologist, but these books came from Adler's spoken—not his written—words. They, therefore, have all the straightforward drive and spontaneous originality of his personal contacts.

Problems in Neurosis, a book compiled with extreme skill by Philip Mairet from Adler's actual case notes, also avoids Adler's stylistic pitfalls. *What Life Should Mean to You*, again, was very well handled and clarified by Alan Porter in his excellent translation; but perhaps the most easy of all to read, because of its brilliant and living style and close approximation to Adler's own way of thinking, is Béran Wolfe's *Understanding Human Nature*, translated from *Menschenkenntniss*, the series of lectures given by Adler in 1913 in the Volks Hochschule, and with Adler's constant verbal co-operation. It is unfortunate that the last few chapters of this brilliant book could not be finished by Béran Wolfe with Adler's co-operation. They were merely a skeleton presentation of lecture notes, unbreathed upon by the genius of its author and his inspired translator. This is a book that each fresh generation will rediscover for itself. In it, Adler had the freedom of movement his mind constantly needed, given point by the verbal felicity of Béran Wolfe. *Understanding Human Nature* has a brilliance and sharpness of outline quite unlike any of Adler's other writings but very like his spoken thought. Béran Wolfe was no mean psychologist himself, and he manages to slip into the taut, nervous phrases into which he has poured the contents of Adler's packed German sentences, the very essence and spirit of Adler himself.

Adler had a genius for personality. Some of his meaning comes through all his books, because he wrote them; but many of his disciples could have defined what he meant, and *did* define what he meant, better than Adler himself.

The Faculty of the University of Vienna entirely failed to appreciate *The Nervous Character*, and their refusal to grant Adler his Professorship upon this work remained an unstaunched wound for the rest of his life.

Later, when the University of Berlin had given Adler an honorary degree, and America had established a Chair of Medical Psychology for him in the Long Island College of Medicine, his own University would have been glad of the slightest excuse to reconsider its former verdict; but when Adler was indirectly approached on this matter and asked to submit anything he cared to show them, with the promise of its acceptance, he would not hear of it.

The rebuff had been felt by him both as final and unforgivable. No honours that came to Adler from other sources, no recognition from countries not his own, ever made up to him for this Viennese slight. It was even more for his father than for himself that Adler felt the deepest disappointment. He knew what his career had cost his father, and he had wanted to crown his father's old age with a local triumph of a kind that he could best understand and appreciate.

Throughout his whole career, Adler received blow after blow from man or fate; he was far too sensitive a human being not to have smarted under each in turn; but smart as he might, no blow that ever struck him could daunt him. Nor was he once put off the path of his intent. Browning's *Epilogue* might have been written for him:

> "*Marched breast forward,*
> *Never doubted clouds would break,*
> *Never dreamed, though right were worsted,*
> *Wrong would triumph,*
> *Held we fall to rise, are baffled to fight better,*
> *Sleep to wake.*"

Adler always fought the better for a challenge; and the pain of his own wounds taught him how best to staunch those of others.

One more cruel sting to his pride was given to Adler in Vienna. After Berlin had granted him the freedom of its city, Adler's own *Wien* slowly came to the conclusion that she must follow suit, and Adler was made an honorary citizen of Vienna. But an enemy, from the group he had left, told the mayor beforehand that if he really wanted to please Adler, he should tell him that this honour was given him as a recognition of his merit as a pupil of Freud's.

Adler flushed deeply at the mayor's ignorant blunder in the speech of presentation; and when it was time for him to reply, said with quiet sarcasm that he must express his gratitude for the great knowledge the mayor had shown he possessed of his work and its origin, but that he must confess he could not lay claim to ever having been a pupil of Freud, since he was merely the founder of 'Individual Psychology'. The mayor, who was an ignorant fellow, remained quite unconscious of his blunder; but Adler's friends did not find it easy to forgive the malice of the informer.

As against the slights and insults Adler received in the city he loved best in the world, must be placed the increasing value set upon him and his work by both his own professional colleagues and the teachers, who were beginning to realize the help that Adler might be able to give them in their own profession.

'We all of us went to Adler's lectures,' Professor Julius Bauor told the writer. 'I doubt if there is any doctor of reputation in Vienna who was not to be found there at one time or another, and we came away with an added value for our job, and a deeper understanding of the human beings we had to practise on.'

The Viennese School of Medicine owed to Adler much of its deft approach to its patients.

The German doctor is always too anxious to impress his autocratic personality upon the patient, and to *tell* him what is the matter with him. The Viennese doctors learned from Adler to find out from a hundred slight mental and physical signs and stresses what their patient was suffering from, and how best to give him the courage to help himself on the road to recovery. Not even the stubborn Viennese University could do without Adler's contribution; and to this day no medical student can take his final degree without being able to state an intelligible account of Individual Psychology, for the University that refused Adler his Professorship on *The Nervous Character*.

The year 1913 was a very important one in Adler's life. In it he gave the course of lectures which were afterwards put together in *Menschenkenntnis* and which did more than anything else he had yet achieved to spread his reputation over Central Europe.

In 1913 Adler and his group made their final definition of the twelve chief tenets of 'Individual Psychology' as follows:

1. Every neurosis can be understood as an attempt to free oneself from a feeling of inferiority in order to gain a feeling of superiority.

2. The path of the neurosis does not lead in the direction of social

114

functioning, nor does it aim at solving given life-problems, but finds an outlet for itself in a small family circle, thus achieving the isolation of the patient.

3. The larger unit of the social group is either completely or very extensively pushed aside by a mechanism consisting of hypersensitiveness and intolerance. Only a small group is left over for manœuvres aiming at the various types of superiority to expend themselves upon. At the same time protection and the withdrawal from the demands of the community and the decisions of life are made possible.

4. Thus estranged from reality, the neurotic man lives a life of imagination and fantasy, and employs a number of devices for enabling him to sidestep the demands of reality and for reaching out towards an ideal situation which would free him from any service for the community and absolve him from responsibility.

5. These exemptions and privileges of illness and suffering give him a substitute for his original hazardous goal of superiority.

6. Thus the neurosis represents an attempt to free oneself from all the constraints of the community by establishing a counter-compulsion. This latter is so constituted that it effectually faces the peculiar nature of the surroundings and their demands. Both of these convincing inferences can be drawn from the manner in which this counter-compulsion manifests itself, and from the neurosis selected.

7. The counter-compulsion takes on the nature of a revolt, gathers its material either from favourable effective experiences or from observations. It permits thoughts and effects to become preoccupied either with the above-mentioned disturbances or with unimportant details, as long as they at least serve the purpose of directing the eye and the attention of the patient away from his life problems. In this manner, depending upon the needs of the situation, he prepares anxiety and compulsion situations, sleeplessness, swooning, perversions, hallucinations, slightly pathological effects, neurasthenia and hypochondriacal complexes and psychotic pictures of his actual condition, all of which serve him as excuses.

8. Even logic falls under the domination of the counter-compulsion. As in psychosis, this process may go as far as the actual nullification of logic.

9. Logic, the will to live, love and human sympathy, co-operation and language, all arise out of the needs of human communal life. Against the latter are directed automatically all the plans of the neurotic individual striving for isolation and lusting for power.

10. To cure a neurosis it is necessary to change completely the whole upbringing of the patient and turn him definitely and unconditionally back into human society.

11. All the volition and all the strivings of the neurotic are dictated by his prestige-seeking policy, which is continually looking for excuses which will enable him to leave the problems of life unsolved. He consequently turns against allowing any community feeling to develop.

12. If, therefore, one may regard the demand for a complete and unified understanding of man and for a comprehension of his (undivided) individuality as justified—a view to which we are forced, both by the nature of reason and the individual psychological knowledge of the urge towards an integration of the personality—then the method of comparison, the main tool of our method, enables us to arrive at some conception of the power lines along which the individual strives to attain superiority.

In 1913 William Stead brought out his prophetic book upon the Hapsburg dynasty, and Adler reading it said to himself, 'I believe this man is right—this *is* what will happen to Austria in case of War!' But Vienna thought nothing of such portents. She had enlarged her great empire by a sudden grasp at Bosnia and Herzegovina; and nothing had happened. Russia, since her defeat by Japan, was considered by Austrian diplomats hardly to matter one way or the other. The old Emperor kept both his traditional friendship with England, and a dignified and carefully amicable relationship with the uneasy William.

The Balkans had just recovered, with the timely help of Sir Edward Grey, from a very serious flurry. The barometer was set fair for 1914.

'How is my *Wien*?' Adler, away for a few days' holiday, demanded of a friend who had joined him.

'Why do you ask such a silly question?' his friend replied. 'Were you not there yourself two days ago? What *should* happen to *Wien*?'

'Well, one never knows,' Adler replied with a little sigh, 'but I am always afraid—whenever my back is turned—that someone will take my *Wien* away from me!'

XII

Adler and the War of 1914

Adler was uneasy over the Austrian threats to Serbia long before 'the punitive expedition', as the Viennese called it, with tragic felicity, took the Archduke's assassination as their excuse for war. Yet he reluctantly agreed to Raissa's taking their four children to Russia in the spring of 1914. He knew that in the truest sense of the word Raissa was homesick and it was but natural that she should take her children—the only tangible fruit of all her dreams—home with her.

What this unexpectedly prolonged separation must have meant to Adler, whose devotion as a father was the most prized of all his spiritual possessions, can be well imagined, although no one knew what was in his heart. After the murders of Serajevo, Adler telegraphed a peremptory summons for their immediate return. He could give no explanation in his telegram; and to Raissa, perhaps a thousand miles away, in the heart of that big, somnolent, unconcentrated country, his abrupt command was unintelligible, and in the light of their relationship to each other, not to be for a moment unhesitatingly accepted. 'Shall wait,' Raissa telegraphed back.

Too late came the explanation; and the flood of war swept between them.

For five months, Raissa and the four children were held back from any attempt to return to Vienna, and their journey—when at last they were allowed to take it—lasted a fortnight and was a terrible ordeal for both mother and children.

When Raissa and her children were at last safely re-established, under the Dominikaner roof, her greatest friend told me: 'A different Raissa had come back from Russia! I cannot explain to you what had taken place, I only knew that Raissa was utterly changed. She was no longer the ex-Russian student, with all that that implied, but a balanced woman of the world, well-dressed, well-groomed, taking her place as wife and mother, with a dignified sophistication that seemed at first wholly strange in her. Her large and generous heart was still the same, but I think it was no longer disturbed or broken. It was as if Raissa had taken a new grip on the world, and now faced life, not with the mad audacity of her youth, but with a chastened and wiser courage. She had gone away wretched—like a human being who had lost his way in the world; and she came back—having fought out her battle in her own soul—like a human being that has found the way to live, under whatever difficulties or provocations. I don't say that Raissa was any happier with Adler, for I saw no reason to suppose that she was until later (when their happiness *was* restored to them), but from the time she returned from that Russian visit, Raissa was ready to play her part with strength and dignity in her own home.' Unfortunately each took different sides in the war, and this accentuated the bitterness of their human bondage—Raissa was pro-Ally; Adler, a Viennese, followed the Austrian side of the war.

What Adler had suffered in loneliness and anxiety for these first six months of the war can well be imagined; but at last those four crowning jewels of his life—and the setting that held them together (for Adler as well as for herself)—were restored to him.

Adler, however, had barely time to feel the joy of this restoration when he was hurried out of his home upon urgent war duties.

He had to serve for two years as a military doctor near the Russian front, first at Cracow and then at Brno. He was then transferred to the little village of Petzenkirchen where he was in charge of Russian prisoners suffering from typhus.

Adler often visited the Pirquet Children's Hospital in Vienna; and it may be that through his work in this hospital, his plan for retraining both child and parent in child guidance clinics attached to the State schools first took hold of him.

One of the staff of this hospital told me that it was soon discovered that Adler had an incredible power of calming children, so that it became the custom for the Pirquet surgeons to send for him when any painful surgical treatment had to take place.

This doctor was so struck by Adler's success in soothing and calming sick children, and by his general bearing in the hospital, that he began to attend all Adler's lectures; read his books; and became a complete convert to Adler's teachings.

'Whatever was asked or expected of Adler,' this doctor told the writer, 'he met with such ease, modesty and kindness that you felt he must be acting upon a special principle unknown to other people.'

One of Adler's most painful duties during the war was to advise what soldiers after convalescence were fit to be sent back to the trenches. This job caused him such pain and anxiety that it influenced his sleeping as well as his waking thoughts. 'It was then that I stopped dreaming altogether for the rest of my life,' Adler told the writer, 'or rather from then on, I taught myself to forget before waking whatever dreams I had had; for I saw that I was trying to deceive myself in my dreams into letting soldiers off from a return to their duties. I still tried to let them off in my waking hours; but at least I knew what I was up to then!'

That Adler should be specially successful in his war work and add to the knowledge of psychiatric discoveries, through his treatment of shell-shock cases and other war neuroses, was only to be expected. It was, however, a great misfortune that during this period he had no time either to take notes of his innumerable shell-shock cases (with a few individual exceptions) or to control this invaluable human material for future reference. Adler ought to have been followed from case to case by a student secretary; but the pressure of work was too dire for anyone to make this their special business, and Adler himself was too incurably modest to try to preserve the priceless skill and knowledge that slipped away from him into oblivion.

Adler's physical endurance at this time was almost a miracle. He worked without cessation for two years, upwards of sixteen hours a day, without a physical breakdown of any kind. No doubt, as he was already approaching middle age, this terrific strain and concentration may have helped to sow the seeds of the heart disease that killed him twenty years later; but Adler showed no apparent signs of strain; nor, when he returned to Vienna to help in the overcrowded hospitals for the last two years of the war, can he have been said to relax his efforts or to shorten his hours, although it is probable that he suffered much less than when he was dealing with the acute and unnecessary agony of young and healthy war victims.

Adler was no hoarder; whatever he had, he gave. He said once, to one of his patients before a long parting: 'You ask me what is the most important thing for you to remember until we meet again; I would say to you, Give! You cannot give too much—give all—all is not enough!'

It was his 'all' that Adler gave to staunch the wound that the world was making in its own breast in 1914; and it was because Adler foresaw that what he had had to give—although it *had* been his 'all'—was not enough, that his heart broke in 1937, when he clearly envisaged a fresh attempt at suicide and wholesale murder upon the part of his brother man.

119

XIII

Gemeinschaftsgefühl: Social Interest

W
hen Adler returned to Vienna in 1916 and found himself
once more with his old group in the Café Central, it was
a strange and significant reunion.
The fortunes of war still stood high; but the sufferings of Vienna
had begun. Beneath the superficial hopes inspired by military
triumphs—chiefly those of their autocratic ally Prussia—lurked an
uneasy mind.

Some of the original Individual Psychological group were dead;
many were at work elsewhere; but all who were there were hungry
for Adler's cheerful presence, and looked to him as always for fresh
life and courage. 'Now, Adler,' a friend called out to him, 'what have
you got that's new to bring us?' (*'Nun, Adler—was gibt's Neues?'*)
Adler looked unchanged; he sat down among them, the same solid,
little figure with the ready smile and twinkling eyes; but they were
soon to find a vital difference.

'Adler was never the same again after the war,' an old friend said
of him. 'He was much quieter and stronger, one soon became conscious that he was no longer ready to squander his good spirits on
any subject that came up; it was as if he had concentrated all his
powers into a single purpose. In a sense he was not graver; but he
used his wits more earnestly.'

'It seems to me,' Adler said in answer to his questioner, but looking
seriously from one to the other round the long table, 'that what the
world chiefly wants to-day is *Gemeinschaftsgefühl*.'

What a platitude in the middle of a war!

Here they were, these picked brains of Vienna, hard-bitten intellectuals, scientists, writers, teachers, journalists—waiting for the
wisdom of a great philosopher; and what did he offer them—a mere
generalization of 'good-will'! A religious word, almost such a word
as a revivalist preacher might be fool enough to shout at a crowd of
emotional women.

But those who knew Adler best listened carefully, for they were well aware that when Adler said: 'What the world needs is this or that,' he would be prepared to give it to them.

The difference between a platitude and a truth is after all only that between an incontrovertible fact *stated,* and a deeply experienced fact *felt.* Adler's thoughts were always only a part of his achievement. If he thought that *Gemeinschaftsgefühl* was the solution of the world's problem it would be because in himself he had worked out its truth, and knew how to obtain it for others.

But the Nietzscheans could not bear it. Whatever else they had joined Adler for—these Will-to-Power men could not put up with this menial goal.

They had gladly accepted Adler's 'inferiority sense', and the advance from a minus to a plus in childhood through its stimulus; the family constellation was no difficulty for them; even the teleological rather than a 'causal' aim they had swallowed, though rather reluctantly; but this tame ethical stress upon a vague word, almost religious in its tendency, was more than their proud spirits could entertain.

'*Gemeinschaftsgefühl,*' poor Neuer cried aloud, 'what a word to use —it does not even exist in philosophy!'

'It is what the world wants,' Adler repeated quietly.

This was, of course, but the beginning of the turmoil; a long and embittered discussion took place. Paul Schrecker and Froeschel rebelled—they were the strongest Nietzscheans, and in the end they left the circle; but Neuer remained.

Slowly, he told us, he began to see what Adler was driving at: there was a law binding man to the universe, moving always in the same direction, and towards a goal that could never be reached, but which never varied; and as man obeyed this law and co-operated with it, he would develop in a direction that furthered universal welfare—but his co-operation with others was the price he must pay for this development. The egocentric goal must be broken up. Social Interest *was* the only goal for mankind; and every human being must be trained towards it in childhood, until it became as natural to him 'as breathing or the upright gait'.

From his earliest infancy, the sharp spur of the inferiority sense to the grown-up world round him was there to urge the child on towards a successful life-plan; but to *be* successful the aim of this life-plan must be the service of mankind.

What Adler was proposing to his group, and what he was working out in his own life and heart, was the break-up of the egocentric goal.

If it was the first part of Adler's programme as an Individual Psychologist to make a self-reliant and courageous human being, it was the second and final part to make this self-reliant and courageous person responsible in relation to all mankind. Someone once said to Adler: 'But do you not believe we can sublimate our powers?' 'Yes,' Adler said, 'we *can* sublimate them—but not in the air—we can sublimate them in the presence of our next door neighbour!'

This was no new idea of Adler's; the group themselves had helped him to formulate it in 1913, when they first drew up their twelve points of Individual Psychology.

What *was* new to them was the weight Adler put upon it, for he knew *now* that it was the one question at issue between man and his fate.

Either man learned in time to conquer his egocentric goal and the isolation that it brought upon him; or he would destroy himself root and branch, not only in the limited way he had already set about it, in 1914, but on a far more complete and irrevocable scale.

Adler's belief in evolution was no passive optimist's. He scoffed at those who blithely suggested that by an incomplete pacifism, ignoring the warring wills of others, the law of evolution could be made to do their work for them.

Adler did not believe that any laws, unless obeyed and co-operated with, worked for human beings.

He thought it as unreasonable to expect evolution to solve man's problems without man's active co-operation as to expect without a sexual union the production of a child.

His goal of 'Love thy neighbour as thyself' was the same as the goal of all true religions has always been; but Adler was prepared to do what no man of science had as yet adventured—to harness his science to a religious goal, in order to train the human being in such a way that the goal could be reached. He was no vague idealist believing in an impossibly perfect human being; but he had seen proved hundreds of times in his neurotic patients, and never once contradicted, that given a retraining of an egocentric human being— in a socially interested direction—you arrived at someone who could naturally avoid the major ills of life.

From this moment, in the Café Central, and with those men who sat round the table, Adler was prepared to alter the direction of mankind. Because he told them that he was, and because they had learned to rely upon him, they threw in their lot with this new idea.

Not at once, and not all of them, for if it is hard for the rich man to enter into the Kingdom of Heaven, it is harder still for an intellectual to give up the pride of his intellect.

Adler required that his friends should give up this pride; not that he ever wanted them not to use their wits to the uttermost of their powers, but he wanted them not to use their wits for the sake of using them, or for their own honour and glory, but for the plain uses of mankind.

The Nietzcheans had at once rebelled, and some of the psychiatrists who had left Freud's circle to follow Adler because they believed him to be the truer and more enlightened scientist, and had set their own futures on the development of his theories, went after them. They had believed that Adler would succeed in making a school of Individual Psychological doctors, a far more practical and powerful school than Freud's psycho-analysts. One of them said to the writer: 'Adler had everything in his power to form such a school. He had only to make his psychology into a school of medicine for us to spread Individual Psychology throughout the world. Even to-day, I am willing to admit that there is no cure for neurosis in a human being other than Adler's psychology provides.

'We all knew that, and we were all prepared to accept what further he had to teach us; but this stuff for everybody—this sudden missionary idea of *Gemeinschaftsgefühl*—how could we deal with it? The medical profession must keep its science above the crowd! Adler should, as a scientist, have known this, and he should have known that if he insisted on spreading this sort of religious science through the laity we, as a profession, could not support him.'

Franz Plewa, a medical student, explained Adler's lack of professional support as follows:

'General practitioners in Vienna have been and still are very much influenced by Adler in the handling of their patients. In educational centres Individual Psychology is still spreading, though often under other names, but in the medical profession materialistic reasons always act against it, even where it is known and accepted. A doctor who practises Individual Psychology must be prepared only to take seven or eight patients a day, instead of twenty or thirty; and until he becomes well known he cannot charge proportionately for these long sittings.'

One of the greatest difficulties to the spread of Individual Psychology is still that doctors are prevented from having an exclusive use of it.

They do not want to share their knowledge of it with the laity. Freudians escape this problem, for their heavy and prolonged training is far too complicated a business for the laity to follow; but Individual Psychology, though far harder in practice, is superficially much easier for the man in the street to understand; and Adler imposed no intellectual tests upon his students.

Adler felt that medical men wanted to turn themselves into a priesthood over his psychology. They tried to keep the knowledge of psychology to themselves, instead of imparting it to their patients; and they also wanted to run away with Adler's ideas, and turn them out with their own imprint upon them.

'Here enter the Plagiarists!' Adler exclaimed on one occasion, with an expressive gesture, when two such doctors came into the room to join a discussion circle.

There was, however, a less venal and more scientific reason which undoubtedly kept many medical sympathizers from working with Adler, and that was their intense difficulty in giving up causal thinking in psychology.

Adler was fond of telling a story to show both how adhesive and how unreasonable causal thinking as applied to psychology can be, and how often it blinds such thinkers to the findings of plain common sense.

A psycho-analyst came to Adler one day and said: 'Now at last I can prove to you once and for all that the Œdipus Complex is an undoubted fact! Our female dog has a male puppy and though both she and the male parent have separate baskets in the same room, the male puppy always chooses to sleep with his mother!' 'Please show me the baskets,' Adler demanded.

When they stood in the room where the dogs slept Adler said, 'I notice that the mother has the larger basket—cannot we find here the reason for the puppy's choice?' S. looked momentarily a little dashed. 'Oh, if you like,' he said. 'Just to show you, I will change the baskets to-night, and put the father in the larger one!' In the morning he admitted to Adler that the puppy *had* slept in the father's larger basket with the father. 'But,' he added triumphantly to Adler, 'shouldn't that prove to you that the puppy has now reached the second stage of sexual growth and become homosexual?'

It was perhaps unfortunate that at this moment of academic cleavage Adler should have changed his café to The Whiff of Tobacco .

This was in itself a severe test for his more prosperous medical colleagues, for The Whiff of Tobacco was, if not actually disreputable, a very humble, nondescript type of café, housed under the same roof as a cheap 'War' kitchen.

Adler, who never had much time at his disposal, found it a great convenience to have his food in the same place as his evening discussions. Perhaps he never realized how much this café and its inmates shocked and distressed his more successful colleagues, or perhaps he *did* realize it and was putting them to a test; at any rate there he sat, and continued to hold his group meetings, with the consequence that many of the more prosperous of his friends and colleagues refused to continue their attendance.

'The trouble with Adler', his old friend Siller the café keeper told the writer, 'was that he was too good a fellow to please his professional colleagues. His heart was too big for him; he never would turn away scallywags!'

His friends, who loved Adler's company, did not always care to share it with an increasing circle of half-cured neurotics, out-at-elbow tramps, or other strange persons. It was disconcerting to look forward to a scientific discussion, on a long Sunday excursion, and find sixty other persons without scientific attainments on the railway station prepared to join in. 'Love me, love my dog,' is not a saying that can be taken too literally with fastidious persons.

Adler's human 'dog' was but too often a mongrel, and sometimes a savage one into the bargain; but Adler never admitted it.

Perhaps the difference between the qualities of one human being and another—in the sense of worth—was not very important to Adler.

'What is man,' he once said to a friend of his, 'but a drop of water? A conceited drop,' he added after a slight pause.

Adler himself never accepted a privilege unshared by others in his company. Nor was he fond of providing privileges or special treatment for other people, though he would do so if he felt there was a real need for it.

'You'll *have* to sit in a front seat,' he said to one of his friends at a lecture he was giving, 'it can't be helped—since you do not know enough German to understand well otherwise!' But the friend felt that it was up to her to improve her knowledge as fast as possible, though Adler himself saw that she got the seat.

Nevertheless in spite of this conviction and practice on his own part, Adler had an indulgent understanding for aristocracy and its special privileges. 'You see,' he once told the writer, 'an aristocrat has some really good traditions—one may not believe in them to-day

—personally I do not believe in them—but *Noblesse oblige* for instance—you could hardly expect anyone to give up such a good idea as that lightly!'

But The Whiff of Tobacco did not lose Adler all his Nicodemuses. There was one of his academic friends in a high position, a fastidious intellectual, who continued to sit with him in The Whiff of Tobacco , and it was through this friend, Professor Furtmüller, whose love followed him to the grave and after, that Adler owed the greatest opportunity of his life—the opportunity of launching through the State Schools of Vienna that practice and training in *Gemeinschaftsgefühl* which he believed to be necessary for mankind.

XIV

Adler's Child-Guidance Clinics

There is a story Adler loved to quote, that when Archimedes discovered the law of hydrostatics, so great was his sense of triumph that he sacrificed one hundred oxen; and that thereafter during his lifetime, whenever a new discovery threatened, the oxen began to tremble.

There is no doubt that both Adler and Freud suffered throughout their working lives from the fears of the oxen, fears which in many cases reached a direct hostility.

There is nothing in the whole history of medicine so upsetting to the ordinary layman as that his sickness or mental troubles should require any improvement in his character. For this reason the tremendous statement, unsupported by fact, that human nature does *not* change (by which is indirectly implied that it cannot change, and that no one would wish it to, if it could!) is too reassuring to be lightly given up. Both Freud and Adler in different ways challenged the truth of this statement.

Freud got off on the whole cheaper than Adler, though he had plenty of opposition to face, and even ridicule, in his earlier life; but the change in the human being required by anyone who accepted Freud's theory was less exacting than the change required in character by the theories of Adler.

People did not much mind having their *libido* released from suppressions, but to shift one's whole basis from a prestige goal to one of co-operation and love of one's neighbour is a lifelong task.

A whole course of Freud's unpalatable freedoms can, however, result in a certain lack of popularity; whereas a faithful Adlerian accepting his task in life as a strict attention to his own business, coupled with a friendly attitude towards the business of others, should find a much wider welcome for his doctrines.

The Freudian doctrines were greatly assisted by the notoriety

127

given to them through their allegiance to the sex instinct; but it is only fair to say that the long training and initiation Freud exacted from his students made them far more valuable as exponents than the open, unsystematized activities of the Aderian students.

Everyone knew what Freud stood for; but it took a great deal longer, and must take longer still now that Adler's own voice is silenced—and with it the voice of the education built upon it in Vienna—to understand what Individual Psychology stands for.

It was not until the war of 1914 ended, and the reign of the Social Democrats set in, that Adler entered upon his kingdom and was able to give the world the practical proof of the value of his science.

His friend Furtmüller, who stood very high in educational centres, opened this field to him. When he was talking one day to the Minister of Education (Glöckel) Glöckel said: 'I am not interested in educational specialists, however learned. I should like a set of practical teachers, who could educate the parents as well as the children into becoming good human beings!'

Furtmüller promptly replied, 'Well, that is not impossible here in Vienna, since I can introduce you to the very man to help you! There is a doctor called Adler, who not only wants what you want, but knows by what steps it can be produced. Why not get him to teach the teachers?'

From this moment, Glöckel allowed and encouraged Adler to attach his child-guidance centres to more than thirty of the State schools of Vienna. A few psychiatrists from other schools also conducted some of the State school child-guidance centres but more than two-thirds of them were under Adler's direct guidance and run by his students. Adler was given a post as lecturer at the *Pädagogisches Institut der Stadt Wien*, where up to the last days of the Schuschnigg regime, students listened with respect and attention to Adler's theories, although the Schuschnigg Government had closed the child-guidance centres in 1939 and no longer allowed the public teaching of Adler's followers.

Individual Psychology will, in spite of this setback, probably owe its immortality to the teachers of Vienna, and their whole-hearted co-operation with Adler's science.

Fräulein Regina Seidler, a faithful teacher and exponent of Adler's, from whom the following notes were drawn, has managed to preserve a little history of these clinics from their start in 1921 to their abrupt and cruel finish in 1934.

She herself worked enthusiastically in charge of the child-guidance circle in her district, from its inception to its close. 'A teacher who has once worked on Adler's theories will never work on any others,' she told the writer. 'They could not do so if they wanted to—because he taught us to understand children, and no good teacher would ever give that up, for his own sake as well as the child's.'

All the *Volks* and *Hauptschulen* in the city of Vienna worked in connection with child-guidance centres. Any child in these schools who showed backwardness, or was difficult in class, was brought by the teacher to the nearest clinic for advice and treatment, so that children from six to fourteen years of age, in the city of Vienna, had access to this special psychological retraining between the years 1921 to 1934. The teachers were trained as well by attending Adler's lecture courses, held fortnightly at Czernin Platz.

Adler never once missed, through all the years that followed, until 1927 when he went to live in America, giving this fortnightly lecture to teachers; and besides the lecture itself, he would take one or two controlled cases for demonstration.

He generally stayed two or three hours upon his lecture nights, and never hurried. Adler was always prepared to answer, with equal patience and thoroughness, any question whether it came from the audience or from the parents of the child.

Once a month Adler took an open lecture for all teachers, parents or others interested in child culture at the *Volksheim*; and on these occasions this large hall was always filled to the brim.

The clinic began by the teacher, under whose teaching the child came, reading out his notes of the case. Adler then talked over these case notes, with both teacher and audience, till the child came in.

This was always a most dramatic moment. For before Adler had set eyes upon the child, he would so describe it, even to its smallest physical habits and appearance, while predicting its whole general attitude, that its entrance and the startling justification its presence gave to Adler's predictions enchanted the audience, like a successful conjuring trick.

In the first series of clinics the parents were admitted, after the case had been fully discussed but before the actual entrance of the child; but later on Adler thought the child might resent the feeling of having been talked over first, so the procedure was changed to the child's entry first, followed, after Adler had dismissed it, by the entrance of the parents.

Most of the Adlerian child-guidance circles followed this practice.

Adler always first discussed with the audience the questions he intended putting to the parents, often foretelling their exact answers.

When subsequently the answers were in fact made, it was held proved that the case was being conducted on the right lines, and that the child's difficulties were caused—or at any rate increased—by a mistaken attitude on the part of the parents.

Adler always warned the teachers to notice what physical reactions the child evinced on its entry; to which parent he went first; whether he would lean against his father or mother, or stand alone; stoop or stand upright; hang his head or scowl; hold out his hand or shrink back.

Adler himself always shook hands very warmly with every child, and treated him, whatever his age or behaviour, exactly as if he were a contemporary and an equal, although in talking to the child he used only the simplest words and, as he also did with adults, very few of them.

Usually Adler's first question struck straight at the core of the child's difficulty. 'Do you help your mother very much?' he would ask a spoilt or selfish child.

The child always reacted immediately to Adler's questions, sometimes by answering very freely and easily, and with evident relish, and sometimes by reluctance or complete silence. The retreat into silence was itself an admission that the child's difficulty had been reached, and that the situation had begun to be understood.

Adler always showed the child his mistaken *attitude*, rather than any outstanding mistake or fault arising from it. If for instance the child was a confirmed liar, a condition most often produced by an over-stern parent, Adler would not mention the child's lies, but he would try to make the child understand that he was highly prized by his parents, and that the sternness was merely an anxious desire on the parents' part that the child should make the best of himself and stand well with the world. He would then show the child that a little more courage and affection on his part, showed to the stern parent, would help the situation all round. When he was talking later to the parent, Adler would make the child's improvement possible by trying to alter the sternness of the parents' attitude; but he tried never to antagonize the parent. 'What you have done for your child hitherto,' he would say, 'was no doubt very good from your point of view; but now perhaps you could try something a little different, and see what effect it has.'

Adler always showed both to the child and parent that the difficulty sprang from the whole personality, and it was there that the change must first become apparent; the symptom would drop off, of itself.

Very often the whole treatment was carried out and the cure achieved without the fault or physical symptom ever having been alluded to. A child with grave urinary difficulties was cured by Adler discovering that she was afraid of burglars in the closet, and therefore never attended properly to her physical habits. He saw at once that she was a fearful child; and the urinary disease and its symptoms disappeared without having once been mentioned between them.

It was the child itself, and not a single fault or illness, that Adler set out to cure.

It was fascinating to watch the child's quick nod, or slow reluctant grin, when Adler's question revealed the core of his being, and he saw for the first time the point of his procedure, and recognized as his own the personality upon which the mistaken behaviour had been based. Adler might sometimes say, in an observant thoughtful manner—never in the least condemnatory, but as one scientist might point out an interesting specimen to another, 'You will always be master in your own house, won't you?' Or, 'You would like to drive that mother of yours between reins, like a horse, wouldn't you?'

Usually after the first question, there would be a long, pregnant pause, which Adler never broke.

He was a past master in the art of pauses; but whereas, with an adult, Adler's pauses were often the rope given his patient in order that he might execute himself without Adler's assistance, his pauses for the child were usually of a tempting and inviting nature, helping him not to feel threatened or hurried, and showing him that the inadequacy of his small vocabulary could be no barrier whatever between him and Adler's understanding.

Children very seldom looked away from Adler, even when they felt embarrassed; it seemed to help them, rather than to add to their embarrassment, to look into those deep-seeing, kindly eyes.

Adler always gave the child a reasonable hope, and with great promptness. He would show the child almost immediately some point in his own behaviour where he *had*, or *might* have, a success.

Then he would proceed to talk out a plan of behaviour so that the child should at once be able to envisage his difficulties on new lines, and in an easier light.

The child usually retorted with a plan for further discussion at the next meeting, and it was always interesting to watch with both Adler

131

and Seif of Munich (a past-master in the art of child-guidance upon Adlerian lines) how eager the child always was to return to them, often asking to bring with him next time the member of the family with whom he least got on, or from whom he suffered the most jealousy and envy. Seif's power of releasing children from tension was so great that the writer once saw a child—a most pronounced stammerer so tongue-tied that it was almost impossible not to believe there was a physical speech obstruction—talk without hesitation to him; and this during their first interview.

When the child had been dismissed with another hearty handshake, Adler gave a talk on the whole case, or on some special difficulty in the case, in an abstract manner: for instance, on 'The Principle of Lying' or 'Stealing' or on 'Bed-wetting', so that the teachers and parents should be able to grasp exactly what general attitude to take towards the whole subject.

The audience used to listen spellbound to Adler's summing up of the child.

The writer, who has seen several leaders of these clinics, including those of other distinguished Adlerians, wishes to put it on record that though every child reacted differently to the treatment, she never once saw a child either distressed or bored by it.

The invariable effect upon children seems to be relief and interest.

A child is sometimes brought in crying, but as nothing is ever forced upon him, and no attention drawn to him, the crying usually soon stops; and is obviously caused by the fear of what may be lying in wait for him.

Sometimes a shy child would remain under the pressure of shyness to the end of the interview; but as the child was neither obliged to speak, nor alarmed by what he heard, the shyness soon appeared to be a mere veil, behind which the child felt himself a secure spectator of an extremely interesting performance, in which he was aware of playing an important part without having to make any effort in order to do so.

There seems no invariable rule as to how contact with a child should best be obtained. With the three most successful exponents of the Adlerian system the author has regularly watched, contact was obtained by all three almost at once, but Adler was both far more slow and far more silent than either of the other two. Seif was always very gentle in his manner, quite unhurried but graver than the others, though his humour was there to be called upon at need.

The third exponent, Ida Löwy, was incredibly quick in her method

132

and questions, but she never hurried the child, and her contact-forming powers were as great as those of either of the other two; indeed she even more obviously held the attention of the child than they did, and received the child's own quickened affection and response in the first glance that passed between them. Adler was the least personal of the three; Seif the most authoritative; while Ida Löwy had a sort of clear—but quite unsentimental—tenderness that seemed to have an instantaneously releasing effect upon the child.

It would be impossible, however, to draw any comparison between their results, because they all three obtained successful results in the shortest possible time.

There was always a follower up of the cases present, as well as a doctor in the case of Ida Löwy, who was not herself a medical practitioner. The doctor was present to be called upon, if any physical treatment or advice were found suitable. The cases varied as to the time it took to cure them, not—as some might think—with the gravity of the child's trouble, but with his power of response to the practitioner and, as was to be expected, the power of the parents to respond to the psychiatrists' suggestions after home was reached. With very brutalized or self-satisfied parents, the child was obviously at a disadvantage in his new orientation as he had been (though in a greater degree) in his old; but it was quite extraordinary to see how often improvement in the child was met by improvement in the parents. Only in cases where the family treatment was hopelessly bad was there any attempt made to transplant the child.

Adler's idea was that a child's home, even when imperfect, was the best school for his development yet found. He would always rather strengthen the child to deal with his difficulty than remove him to a place without difficulties, or even with fewer difficulties; but about this—as indeed about all other problems—Adler always relied upon common sense.

Where he had made certain that *no* development could take place in the child because of the evils of his family life, he would advise a complete change of environment, at least for time enough to put the child on his feet and to overcome his worst difficulties.

XV

Humour in Psychology

'One chapter', Adler told the writer, 'in the book we are going to write together about my life, I should like to have called "Therapeutic Jokes".'

It was a great deprivation that during his lifetime we never had the opportunity to enlarge upon his jokes, so that the author felt insufficiently prepared after his death to tackle the subject. However, an opportunity occurred some time later when meeting Herr Frankel, the engineer, who was one of Adler's most intimate boon companions, at least to discuss the subject. We had two long talks together in a smoky café overlooking the Donau Canal in *Wien*, just before the German occupation.

Herr Frankel was, I like to think, almost a product of Adler's jokes.

He was the most genial, the most courageous, the most cheerfully and benevolently funny of human beings; and though the time we met was the break up of all he had lived for and loved, and his very life itself was at stake, he entered into the memory of his old friend's jokes as if nothing but sunshine and security spread themselves out before him. 'I'm afraid', he said, 'I can't be of much use to you about Adler's therapeutic jokes because you will readily understand that he based his jokes on each individual patient's special needs. They were a private affair between himself and his patient, and Adler never repeated them in public. Sometimes a really cured patient might let out a joke or two at his own expense but not the vain ones—and most of us were "vain". However, I can tell you some of the jokes Adler loved and laughed at; and I think you will see that they were always ones that got the better, through wit, of a difficult situation. I may say too that I never heard Adler tell an unkind joke or one directed at the expense of any of his companions. He would often cut in with a joke if he thought the conversation was getting heated, or too personal in any way. He used to say jokes were the best form of conversation because they entertained and did no harm and that very few long conversations could escape both these pitfalls.'

All jokes suffer from being torn from their contexts; still in each of the stories that follow there is a whiff of Adler's sceptical and yet tender enjoyment of the oddities of mankind.

A man of genius, in his divination of facts as well as in his prophecies on things to come, is always a little ahead of the rest of the world; but if he is wise as Adler was wise, he tries to hide his knowledge.

The light-hearted Vienna of 1914 considered that war with Serbia would be a most satisfactory solution for various outstanding political pin-pricks. 'A punitive expedition', the Viennese called it, with tragic felicity—not anticipating that they themselves were to be the 'punished' throughout futurity.

'There is going to be a war,' Adler told his group of Individual Psychologists when the assassination of Franz Ferdinand took place; 'and in my opinion, it will last a long time and famine will be one of its results. Let us show a little foresight and add to the stock of food by growing vegetables wherever there is any ground for them, and perhaps by breeding rabbits, since they breed swiftly and in large quantities.' One of the group, a not wholly satisfactory character, took up the latter project with enthusiasm. A piece of ground was discovered in a distant suburb, with a small hut or summer-house attached to it. This was to be the rabbit farm. Funds were collected from all the group, Adler in particular being lavish in his offerings, and the volunteer member started off to buy the parent rabbits.

At each meeting the producer appeared with more and more glowing accounts of the rabbit farm. A few pairs of these industriously prolific animals had more than met the demands made upon them. Further funds were now needed to supply sufficient food for the little ones. At last the group suggested an excursion to see the results of this successful experiment. Unfortunately, just at this time, a disease attacked the rabbits and their caretaker begged that the visit should be postponed.

Several times over a date was fixed, but foxes, rats, a heavy rainfall, blow after blow descended upon the colony of rabbits the moment any suggestion was made to visit them by the group. At last, feeling a little suspicious, several members of the group decided to pay a visit to the farm without giving any notice to the caretaker. This they did, but there were no rabbits—not even the original pair of meri-

torious parents. The farm, however, was occupied by three illegitimate children of the caretaker. Adler was fond of telling this story.
'After all,' he would finish with a twinkle, 'he *had* produced a family,
though not quite of the kind we had a right to expect!'

When Adler was on special war duty in Cracow, a Polish Jew
deserted to the Austrian side and became one of his patients. 'How
long were you in the Polish Army?' Adler asked him. 'I joined up
three days before I gave myself up to the Austrians,' the Jew replied.
Adler looked surprised. 'I was also in the Russian-Japanese war,' the
Jew continued, 'that time I was made prisoner after two days!' 'But
how did you manage that?' Adler demanded. 'I should like to see the
war I would take part in for more than two days,' replied his patient.
In repeating this story Adler said with a smile and a sigh, 'If only all
soldiers had the same good sense!'

However, it must not be supposed that Adler was a pacifist. He
believed that man must always be prepared to fight for what he
valued; but he also believed that in a socially interested world, run
on good neighbour principles, a man could keep what was of value
without having to fight for it.

An Austrian general once told Adler, 'I find that Jews make very
good soldiers, but they are difficult to get hold of!'

Adler was fond of the following story. A boy came late to school
one day and his teacher asked him why he was late. The boy replied,
'It was so slippery that I took two steps backward for every one I took
forward.' The teacher asked, 'Then how did you get here at all?' 'I
turned round and went home,' said the boy.

Early in the days of the Nazi regime when Jewish children, though
under a cloud, were still allowed to attend the same schools as other
children, a Nazi teacher asked his class, 'Why did the Germans lose
the war?' The proper answer to which, from his point of view, being
'They did not lose it—they were betrayed by the home-front.' No
one, however, quite dared to answer such a tricky question. At last a
little Jewish boy held up his hand. 'Well,' demanded the teacher, 'and
why was it?' 'Please, sir, because of the wicked Jewish generals!' the
child replied. 'Boy,' threatened the teacher, 'we Germans *had* no
Jewish generals!' 'I beg your pardon, sir,' faltered the child, 'but I
meant the wicked Jewish generals on the Allies' side!'

Another of Adler's favourite stories was about an argument between a Catholic priest and a rabbi, both of whom wished to find a
way to unite their religions. The priest said: 'We have Easter—you
have the Passover at the same time. Why not give up the Passover

and celebrate Easter with us?' The rabbi replied: 'That won't work! It was the feast of our deliverance from Egypt—we simply couldn't give that up!' 'Well then,' urged the priest, 'we have so many fasts—and you have only one—why not strike out your only one?' 'That's impossible too,' replied the rabbi, 'the Day of Atonement is the greatest of all our observances.' For some time longer they went on in the same strain; finally the priest lost patience and said: 'Well, suppose you start making the proposals now, and see if you don't find me more reasonable than I find you!' 'All right, then,' agreed the rabbi, 'before anything else is suggested, let's agree to get rid of the whole story about Jesus Christ!'

The following passport stories, Frankel said, had greatly amused Adler. A passport officer asked a Jew desiring to emigrate, what was his religion. 'I am a Christian,' the Jew replied firmly. 'Surely not,' objected the passport officer, 'you look like a Jew, you speak like a Jew, and you have a Jewish name.' 'That may be,' replied the other, 'but I eat pork and I don't believe in God, so of course I am a Christian.'

One day after the rise of the Nazis two Jews were overheard actually cursing the Führer out loud in a public café. A young Nazi immediately dashed across to their table, threateningly demanding how they dared to do such a thing. 'We don't mean *your* Führer,' the Jews told him soothingly, 'we were cursing our own Führer Moses!' 'But why ever should you do that?' the Nazi demanded still suspiciously, 'why do you wish to curse Moses?' 'Because if he hadn't led us out of Egypt, we should have British passports,' replied the Jew.

Two Jewish horse dealers, who happened to be partners, but who with reason greatly distrusted each other, went to their rabbi and asked him to take care of their money for them, and never to give any to either of them without the other being present. One day a chance came to one of them to make a favourable purchase on the spot. He rushed to the rabbi saying, 'Give me the money at once! I know my partner isn't here—but he is only down the street and he will beckon from his window to show you that he agrees to the deal!' The rabbi saw the partner excitedly waving in the distance, and gave up the money. The man made off with it, and was never seen again by either the rabbi or the partner. The partner complained bitterly to the rabbi that he ought not to have given up the money, and declared that he had merely waved from his window in order to stop the sale. The rabbi said, 'Yes, but you see I didn't give him your money at all. I remembered that I had promised you not to do so, and the money that I gave him was therefore my own.' The partner, now much relieved, exclaimed, 'That's all right then! Now give me over all the money we left with you!' 'Oh, no!' said the rabbi, 'that's out of the question. It was a bargain. I was never to give one of you the money without the other being present!'

These jokes may or may not have been used as part of actual treatments by Adler, but the atmosphere of such joking Adler often found very helpful in relieving the tension of undue emotion, often arising in all psychological treatments. He never, however, joked with his patients over their difficulties unless he saw that they could take a joke without being wounded by it: but sometimes they took what he said without understanding the humour that lay behind it.

A patient who never took much pains over her personal appearance, or about the meals which she set before herself or her household or indeed about any other kind of household order, was once astonished by Adler's conduct in a restaurant to which he had specially invited her to dinner by herself. 'I never should have believed it of him,' she told a friend. 'He actually sent his steak back six times to be cooked over again! I had no idea he could be so particular and give so much trouble!' But the friend to whom she told this story knew that Adler never minded how simple his food was or gave any unnecessary trouble about its service for himself, and realized that Adler had meant to show his patient, by a practical demonstration, how important it was to get material things right, and not to evade a responsibility which belongs to all of us alike.

On another occasion, when he saw a patient to whom he was much attached but who he believed was narrowing her life unnecessarily, and in a dangerous manner, he slowly walked towards the corner of the room in which they were sitting together, looking back at her over his shoulders from time to time until he had reached a point where he could move no further and was completely cut off from the rest of the room. 'And where shall I go from here?' he asked her.

Once after one of Adler's lectures a very authoritative and antagonistic lady came up to Adler and began to disagree violently with what he had been saying. Adler listened to her patiently for some time, and then said with a charming smile, 'I find you are wholly right, and therefore we need not continue this discussion any longer, but can say a friendly farewell.'

The lady urged that there was still more to talk over, but Adler shook hands with her firmly, saying, 'No, I understand now all that it is necessary for me to understand, so we will say good-bye!'

HUMOUR IN PSYCHOLOGY

The lady departed reluctantly, and Adler's friends reproached him for letting her believe that she had convinced him. 'Why, you threw away your lecture!' one of them exclaimed. 'Yes, I know,' replied Adler with an indulgent smile, 'but you see I only had to be right once!'

No one who had ever worked with Adler could doubt the depth of his sympathy, but it was always mixed with the strong antiseptic of common sense. Nor would he easily pass over with his patients any wish of theirs to evade a direct issue, or accept the admission of an ignorance he believed that it was within their power to clear up. When a patient said, 'I'm afraid I can't explain this to you,' Adler would reply, 'I assure you, you explain yourself very well without trying!'

Once a patient asked him, 'Shall I be a Socialist or a Nazi? I can't make up my mind!' Adler replied, 'You must certainly vote either one way or the other, or you will be a neurotic!'

Of a man who constantly postponed his decisions, Adler remarked, 'Anyone who takes so long to decide has already decided that he will do nothing!'

On another occasion he told a friend who had to make rather a difficult decision, 'When you hesitate about a decision it is always because you wish to remain where you are.'

Many people have criticized because they failed to understand Adler's handling of the part played by the 'unconscious' in a patient's symptoms. Adler, in contradistinction to Freud, referred to the 'unconscious' as 'the not understood'. He believed as other psychiatrists believe that a great deal does take place beneath the level of a patient's active consciousness but he also believed that this 'unconsciousness' masked motives that the patient feared or was unwilling to reveal to himself, and therefore as it were kept them away from his own consciousness in order to evade having to control them. Adler believed that human beings—other than those who were incurably psychopathic—were always motivated by controllable forces, and knew that they could control them if they understood them; but they simply preferred for reasons of their own *not* to understand them. His treatment therefore consisted in helping a patient unmask those hidden motives until he saw both what they were and what they were preventing him from being able to accomplish with his unfettered powers.

Adler loved Goldsmith's 'Elegy to a Mad Dog' and often quoted with relish:

139

The dog, to gain some private end,
Went mad and bit the man,

with its final *volte face,* 'The dog it was that died'.

For Adler always believed that the neurotic's final and most cruelly persecuted victim was himself.

Adler's whole treatment was based on the fact that though neurotics might have perfectly true grievances and grudges against life, they were capable of giving their contribution to the world even with these handicaps, if they would stop putting all their strength and drive into exploiting their weaknesses rather than in seeking to overcome them by freeing their courage towards co-operative living. 'Courage,' Adler used always to say, 'is the health of the soul.' Instead of trying 'to free the *libido*'—which is nothing but the patient's unreleased self-will—as Freud's system indicated, Adler would always try to release the courage of man's soul in order to link it with the love of his neighbour—or, as he called it, the Law of Social Interest.

The main difficulty in Individual Psychology is that though almost all patients want to be braver and welcome the powers they feel set free in them by an Adlerian analysis, they find the second half of their task—the directing of these new powers away from egocentricity and personal prestige towards the love of their brother man—a much longer and less attractive process. 'Yet', Adler used sometimes to say a little sadly, 'the turning from a minus towards a plus is only one side of the medal—the training towards good fellowship is an equally important half!'

XVI

After-War Years and Friendships

When the war was over in 1919 Austria found herself facing the still more terrible consequences of the Peace. Adler had long foreseen the future doom of his country; but characteristically, as he had no power to deal with its tragedy, he spoke of it as seldom as possible, and then only to those, generally foreigners, in whose discretion and tolerance he could trust.

Adler never cared to talk much about those first two awful years after the war. Vienna was already straitened and freezing, with her food supplies negligible, and now she was left with a few hundred miles of stony mountains instead of a great empire, to supply all her vital needs.

Her hospitals were full of children with softening of the bones; 72 per cent of her new-born babies died of tuberculosis from malnutrition; and complete financial disaster stared her in the face.

What Vienna was like from 1919 to 1921, the author of this book knows very well, for she lived there from 1920 to 1924.

Before the stabilization of the *krone* the small *rentiers* of Vienna with an income of four hundred pounds a year could buy one loaf of bread a month upon this income. A friend who had been left fifteen hundred pounds by a relation spent half his legacy upon his tram fare to the Bank in order to receive his fortune; and a glass of beer and a sandwich, which he took while waiting for the signatures to the transfer, took up the rest of his little heritage; so that he walked home no better off than when he started.

The square outside the main railway station of Vienna was grass grown; and one cab, with a bony horse, waited outside it, generally in vain, for a possible fare. The principal thoroughfares were full of holes. Foreign motorists (there were no Austrians who could afford cars) were asked by public notices to drive very slowly, as the populace were too starved to be able to move quickly enough to avoid being run over. The patients in the hospitals had to be crowded into

141

one ward in the winters of 1919 and 1920 in order to spare fuel; and
the bandages were made of paper. Sick children were fed on acorn
coffee and boiled carrots. For a short, but nightmare period, there
was no chloroform.

The chief child's surgeon came to the author with tears in his eyes
to beg for rubber gloves: 'I cannot get any more in Vienna,' he said.
'Unless you can get them for me all my hip-diseased children must
die—I cannot operate without them! I have only twelve pairs left.'
They were obtained for him, and some of the children did not die.

The American Red Cross was largely responsible for their salva-
tion; the Dutch Red Cross was as quick on the trigger, and did a
continuously magnificent service; the Anglo-American Friends with
the help of the British Government was wonderfully organized and
run in co-operation with the Austrians themselves by Dr. Hilda
Clarke. One Scottish girl—a Miss MacAndrews—whose name should
go down into history as a practical heroine of Romance, put all her
savings into a prize bull and brought him out with her to Austria,
where his redoubtable paternal powers and the good use to which he
put them saved the lives of hundreds of children dying for lack of
milk in the hospitals.

Adler gave his services in every direction unstintingly wherever
and however he could. Vienna was his centre but the doors of the
world were once more open to him, and he was constantly being
called upon for lectures in Germany and Central Europe. He had
an enormous practice, but few of his patients could now afford to
pay him more than sixpence a consultation. Many of them he took
—as other Viennese doctors did—for nothing.

Many doctors' own children were starved to the bone; but butter,
eggs, and milk were practically unobtainable in Vienna, except by
millionaires, who bought them at fabulous prices, or through Foreign Missions, whose supplies came from their own countries and
were supposed to be limited to their personnel.

Adler's family did on the whole rather better than most, for some
of his country patients paid him in kind from farms or big estates;
and his eldest brother, who had a large and well-stocked place, was—
as he had always been, though rather resentfully and grudgingly—a
real Providence to his whole family, even including that rebellious
and hitherto successful Prodigal—Alfred, and his children.

Raissa and the children acted cheerfully and courageously throughout all their hardships.

They had no help now from Russia, either actual or potential; on

AFTER-WAR YEARS AND FRIENDSHIPS

the contrary Raissa's whole family and its fortune were involved in the Bolshevik revolution. Raissa was faced with the life-tragedies and destitution of all her Russian relations and most of her girlhood friends.

Adler stood by her to the limit of his powers; but as anyone knows who has had to meet similar situations, the little that an individual can do, however heroically charitable he happens to be, is as nothing in the face of the economic disruption of a State. Adler had his own family to provide for and to steer through their early years; and the monetary collapse of Austria destroyed his savings. Both care and sorrow, with a sense of complete material instability, made a long visit to the Adler family. However, they were in many ways far better equipped to meet their difficulties than most people.

They were not egocentric, and their tastes were simple; but what perhaps kept up their spirits most, and was of most use to others, was their unconquerable courage. Both Adler and Raissa shared this quality equally; neither of them was to be daunted by the Unknown in any of its forms or however roughly it broke upon them; and they had taught their children the same lesson.

The Adler family rode loose to life, and if unhorsed could remount without assistance. The two youngest, Kurt and Nelly, were too young to share the same responsibility as the others, but there is no question that the two older girls helped their parents by an equal courage and sacrificed their own wishes—ardent as are the wishes of youth—unflinchingly.

They were able to keep their flat in the Dominikanerbastei, as under the Social Democratic Government rents were not allowed to be raised. Adler worked as he had always worked, in a sort of effortless rhythm that exacted little from himself, and nothing from others.

Slowly the black clouds lifted; the *krone* was stabilized, the Austrian loan went through, tourist traffic began, and the charm, the disinterested courage and gaiety of the Austrian people did the rest: Not even during the most agonizing period of starvation and cold did the honesty and courage of these indomitable people relax. The blood came back into the veins of Austria. Since then a far worse disaster has befallen them. Their integrity as a people has been destroyed. Their heritage and tradition has been forced under the heel of a cruel and barbaric conqueror. Vienna is a whispering cemetery. The enemies of peace have proved far more cruel to her than the enemies of war. But it is difficult even in modern times, with all the resources of science put to ignoble uses, to destroy the spirit of a race.

AFTER-WAR YEARS AND FRIENDSHIPS

Those who knew and respected Austria in the days of starvation and economic ruin, after the war of 1914, have not lost their faith in her powers of recuperation after the worse war of 1939, and now need never believe that her heroic and civilized people will lose their immortal heritage.

The spirit has resources of its own that no alien hand, however brutal or however powerful, can destroy.

Adler and his family were typical Viennese; no time was too bad for them to ski in winter, swim in summer and make music all the year round.

Their circle of friends grew larger and larger, and soon became international. Their main difficulty, now that Adler had become famous, was to keep their social life from submerging them altogether.

Fortunately they had all learned in a hard school. Work came first, and nothing as far as Adler was concerned was ever allowed to interfere with it.

In 1919 he made one of the great friendships of his life, a friendship that both influenced and reinforced his future work.

Dr. Lydia Sicher, herself a well-known and greatly respected Viennese psychiatrist and doctor, brought him one of her patients whom Adler successfully cured. Both Lydia and her husband—Professor Harry Sicher—became Adler's most true and devoted friends and adherents. Dr. Lydia Sicher began to make an intensive study of Adlerian psychology, and took up the use of it for her patients, with great success. A volume could and should be written upon Adler and his friends: those that he lost and those who gave him an increasing and unbroken fellowship. The Sichers both belonged to the latter category.

Dr. Lydia Sicher united a brilliant brain with a dauntless spirit; she was therefore exactly the kind of human being who most appealed to Adler. Both as a doctor and as a lecturer, Dr. Lydia Sicher's work was of the highest quality; she possessed many of the characteristics that Adler found most helpful both to the spread of Individual Psychology and to himself personally. Her humour was of a dry and bracing kind, and never failed her. She had all Adler's love of the concrete fact shorn of verbiage, and a staunch fidelity to complete accuracy both of word and thought.

Harry Sicher, her husband, was a skilled dentist and anatomist; he was a Professor of Vienna University and an acknowledged head of his profession. His personality was quite different from that of his

144

wife; he had an easy nature, and a fund of first-class jokes. His high level of intelligence as a scientist with something in him, simple and effortless, made him peculiarly sympathetic to Adler. Harry Sicher's interest in Individual Psychology was different from his wife's; and differently applied. Lydia Sicher based her whole professional life upon it, while to Harry Sicher it was a useful approach to the personality of his patient. He certainly succeeded in giving his patients a complete confidence in him, as well as freedom from anxiety; he did this no doubt partly by the extreme skill in which he wholly avoided or greatly minimized pain or even inconvenience for his patients; but there was also something quite apart from this—a skill and friendliness of personality that he had obviously developed from his understanding of Adler's psychology. Professor Sicher's future career in Chicago, as an anatomist of the first rank, has become internationally famous.

Lydia's successes with her patients were remarkable. She was unflinchingly honest, and perhaps to an ordinary acquaintance might seem brusque and unsympathetic; but beneath the surface, and not very far beneath either, Lydia Sicher's desire to help, and her companionable and dependable personality sprang to meet human need. She was incapable of shirking any effort to relieve pain, or to bring common sense into the mind of her patient. As a friend, she gave without stinting. A word of praise from her had all the force of her personality behind it, and rang so true that the recipient was nerved to fresh efforts by it. A glance of her clear fearless eyes moved halting souls towards fresh endeavours. A quick strong clasp of her firm hand was a living symbol of the worth of human fellowship.

These two friends, from 1919 on, enriched the rest of Adler's life. They stood by him through thick and thin, and fought his difficulties as though they were their own. Lydia Sicher and Franz Plewa— a young medical student—were trained by Adler himself to take his place in Vienna. Their whole-hearted co-operation and understanding of his psychology was a source of continual satisfaction to Adler.

Both worked under him when he was in control of the Psychiatric Ward of the Mariahilfer, Franz-Josef Ambulatorium in Vienna; and when Adler left Vienna, Dr. Lydia Sicher held Adler's appointment, and Plewa continued to assist her. More than three thousand cases passed through their hands in the ensuing years and were treated by them with Individual Psychological methods. They therefore had an unrivalled knowledge of Adler's theories, and of the treatment he applied to a wide variety of mental disease or instability.

Besides this regular hospital appointment Adler was consultant for several mental hospitals in or round Vienna; and many general practitioners and surgeons had such a high regard for his power of diagnosis that he was often called in to give his opinion in doubtful medical or surgical cases, quite independently of any connection with psychiatry.

When asked to what he attributed his success in diagnosis in fields other than his own, Adler would say with a sly twinkle: 'Perhaps because I happened to notice that there was a patient behind the disease.'

When any of Adler's own patients had physical symptoms, Adler was always interested in them and never failed to give practical and helpful advice. He was very quick, too, to spot any hidden trouble or incipient disease of a dangerous kind, and always insisted upon an immediate visit to a suitable specialist.

Adler was very strict as to the rights and duties of his own profession, and never allowed psychiatric treatment by a layman without association with a doctor to take place under his name.

Although he encouraged the training of lay psychiatrists to undertake psychiatric treatment of children, and in special cases even of adults, Adler preferred any grave form of neurosis to be treated only by a doctor who was also a psychiatrist.

Ida Löwy of Vienna was one of the finest and most successful child psychologists. She was an unforgettable and international figure in the Child-Guidance clinics, as well as being, until her psychiatric work took its place, a music teacher by profession. Adler himself trained Ida Löwy and she was perhaps the most wholly imbued with Individual Psychology of any of his friends or adherents. With Ida Löwy, Social Interest *was* as natural as breathing. Her influence over children, and indeed upon all who came into contact with her, was a unique experience.

Her spirit seemed to penetrate into the core of a child's difficulty with the swiftness of lightning; but unlike lightning, her influence moved with the penetrating gentleness of a completely disinterested love—an impersonal, unexacting love—that won an instant response from the child. To watch Ida Löwy conducting a child clinic was to see for the first time how human nature *can* be changed; and what the power is that can change it.

What Ida Löwy brought to the child was an understanding so complete and sincere, and so wholly without any sense of moral or superior judgment, that the child could not fail to slip into this sunny sphere of understanding with relief. For the first time, the child was face to face with the logic of its own difficulties, and saw in a flash the simplest way to master them.

Ida Löwy must always have been a child lover, and no mean natural psychologist; but she owed the ability to use her powers successfully to her own response to Adler's treatment.

She had suffered much from anxiety neurosis in youth, and had had a life of suppression and poverty. Perhaps also the early success of a younger and prettier sister who came into possession of all the primary gifts of life at an early age may have made Ida still more uncertain of her own powers. Adler said once tenderly of Ida (making a play upon her name 'Löwy' which means 'Lion'), 'Such lions often need a little shove to start them off, but when they get it—they go very far!'

Ida Löwy went very far; she worked undemoralized up to the gates of Death; while she lay dying of cancer, she heard of the occupation of Vienna by the German Reich and knew that it meant the end of her people, and of all possibility of continuing the work to which she had given her life.

The writer saw her take her last clinic only a few weeks before her death, with an unruffled spirit and with no outward sign of pain or even discomfort, though death was written in her face.

For five hours Ida Löwy sat by her little table, with a cup of tea on it, placed there by an anxious friend, which she forgot to drink. Each child in turn came to her loaded down with the weight of its special anxiety; and turned away with shining eyes and a lighter heart.

Not even Adler could have had many such friends as Ida Löwy but it is safe to say that only Adler could have had such a friend, for it was from him that she had learned how to become a 'whole human being'.

XVII

Adler's two great Teacher Students and their Work founded upon his Psychology

---

Nobody who has not lived through the after-war years in Vienna can imagine how difficult it was to launch, at such a defeated and devitalized time, any new activity. Above all, to launch it in a community that was on the verge of starvation, and suffering from all the symptoms of foodlessness and extreme cold.

Between 1919 and 1922 the vital services of life were almost at a standstill in the city of Vienna. Hospitals, markets, food supplies, gas, electricity—every need of a great city's normal life was working at the lowest possible pressure. There was hardly any means of locomotion other than the battered pre-war trams, deprived of sufficient current to do more than jerk and crawl through the neglected streets, with constant stoppages.

The telephone service was wholly problematical. Wood and all fuel, except for Foreign Missions, were almost unprocurable, and prohibitively expensive. Only those who could carry it back from the Wienerwald on their shoulders could get wood for the carrying; and some of these died under its weight on their way home.

Adler needed to be the heroic optimist that he was, impelled by a selfless love and generosity, in order to launch his new service in the depleted schools, through ill-nourished teachers, to worse-nourished children.

Nevertheless, Adler launched it; and his faith in the teachers was justified. In 1920 he was appointed head of the first Individual Psychology clinic for problem children at the Kaiser Franz-Josef Ambulatorium, Vienna.

Perhaps his science could not have succeeded with a less cultured background or in any city with less courage and creative power than Vienna. Perhaps the *Wien* that Adler had so loved and cherished, and from whose lack of appreciation he suffered all his life, nevertheless gave him, in her worst hour, an immortal gift—a gift that he would have prized far beyond any personal one—by allowing him a field upon which he could prove to the world the success of his discoveries.

From the ruins of her old luxury and grandeur, Vienna built up this new thought-life of one of the greatest of her sons.

Adler created his psychology; Glöckel set it free to act; but it was upon the teachers that the success of this new system depended. Nor did Adler ever fail to give them the fullest possible credit for the triumphant success of his psychology acting upon human material. 'The Teacher', Adler used to say, 'is the long arm of the family. He can reach the child, at a time when it has passed beyond its parents' control.' He used to add: 'To teach all the parents in the world how to bring up a child is too ambitious a task for Individual Psychology. There are too many parents and all are not willing to come to us; but there are not too many teachers; and I have always found teachers ready to find out how to make their own work more successful by learning how to understand the child.' The Vienna teachers, however starved and listless, were a noble band who had in their hearts a disinterested love of their profession, which made them peculiarly accessible to Adler's teaching. It cannot have been mere chance that gave to Adler two of the best teacher-recipients and leaders in Ferdinand Birnbaum and Oskar Spiel that anyone could possibly have found; and it is probably not too much to say that without them Individual Psychology could never have had so sound and enduring a success. No life of Adler would be complete without a·description of them and of the work they did for Individual Psychology.

Spiel, the first of these two men to discover Adler, came to the Berlin Conference on Individual Psychology which was organized and carried through with triumphant success by Frau Herz and Frau Orgler.

Adler's lectures at this Conference were the foundation for his book *Der Sinn des Lebens*, only translated towards the end of his life, and known in English as *Social Interest: A Challenge to Mankind.* They were also Adler's answer to Freud's just published *Das Unbehagen in der Kultur*, a deeply pessimistic book which seemed to Adler to take the moral law out of the Universe and to be a direct attack upon the value of human life. It is in this book that Freud shows his anti-social bias by asking the question 'Why should I love my neighbour as myself?'

Adler always spoke and wrote best when he was challenged, and at

149

this conference his course of lectures was extraordinarily successful, and his audiences grew larger and larger, spreading his psychology very widely over Germany. Unfortunately, however, Adler's psychology could not take deep root in Berlin on account of the political unrest that preceded the Nazi regime and the dread return of militarism, with its corollary of authoritative education.

Spiel, a Viennese school teacher of great ethical intelligence, found in these Berlin lectures of Adler's a spiritual release and a source of fresh hope for the future of mankind.

Spiel was to become one of the most successful and capable exponents of Adler's psychology. He had already been studying Freud, and attending the School of Psycho-Analysis for a year, with increasing dissatisfaction. 'I could not find', Spiel told the author, 'anything I could apply to my work as a teacher. Freud's theories were too complicated for any child to understand, and far too sterile ethically to be of any use to children, even if they could have understood them! The moment I heard Adler's opening lecture, I realized I had found the key to my difficulties. This is what I wanted for my children. I had been struck already by the articles of Künkel and Kronfeld in the *Internationale Zeitschrift für Individual Psychologie*. Both had a nearer approach to Adler, and it was my interest in their writings that brought me to the Berlin Congress.

'I had of course often heard in *Wien* of Adler's child-guidance clinics, but I had hitherto supposed that his psychology could only be a help in directly abnormal cases. I had not realized the universal value of Adler's teachings, or that they could be applied to every child, and by every teacher.

'This Berlin Congress was a revelation to me; perhaps I was even more convinced of the practical truth of Individual Psychology and its bearing upon my profession by the lecture of another teacher than by Adler himself, since I knew Adler to be a genius and was not sure if his dynamic powers were not due more to his personality than to the theories themselves. But when I heard one of the Munich teachers lecture upon Individual Psychology I was convinced by the weight of the facts alone. Here was a man who gave us the practical application of Adler's theories upon his own scholars. Nor was this man a singularly effective personality; except by the ability with which he handled his facts, he might have been described as the ordinary provincial teacher. Yet after I had heard him, I knew that I must from henceforward be an Adlerian myself, and devote all my powers to mastering this new science.'

150

ADLER'S TWO GREAT TEACHER STUDENTS

On his return to Vienna, Spiel took his experience and the decision he had reached through it to another teacher, his greatest friend, Birnbaum.

Birnbaum listened with cautious interest, and answered: 'Let us go then, and hear Adler speak at the Volks Institut together, before we commit ourselves further. Hitherto I have avoided his lectures there as they sounded so popular. But if we find he really has something we can act on, I will throw in my lot with yours and we will work for him together.' They left the Volks Institut, after hearing Adler's lecture, equally convinced and enthusiastic adherents of Individual Psychology.

Birnbaum was an educationalist of a very high order; and it was upon the work of these two men, acting together, that the success of the Adlerian doctrine in the schools of Vienna subsequently rested.

They were both men enthusiastically in love with their profession, and completely disinterested as to its rewards.

Adler became deeply attached to them, and always admired and drew attention to their work with pride and affection.

These two devoted and intimate friends, Spiel and Birnbaum, had wholly different natures and human attributes.

Birnbaum was a typical German in the best sense of the word, an infinitely conscientious and accurate man, a great organizer, understanding to the minutest detail how to carry out a theory. He was a man who never said or did anything that he was not equally prepared to explain. His every thought had the clarity of a jewel. He never rested until he had found an exact definition; and his powers of work were inexhaustible.

Birnbaum had a rugged exterior, and a temper slow to rouse but of indomitable courage. Very few things angered him, and nothing daunted him.

At the time when he put in his Professorship thesis, to mention Adler at all was damning, if not actually dangerous. Birnbaum founded his thesis upon Adler's doctrine, and mentioned his name placidly at every turn of his argument.

So struck were the judges by this disinterested integrity that they decided to give Birnbaum the Professorship in spite of their political cautiousness.

'He is too honest and courageous a man to lose,' one of his judges admitted. 'Let us pass his thesis and accept the consequences.'

Birnbaum was a true leader, and in himself a great man; but he never had even the wish to use his powers for personal success or

151

beyond the range of his own particular job; nor did he have time to realize what he had in fact accomplished. Birnbaum was not one of Adler's most intimate friends, but he was certainly one of his most real and valuable ones. He always took Adler as he found him, with a trust so absolute and so unwavering that nothing ever shook it.

The mischief-making and back-biting so common among the disciples of great men never troubled or even reached Birnbaum. He and Adler thrashed out together whatever differences of opinion they had in their common problems, with unruffled good humour, over a long stretch of years. 'I never found Adler difficult,' Birnbaum told the writer, 'nor do I believe anyone who had common sense or humour ever quarrelled with him. Those of his friends who complained that he was dominating or quarrelsome must have been thin-skinned indeed—or perhaps too vain to be quite honest. I do not suppose that Adler would have been gentle to dishonest persons —unless he were treating them! He was a man who liked plain speaking between friends. He always meant what he said, and expected us to do the same. With such a man *anyone* ought to be able to get on.'

Spiel was perhaps even nearer to Adler's heart than Birnbaum, for he was a true Viennese, as Adler himself was, a man of extremely easy and elastic nature, with great contact-making powers. No child could ever have failed to feel at home with Spiel, though Birnbaum would very likely have awed him. Spiel had as much natural dignity and selflessness as Birnbaum but they were of a much less imposing and visible kind. Like Adler, he never gave anyone a sense of hurry or pressure, and was without inward tension.

These two men worked Individual Psychology into a practical teaching system which spread among the schools from district to district. They carried on in their own school extensive note-taking; and followed up their pupils' subsequent careers with tireless exactitude.

If the freedom to develop human nature educationally survives, it will be largely upon the systematic selflessness of these two great men that its future rests.

Their case notes and class histories exist, and exist safely in book form. Unfortunately the political regimes of Dollfuss and Schuschnigg were inimical to their publication in Austria; and Nazi Germany was even more strict against any expression of a liberal education.

They had, therefore, with great difficulty and at an expense that neither could afford, to get their work translated how and where they could, and then finally transplanted into another country.

Spiel's book will appear, it is hoped, and in a suitable form, before very long. This book of theirs, quoted extensively in Lewis Way's Pelican *Adler*, will act as the most important textbook that exists of the Adlerian system applied to child-education.

It is a revelation of what has been done, and therefore of what *can* be done, in setting free children's personalities, without fear of future neurosis or delinquency, to live a normal life in the service of their community.

In spite of the desperate poverty and general devitalization of Vienna after the war, the child-guidance clinics spread very rapidly, from their earliest inception in 1919, until they were attached to more than thirty schools; while Adler's own Demonstration Lectures were attended by teachers from over fifty schools in Vienna or from the surrounding suburbs.

In the second and twentieth districts alone there were nine of these clinics, conducted by Adlerian teachers.

The peak years of this system of education, before politics disturbed its foundation, were 1927 to 1931. Adler's influence over this period upon the child-life in Vienna could hardly be exaggerated.

People from all over the world were waking up to the part that Vienna was playing in education, and to this new method of dealing with the greatest problem of mankind: the successful training of a human being.

From every country teachers were heading towards Vienna, in spite of the language barrier, to study the Adlerian system at firsthand and pick up what they could for their own countries.

The spirit of Individual Psychology was already moulding the thought of international educationalists, and the almost yearly Educational Conferences and Congresses held in the summers greatly strengthened Adler's influence.

Under Glöckel a practice had been introduced into the *Gemeinde Wien* schools to give the children certain hours a week for free discussion in class upon any topic of general interest, the subject to be chosen by the children themselves.

Adler's own life at this time was so full, and the calls upon his time so urgent, that he was only once able to visit the school where Spiel worked, in order to see for himself his thoughts put into living flesh.

Adler attended one of these free discussion hours. It happened to be the last, of a class of boys of fourteen who were about to leave their school and go out into the world the following week.

Spiel's fifty boys had chosen for their final discussion 'The Meaning of Life', perhaps promoted to it on this occasion by Spiel himself, and his deep admiration for Adler's *Der Sinn des Lebens*.

Adler sat silently in a corner of the big classroom, listening intently to the discussion that took place.

These were boys, formed by his theories, who had been trained in courage and co-operation; boys who had learned to use social interest instead of egocentricity for the goal of their whole beings, until it had become an unconscious happy process, freeing them alike from tension and self-seeking.

To Adler it was a new and marvellous experience, for he had never seen before the children of his mind take on flesh and blood: their spirits endowed with his spirit; their eager voices pouring out the very stuff of his heart.

It was an historic occasion, if history were really a study of the spirit of man, rather than of his outward possessions and his unhappy struggles to retain them.

Here sat the creator, and this group of ardent, happy, manly boys was his creation. Spiel told the writer, 'I had never heard the boys speak with more manliness and good sense. I could not have wished for a better discussion, or for one more wholly based on common sense. Each boy took his turn, and each had something to say that was worth saying.'

When the hour was over, Adler got up in absolute silence, too moved for speech, and wrung the hand of his interpreter; an interpreter who had acted as a true and sound bridge between Adler's own thoughts and their human receptacles.

'He never spoke of it to me afterwards,' Spiel told the writer, 'nor I to him. But I had the feeling that it was one of the happiest hours of Adler's life; and I *know* that it was the happiest of mine!'

Seven years later, Spiel held a reunion for this class of boys, and every one of them came to it.

It was an hour of great poverty and distress; but even at so dire a period only one boy out of the whole class was unemployed, and he was to find employment again within the month.

This was a proof of Adler's theories. The world had need of such human material as they could turn out.

When in the years to follow the authoritative regime blotted out all that it could of freedom and self-development in the schools of

154

Vienna, Fräulein Seidler said to the writer, with a quiet smile: 'There is one thing they have not been able to do; although they can rob the children of their intellectual liberty and free self-development, unless they dismiss every teacher in the *Gemeinde Wien* they cannot rob the children of what the teachers have learned. What Adler and his theories made us—we remain.'

XVIII

Adler's Main Contributions to Thought

Any serious student of psychology should read Professor Ansbacher's first full and systematic presentation of Adler's writings, *The Individual Psychology of Alfred Adler*, edited and annotated by Heinz L. and Rowena Ansbacher.

No such clear and thorough compilation of Adler's psychology, chronologically presented, has as yet appeared. It is a landmark in psychology.

The Ansbacher quotations from Adler as well as the comments made on them are extraordinarily well chosen and substantiated.

The comparisons drawn between Freud and Adler reveal as never before the basic cleavage between these two great thinkers. Ansbacher brings out with penetrating skill the similarities between Adler's discoveries and the present-day views of modern psychology based on the social sciences.

Nor can one afford to overlook two other important books written on Adler by Lewis Way, *Adler's Place in Psychology* and his more recent Pelican *Adler*. All three of these books throw fresh light on Adler's main contributions to psychology, which I have grouped superficially and for convenience in this chapter under the following headings:

I. The inferiority feeling, or as it is more generally but less correctly termed by the general public, 'The inferiority complex'. This—of all his discoveries—is the one most popularly connected with his name. 'I am', as Adler used to say smilingly, 'the legitimate father of the inferiority complex.'

II. The family-constellation theory, upon which much of modern child guidance is based.

III. Adler's special treatment of 'Neurosis' founded upon his theory that 'Neurosis is the *exploitation* of shock', and an effort upon the part of the patient to escape the normal responsibilities of human life.

156

ADLER'S MAIN CONTRIBUTIONS TO THOUGHT

IV. His theories on Delinquency—which the author has attempted to make plain in his treatment of the convict and other criminal patients. See Chapter XXIII.

V. Dream Theories. See *Social Interest*. Adler.

VI. Early Memories. See *Social Interest*. Adler.

VII. The Masculine Protest. *What Life Should Mean to You*. Adler.

VIII. Four General Types of Human Beings. See *Social Interest*. Adler.

IX. Three Life Tasks. See *Understanding Human Nature*. Adler.

X. Laws of Social Interest. See *Social Interest*. Adler.

I. Inferiority Complex

Adler taught that every human being's main instinct strives towards an advance from a minus or inferiority feeling towards a plus or superiority feeling; and that the difficulties of life, or the inferiority of organs themselves, can always be compensated for by the individual's own efforts to overcome them.

Adler's first well-known text-book *Organ Inferiorities and their Psychical Compensations*, was largely accepted as a classic by his medical contemporaries.

An inferiority feeling in the young of the human species was, in Adler's mind, never a failing or defect, nor in any way comparable to a neurosis, since the child is *really* helpless; and his physical and mental inferiority are facts of nature and not any attempts upon the child's part to evade responsibility.

It is not unless the child *uses* this fact of his inferiority as an alibi to prevent himself from carrying out the contributions within his power that the inferiority *feeling* becomes a 'complex', and prevents the child's normal development.

Adler taught that to prevent a negative or neurotic tendency in the child, he should from the first be encouraged to make his contribution towards the family well-being. When asked at what period a child should begin his contribution towards life, Adler said 'Within the first half hour'.

Out of the child's first sense of inferiority, Adler believed he began to form his life-plan—in an urge to overcome his limitations. Naturally the child is not in a position to form a wise life-plan from the facts at his disposal at this period but we may very soon see if he deviates in any dangerous way from the normal by his behaviour. 'How can you tell if a child is neurotic or not?' Adler was frequently asked.

157

'By whether he is troublesome or not,' Adler would promptly reply. 'Any child that gives trouble without due cause *is* a neurotic child.'

A neurotic child always cries for what he wants instead of trying to get it by his own efforts, and attempts to dominate others by his weakness. Sometimes the child uses coaxing methods, sometimes rages—sometimes a passive type of goodness in order to subjugate his elders. Slavish obedience on the part of the child is extremely dangerous to him in later life, since he must sooner or later be forced into emergencies where he has no commands to depend on, and where the habit of unreasoning obedience makes him easily flustered or drives him into a panic. Wise encouragement and a gentle guiding into situations where the child *can* make a success for himself, without undue expenditure of effort, soon set the neurotic child back upon the paths of responsibility and courage.

The delinquent child, Adler pointed out, is also easy to spot. This is the child who insists on having his own way to the detriment of others. When a child habitually hurts other people in order to get what he wants, he is a potentially delinquent child. All children occasionally make this blunder just as all children occasionally cry for what they want; what distinguishes the potential neurotic or potential delinquent child from the normal one is *persistence* in these wrong methods of overcoming difficulties.

Adler taught that the child's life-plan is formed in the first three to five years of its life. Often even at three years old this pattern is completely formed, but it can at any time be altered, since it is formed upon the child's opinion of himself and others, and wherever the child, either by wise persuasion or by a discovery of his own, succeeds in altering his opinion of himself and the world round him to a more normal and courageous one, his life-plan will also change to suit his new outlook. He will have achieved a firmer and more courageous life-pattern, although perhaps never a wholly different one.

The part played upon the child by parents, teachers and contemporaries will all help or hinder the child in creating his life-plan— but he himself is the creative artist, and has to accept the full responsibility for his own acts. The materials others have provided for him —but the pattern is his own. Adler held that a child may be a 'spoilt' child where there are no traces of outside spoiling; nevertheless it adds terribly to any child's handicaps, when outside spoiling is there to increase his wrong view of life. Adler taught that alternatives and developments can be made in the life-plan at any time in a man's history, but naturally prevention is far easier than cure, and where habits have not had time to shackle the child's spirit, he has more freedom for a fresh development.

Adler used to relate in proof of this theory that during the war he had two patients, who on the same day had to have their right arms amputated at the shoulder; two years later both visited him in Vienna, by chance in the same week. One of them said to him: 'Dr. Adler, I am helpless without my right arm. I cannot work; marriage is out of the question for me; I am a log of wood—not a man!' The second said: 'Dr. Adler, I find I can get on beautifully without that right arm. I have a better job than before I lost it. I am married and have a fine boy. I sometimes ask myself why nature provides us with two arms when one suffices!'

II. Family-Constellation

Adler discovered that one of the most influential factors in the forming of the child's life-plan is his place in the family-constellation. People often wonder why one child in a family, born of the same parents with the same heredity as the other children, brought up in the same environment, treated perhaps with the same individual care and attention, nevertheless develops wholly differently—you can have in the same family a 'good' child and a 'bad' child, a courageous, wise and self-reliant child, and a cowardly, foolish and dependent child, and yet every factor in the children's upbringing appears to be the same. But Adler pointed out that *not* every factor is the same, since one child is born before or after the other, or he is an only child without a contemporary, and it is just upon this fact— whether a child is an eldest, a second, a youngest, or an only child— that much of his future attitude towards life depends.

An 'eldest', Adler discovered, was generally a dependable conventional, authoritative, law-abiding child, standing by its parents in its protective and sometimes domineering attitude towards the younger children; but this is by no means invariable as the pattern of an eldest—since the child may take what Adler has termed its 'dethronement' by a second child so much to heart that it becomes discouraged, loses all self-reliant powers, and refuses to accept responsibility; but an 'eldest' to whom his parents have given a wise and loving explanation of his followers in the family, so that he feels he has an equal stake in their well-being, is unlikely to lose courage or to fail in keeping his headship. He *is* the eldest, which means that he is at least one birthday ahead of the interloper; although a fiercely ambitious, pace-making 'rebel' of a second child may give an 'eldest' a hard time of it.

The second child, Adler held, was usually a rebel; authority is unlikely to have any charms for him, and he is more likely to egg on his younger brothers and sisters against the eldest and the parents than to do much conventional governing on his own. The second child is often a shatterer of conventions: a discoverer and a thruster into the unknown. He is, as it were, born 'modern'. He may not have more creative gifts than the other children, but he is spurred on by his desire to overtake the eldest, into a more decisive and practical use of the gifts he has. On the other hand a 'model' eldest may set so high and severe a pace by his dazzling qualities plus his privilege as first-born, that his second out of sheer despair at coping with such superiority may become either an extremely naughty and difficult child or even run off the rails altogether. He may also become apathetic and a day-dreamer, living in an unreal world and retreating from the normal life of his fellows. If the eldest is a scholar, this discouraged second will probably refuse learning and become an athlete, if his eldest brother has not already shone in that particular field. He will, in almost every case, unless very wisely handled and understood by his parents and others in authority over him, act in an extremely perverse and obstinate manner, especially if he is quickly followed by another strongly individual and pace-making child. Boys are often discouraged by energetic and successful sisters. The position of one boy in a family of girls, or of one girl outnumbered by brothers, has also its special difficulties and dangers. A 'youngest' of either sex has a quite peculiar place in this 'constellation' of the human family. He may, knowing himself hopelessly out-distanced in point of time, and probably size, by all the other children, feel himself greatly discouraged, and that his only chance of obtaining notice is by becoming a buffoon, or a family pet. (Youngests often take up the career of entertainer in later life!) Or he may be too discouraged to develop fully upon normal lines. If his elders have all shown themselves to be brilliant successes in too many fields he may suffer from work or career difficulties all his life. On the other hand the youngest, having the greatest need of courage and independence, and never being threatened by a successor, may develop—like the third child in the fairy tale—and be the most successful of them all. It is always the youngest prince in the fairy tale who out-distances the whole family and carries off the princess. This the youngest very often does in real life as well; but much depends upon the wise refusal of his parents either to make a pet of him because he is the youngest, or to allow any authority on the part of the elder children to damp his courage. It may sometimes be the elder children's duty to protect the baby from real danger, but it is never their duty to hector or domineer over him—this would result in taking away all his initiative, in later life. Needless to say all cruel teasing should be put a stop to by the parents, while at the same time no healthy give and take among the children should ever be interfered with, even if at times it takes rather a rough form for the youngest.

On one occasion, while Adler was looking on, a youngest of little more than a year old was being thumped and banged about in a small go-cart round and round a plot of grass by his elder brother— the expression upon the baby's face was ecstatic. One of the by-standers wanted to intervene, fearing the child would be thrown out, but Adler after watching the game carefully for a moment saw that the child was in no real danger and remarked reassuringly: 'That eldest looks where he is going; I think he can be trusted to see that the baby comes to no harm.'

Adler always advised a common-sense view of the dangers to which children are exposed. Small obstacles within their power to overcome, he thought they should always be encouraged to tackle; small infringements of natural laws can only result in small penalties, and experiencing them improves the child's judgment and power to face life; but Adler was most insistent that nothing should be allowed to happen to a child that could prove a serious handicap to his rudimentary powers, or act as a discouragement to his expanding spirit. Experience had convinced him that a normal child can recover from shocks or accidents without adverse spiritual results; but the potentially neurotic or delinquent children might very well use such accidents as escapes or retreats from the healthy challenges of life.

III. Neurosis

Adler always treated children upon success and encouragement lines; but in his treatment of adults the dread moment of 'unmasking' had to come, when the patient had to see for the first time what his real likeness was. His usual reaction was an emphatic 'No!' and a heightened feeling of conviction that he must be the right judge of himself, and Adler's opinion of him wrong.

Adler always dealt very unemotionally and almost casually with his patient's first horrified opposition. 'It is only a question of how to use your ingredients,' he would say reassuringly. 'You tell me what results you find—and I tell you why you find them—you should not be offended. If I tell my cook, "Perhaps a little less sugar next time—or a little more," she is not annoyed with me. You are not at all an inferior person but I do tell you that you are putting your powers upon a useless rather than upon a useful side of life. You see this already for yourself—or you would not have come to me! I will tell you a story so that you can see better what I mean. A butcher's assistant once said to the butcher: "Your nails are black." "I can easily remedy that," replied the butcher. "I bet you that with my own chopper I can remove that line of black!" The assistant agreed to the bet, and the butcher seized his chopper and chopped off his nails; unfortunately he took off the top of his thumb with them. "I was right!" he exclaimed, in spite of the loss. In a sense,' Adler would add, 'the butcher *was* right, and you also are right when you think that you know how to treat yourself better than I know how to treat you—but you are right at the expense of your thumb.'

IV. Delinquency

(See Chapter XXIII—'Adler on Criminals'.)

V and VI. Dreams and Early Memories

Adler was unable to accept Freud's theory of the invariability of the phallic symbol in dreams; he found instead that his patients presented in all their dreams some clue to their individual life-plan.

Adler taught that dreams were the patient's way of spurring himself on towards his accepted goal, or of warning himself off obstacles to it.

In the same manner he believed that a patient's earliest memory was important, as an indication of his aim in life, not from any intrinsic value the memory might contain, or even because it was the patient's earliest memory, but because it was his *choice*. 'Even when a patient lies it is of value to me,' Adler would say, 'it is *his* lie and nobody else's! What he cannot disguise is his own originality.'

Adler attached great importance as to whether his patient had an aural or a visual memory, or if (as in some cases) he seemed to have both. Adler thought that to have both equally was a sign of great creative power and that the patient should become (if he were not already) a creative artist. 'You will no doubt suffer more than most people,' he told one of these patients, 'but I think that you can also give more.'

Adler was delighted with a saying of Thoreau's, 'Nature is always on the side of the most sensitive.'

VII. The Masculine Protest

Dr. Alexander Neuer states that Adler's theory of 'masculine protest' was brought out by him, in point of time, before Freud's 'Castration Complex' to which it has often been compared. The two theories, however, were not only different in time, but also in origin; and the deductions to be drawn from them are wholly different.

Adler taught that women had an equal value to men, but not necessarily the same value. He greatly liked the saying of Erasmus, 'Women have different biological functions from men, but they should have the same education and the same virtues.'

Adler believed that the potential powers of a woman had always been equal to those of men, but that the false evaluation forced upon them by the physically stronger male sex had discouraged women, so that except in favourable circumstances they were often unable to produce equal results. He often pointed out that in those careers where the male sex had not claimed superiority, women more than held their own, such as the stage and dancing.

Adler believed that this false sense of inferiority was a great handicap to the development of the human race, since it not only prevented humanity from using more than half of its powers, but it seriously impeded the good-will between men and women. Because of their conscious or unconscious resentment and their deep sense of deprivation, women often refuse marriage altogether, or become frigid and unsatisfactory sex-partners to their mates. They often also make up for their lack of permitted scope by becoming parasitic, and overstress their sex in order to control their male admirers. On the other hand many strong and useful women, warped by their inability to practise the careers of their brothers or to enjoy their social freedom, become domineering and tyrannical whenever any of the power they longed for is put into their hands. Homes are often wrecked by the emotional explosions of suppressed and disappointed women. The maternal instinct is too often exploited by them and over-emphasized in order to make up for their lack of a genuine sex life.

'No human being,' Adler pointed out, 'can bear to be dominated by another.' And when Adler said '*can* bear' he meant as well 'should *have* to bear'.

Adler applied his term 'masculine protest' to men as well as to women. He taught that some men may feel that they must stress their manhood in order to feel sure of their superiority to women, since they may not have grounds for feeling sure of it as human beings; while the term is equally applicable to women who some-times over-stress their powers as human beings in order to escape an imagined sex inferiority. 'Neither sex should assume a higher value than the other,' Adler used to say, 'but certainly if nature has a favourite, it is the female, since she grants to the mother the closest form of co-operation. It is a choice, whether a male or female co-operate in the act of sex; but it is a matter of life and death that the mother and child co-operate in their long dual-life before birth and in the act of sustenance after birth.'

Adler believed that the masculine protest was largely responsible for war, hate, slavery, and most of the world's greatest evils. This belief made him curiously kind and understanding to domineering and tyrannical women patients—much as he disliked any form of human tyranny—because he believed they were suffering from an unfair sense of inferiority.

Raissa points out that Adler's having been born and brought up in a *petit bourgeois* family (in spite of his constant early proletarian associations) made it most difficult for him in their early married life to understand what freedom and cultural resources meant to women. This was the first great drawback to their happiness, for Raissa had been born into the intelligentzia class, and always claimed complete independence as a natural right.

Adler had the advantage of a knowledge of human beings—both male and female—drawn from three important strata of social life. He was brought up in the streets; shared the background of the bourgeoisie in his family life; and married into the intelligentzia.

In his maturity, and always in his practice, Adler gave women the fullest possible recognition and urged them towards every form of self-reliance and the development of all their powers.

He acted in the same way in the education of his daughters. Raissa perhaps had taught him more than she realized by her insistence upon a woman's equal status.

In order to understand the full worth of Adler's attitude in his theory of the masculine protest we must take his own experience as part of his discovery. Adler had fallen in love with Raissa for her free spirit, her independence, and her courage; but he was to find himself (confused by the impedimenta of his strict and old-fashioned upbringing) jealous as a young man of all these qualities. No man stood between Adler and the core of his wife's heart—(though for many years he took the shadow of an early love for its substance)— but it was almost impossible for him to believe that only a cause, and that a political cause, could take the place he believed he had a right to possess in Raissa's heart.

Freud believed that it was the physical lack of the genital organ in woman that causes her sense of inferiority and consequent resentment against man, but Adler, with his far greater sensitiveness to the human spirit, realized that women are more than compensated for any sense of physical frustration by the part nature has given them as the bearers and bringers forth of life. It is woman's status as a human being—not her sex organs—that causes her to rebel and to feel deprived of her rights. Raissa as a mother was satisfied. Raissa as a human being deeply resented any inequality or limitation thrust upon her by Adler's young jealousies and rigidities. These had to be broken down in him; and Adler broke them down. He became a champion of women's rights, perhaps the greatest champion that women have ever had—because the least wholesale and the most searchingly practical.

Adler was often asked to examine by intelligence tests the relative mental capacities of boys and girls. His belief in the accuracy of intelligence tests results was by no means entire, although he thought such tests had a certain value for actual knowledge at a given moment; but he thought no child's potentialities could be measured by any mechanical test.

At the moment the test was taken the child might not be at its best, or some factor in its environment might be threatening its inner stability. His examination of sex equality by these tests, however, brought out one interesting result.

He found, as other experts in the same field have also found, that girls frequently out-distance boys up to adolescence, and then fall behind; but there were exceptional girls—to be found in all the schools and colleges he examined—who kept their pace without losing ground, to the end. To find a common factor in the cases of these exceptional girls became Adler's aim, and by constant questioning he at last arrived at a common factor. These specially intelligent girls, he found, had mothers who had successfully practised careers of their own. As a consequence, the daughters suffered from *no* masculine protest and, feeling no discouragement at the thought of their futures, were free to use their full powers.

Some schools of psychiatry believe that Adler shirked the whole part played by sex in human life. The fact that he believed not only in the possibility of, but in the improvement of the human race by monogamy, highly aggravated others. Nevertheless, it would not be true to think that Adler overlooked the part played by any instinct; he was merely unwilling to divide one instinct from the 'whole'; and he certainly believed that all the instincts were controllable by, and harnessed to, the spirit of man—and that his senses were his servants, not his rulers. Exactly what he thought about sex can be found in *Social Interest* where it plays its part in the whole system of Adler's psychology; and in the *Nervous Character*, where sex is shown with desperate thoroughness in relation to Adler's theory of the *Gegenspieler*, the person 'played against' in early childhood, and re-introduced in later life—in the duel of the sexes.

Where Adler differed from all other psychiatrists upon the subject of sex was that he never divided it from any of the other instincts, or from man as a whole. He believed that sex is often used as a stalking-horse in neurosis, and that a patient who develops sex obsessions or perversions does so in order to protect himself from carrying out the normal duties and obligations of life. A sex-maniac was for Adler simply a person who chose sex as an escape from something else that he feared or disliked more. For instance, a sexmaniac cannot earn his living or become the father or mother of a family.

Adler's favourite question to a neurotic was, 'What would you do if you had not got this trouble?' and according to his patient's answer, he usually found what the patient was trying to avoid.

The co-operation involved in a 'task for two', as Adler termed marriage, was what such people really wanted to avoid—not a physical difficulty. That there might be an organic defect in the sex organs Adler never denied, and would always, in doubtful cases, look for one, but he seldom found that there was an unsurmountable physical difficulty, once the psychical pressure was removed.

Homosexuality and Lesbianism Adler always treated as lack of courage. These were but ways of obtaining a slight release for a physical need, while avoiding a greater obligation. A transient partner of your own sex is a better known road, and requires less courage, than a permanent contact with an 'unknown' sex.

166

VIII. Four General Types of Human Beings

Adler believed that every individual differs from another, and that there are no mechanistic or physical tests that can deal adequately with these variations. For purposes of classification, however, he was willing to group human beings under four general types, though he always stressed that there were in each case individual differences:

1. Those who domineer over others and seek to act as dictators.

2. Those who seek their success line in a parasitic direction, leaning upon others and refusing to carry out the obligations of life by themselves.

3. Those who retreat both from their obligations and from other human beings alike, and very often end in a final retreat from life altogether—that of suicide.

4. Those who accept co-operation with others, and act upon this social sense.

Adler always gave as a common solution of these three first types —the knowledge and practice of social interest. This Law of Social Interest or 'Love thy Neighbour', as Adler used to call it, was the core of his teaching, and, he believed, the only cure for either neurosis or delinquency.

IX. Three Life Tasks

Adler taught that men cannot be judged from within by their 'possessions', as he used to call nerves, glands, traumas, drives, etc., since both judge and prisoner are liable to misconstrue what is invisible and incalculable; but that he *can* be judged with no danger from introspection by how he measures up to the three common life tasks set before every human being between the cradle and the grave: work or employment, love or marriage, social contact. Anyone living up to these three tasks successfully, although imperfectly, will have no serious mental or nervous breakdown. Such a man is, to all intents and purposes, a good approach to a normal human being; but anyone who cannot stand up to these three life tasks or who fails in any one of them is to that extent less normal, and more threatened by the mischances and dangers of life. If he fails in all three he is certain to come to grief; in fact he has already done so—since he has failed to play his part as a useful human being.

X. The Law of Social Interest

I.e. Love of thy neighbour. The law of social interest well practised can free the latent powers of a human being and help him to
overcome the egocentric aim out of which all neurosis is born. Adler
believed that when the law of social interest is understood and every
human being's education based upon it—the love of our neighbour
(which is the goal of all true religions) will become 'as natural as
breathing or the upright gait'. (The reader is referred to the book
Social Interest: A Challenge to Mankind).

A collection of Adler's psychological discoveries under the title
The Individual Psychology of Alfred Adler, compiled and annotated
by Drs. Heinz and Rowena Ansbacher of Vermont University,
has just been produced in America, and is about to appear in
England.

This anthology has been collected from Adler's books and pam-
phlets written between 1904 and his death in 1937.

Many of the extracts taken from Adler's early works have never
before appeared in England.

Here at last we see Adler's actual discoveries dated chronologically.
The momentous break with Freud is accurately told and placed;
while how early in the history of the Freudian circle Adler's basic
differences began to show emerges from notes taken from discussions
between Adler and Freud during the break, and in subsequent
quotations. The chronological history of Individual Psychology is
made plain step by step.

Nothing in the deep originality and full significance of Adler's
philosophy has been omitted.

The words are Adler's own; but chosen and commented on in a
sequence and with a coherence which were too often missing in the
torrent of speed and activity with which Adler lived his working life.

The simplicity of Adler's words, the subtlety of his thought, the
creative drive and directness of his practical psychology, cannot fail
to reach the common sense of any intelligent reader who reads this
book.

XIX

'Break with the Pedants'

In 1925, after the Austrian Loan was an accomplished fact, the blood began to run back into the veins of Adler's beloved *Wien*, and the Child Guidance Clinics, now fully established in connection with all the *Haupt Schulen* of Vienna, became famous throughout the educational world.

Adler's reputation was greatly increased by this international recognition, and he was asked to give educational conferences in many other countries; but it was at this time that the Adlerian Group in Vienna itself received its sharpest check.

Adler's younger followers, apparently unbridled by Adler, quarrelled more and more openly with the older members of the group: many of these were scholars and thinkers of achieved reputation who had risked much to leave Freud's group for that of Adler.

This quarrel was founded upon the sharp-set political cleavages of this period. Many of the younger group of Individual Psychologists tried to link their psychology to Communism, while the older members, although most of them had been Social Democrats before the War, were violently averse to Communism; some even had veered sharply towards the Right, and were in danger of becoming reactionary.

Adler himself rejected alike all extremes, and would probably have agreed with Nietzsche that 'there is an element of pathology in all absolutes'. Adler may have felt that the older group were unfairly persecuting the younger recruits, by trying to make an exclusive use of their greater knowledge and already won scholarly achievements. Perhaps too his own elder brother complex stabbed back at him. At any rate he failed to support the older group.

This set-back to the Individual Psychological Society was a tragic business. Several of Adler's private and most intimate friendships were permanently broken by it. Professor Allers was one of these influential friends. He had become a member of the Church of

169

Rome, and had adjusted much of Adler's psychology to the faith he had accepted, though many Adlerians think without due recognition of from where his discoveries had emanated.

Professor Oppenheim was another learned member of the group, personally devoted to Adler; this friendship came to an end with a resounding crash. Professor Oppenheim ran through the streets of Vienna with tears streaming down his cheeks asserting loudly, to all the friends who crossed his path, that Adler had been cruelly unkind to him and betrayed their friendship. Wexberg—writer of an early and extremely able book on Individual Psychology, now settled in New Orleans, where he has become widely celebrated for both the theories and practice he had acquired in Vienna—joined in the quarrel.

The wrongs of Professor Oppenheim, and the irritation produced by the aggressive tactics of the younger group, roused a great deal of adverse criticism against Adler's handling of the situation. A public meeting was held, ostensibly in order to discuss a lately published book of Dr. Schwarz, and to give him an opportunity to explain upon what grounds he differed from Adler on some physiological points; but the half hidden warfare soon broke out between the two groups, and tempers rose to meet the larger philosophical and political issues.

The book was open to a good deal of criticism, and probably got it from the youngest members. Schwarz had always been particularly bitter against these younger men, and had picked out Victor Frankel (now Professor of Psychology in Vienna) and Manés Sperber (now one of our leading novelists) for his bitterest barbs.

Schwarz on this occasion led the attack against the younger group; but it was Allers who made the most memorable contribution. His speech stated fairly, and with great dignity, the various affronts the older members had received, and was much applauded.

There appears to be some doubt now as to who was the actual leader of the younger group; but the writer was told by several of the older members who had been present on this historic occasion that the most offensive speaker was Manés Sperber; and that when Allers had finished his speech, this boy sprang up and tore it to tatters.

Manés Sperber was certainly the most gifted as well as the most irritating of Adler's younger followers. He was, however, accepted with great affection by the whole Adler family, and for ten years visited them almost daily. Adler loved him and knew him as a gardener loves and knows the most delicate of his plants; while Professor Allers, though a much valued friend, was already an acknowledged success, and an able scholar respected throughout Viennese intellectual circles. Probably Adler thought to himself, 'Allers needs no protection from me. He is taking an orthodox view, behind which he can entrench himself quite safely, with the approval of all his friends. On the other hand, my young scamp is always being sat upon by these bigwigs! No doubt he has made a mistake, but if I add the weight of my reproaches to theirs—the boy is finished! He might be too discouraged to hold up his head again!'

Professor Allers responded with quiet composure to Manés Sperber's intemperate attack; then, turning to Adler, he asked him to undertake his defence. To the dismay and astonishment of the whole audience Adler got up and said, 'But perhaps the boy is right!' and sat down again without further comment.

There was a terrible pause; and then Professor Allers, Dr. Schwarz and several of their most indignant sympathizers walked out of the building, never to return.

On the face of it, Adler's behaviour at this meeting appears inexplicable; but looking beneath the surface to the sources of his action, it is easy to see that this public meeting may not have been as innocent as it seemed—a mere dispute between two rival points of view—but a previously arranged trap to catch out, and then expel, the whole troublesome brood of young rebels, while dragging Adler himself into a fixed system of thought which he may not have felt fully prepared to support. 'He gave us up for a little frog!—a nothing!' Professor Oppenheim told the writer. 'Adler forgot how powerful we were, and that it lay in our hands to spread or to retard the science of Individual Psychology!' But did Adler forget this fact? Or did he remember it only too well? Did he not look back on the long years when, in Freud's circle, his own discoveries had been held back and he himself checked or ignored by a higher authority?

This was one of the great spiritual landmarks of Adler's life, when he realized that he must break up even a respected and valued form in order to keep a still more valuable new spirit.

Professor Nowotny asked Adler at this time why he had ruined his chances with his academic following by his 'missionary spirit' and still more why he refused to insist that proper respect should be shown to acknowledged experts in his own psychology. Professor Nowotny remembered Adler's reply for thirty years, although it still dissatisfied him. 'Adler said,' Nowotny told me, ' "We musn't make our psychology too hard for the people to understand." '

There were only two unchanging claims that Adler made for

171

Individual Psychology; one was that it must be *sub specie aeternitatis*; and the other that it must be understandable to Everyman. Beyond these two aspects of the truth Adler, like Keats, kept a 'negative capability' free from all questioning.

Adler thought that pedants, however right their statements might be, suffered from a cardinal defect—they wished to chain Time to their own chariot wheels; and they forgot that there was room in eternity for many answers, and that it might not affect the value of these answers should they remain anonymous. If Adler was vague as to the future development of truth, he was all the more strict as to the acceptance of ascertained fact. 'We scientists are midwives at the birth of this child, Truth,' Adler would say, with a spark of fury in his eyes, 'And if I see anyone sabotaging its birth—then I become dangerous!'

Adler 'hungered for the souls of men'. He wanted to bring into every man's practical experience the moral law of the universe, hitherto seen only in flashes or through the example of exceptional human beings but, nevertheless, actually a law upon the carrying out of which man's future existence depended.

Many of Adler's critics have believed that he was both ambitious and quarrelsome. Ernest Jones even claims, in his perhaps unconsciously revealing life of Freud, that Adler was 'surly'—a criticism that is laughable to anyone who knew Adler well. Adler's friends were legion and he was the kindest and gayest of companions. All his actions, public or private, contradict such criticisms. No ambitious man would have thrown away every aid he could have counted on towards personal advancement or success, nor failed to number among his intimates anyone able to protect or re-enforce his fame. Adler's cures were notorious for being short and successful. He frequently took his patients, if he knew them to be badly off, for nothing. His studies in shell-shock during the war years, 'miracles of cure', as one of his doctor colleagues called them, Adler never took the trouble even to note down. He was adept at conciliation and could not be called quarrelsome, although no doubt as an opponent he was formidable. He could always be harsh to dishonest people; and he was direct in speech, as he was in all his dealings. Where he found malice or pretension he could be merciless. But his benevolence was inexhaustible and his unending patience with boring or exacting people was incredible. Unlike his great opponent Freud, Adler 'suffered fools gladly'. Perhaps his estimation of mankind was not sufficiently high for him to be often disappointed.

'BREAK WITH THE PEDANTS'

After this break with the pedants in 1925 it was noticeable that there was a still further simplification in all Adler's teaching methods. It was then that he started his fortnightly Child Clinics at the Volks Institut which drew larger and ever larger audiences.

His public lectures and writings became easier to follow than before, and received even more severe criticism from his former distinguished adherents. One of these, whom the writer visited just after Adler's death in 1937, could hardly contain his spite and bitterness. He poured forth a diatribe of indignation and contempt upon the memory of his old friend; but suddenly stopped abruptly, and saying, 'Don't go! Wait one moment!' he hurried out of the room, returning with a battered old hat in his hand, green with age. 'Adler used to wear this,' he explained in a softened voice, 'long ago he ought to have thrown it away. My wife asked him to let us have it when he had stopped wearing it. You see, it is still there—the shape of his head—and I have never been able to make up my mind to throw it away.'

Having heard such fearful tales of the part played against the pedants by Manés Sperber, it occurred to the writer that it might be as well to meet this young agitator (for he was still young) in the foreign country to which he had fled before the oncoming of the Nazis, in order to see for herself how black the devil was beneath the painting. Manés Sperber was living in great danger and in the utmost poverty, and was flung a few months later into a concentration camp, where he barely escaped with his life. Somehow, in spite of the extreme poverty of his surroundings and the breathless urgencies of the hour, we found in him an inner security and a spark of spiritual courage that promised to survive his menaced future; still, we had no idea then that he would become the renowned author of *The Wind in the Flame*, better known in America as *The Burned Bramble*, perhaps the best novel that has yet been written on the twin terrors of the Nazi and Communist régimes.

Sperber had parted from Adler in anger because Adler refused to support his then political views. Yet, in the short half-hour we were with him, he made a great and lasting impression upon us. 'More than my life I owe to Adler,' Sperber told us with deep feeling. 'I am glad that you came to tell me about his death. I loved him. There was no one like him.'

Listening to this man, and comparing his quiet courage in those desperate days with Adler's scholar friends whom he had left behind him, in comparative security, men who had hastened to assure us

173

how little Adler had stood for in their lives, and what substantial grounds they had had for rejecting him—we could not escape the thought that if Adler were once more asked to judge between Manés Sperber and the Pedants, he would have said, with even greater conviction, 'But perhaps the boy is right.'

XX

The International Journal of Individual Psychology

No history of Adler would be complete without mention of his favourite and one of his most successful activities, *The International Journal of Individual Psychology*. This *Journal* was started very early in the life of Adler's first free group, after he left Freud's circle; and it soon became widely known throughout Austria, Germany, Czechoslovakia, Jugoslavia and Holland; indeed wherever the German language was read. Its editor, Dr. Ladislaus Zilahi, was one of Adler's greatest and truest friends.

Zilahi was, even apart from the *Journal*, into which he poured the greater part of his life, an exceptionally able human being. He was a staunch Catholic, and at the same time an extraordinarily free and elastic-minded man.

His integrity was like a rock; but he had a charm of manner and spirit that made even his opponents his friends. He was a scholar, and had a special knowledge of Austrian jurisprudence. Besides his editorship of the *Journal*, Zilahi was one of the Vienna *Telegraf's* foremost writers of lead articles.

Adler saw him daily over a span of years, and had a deep personal affection for him, shared by the whole Adler family.

Nothing in his work-life gave Adler more pleasure than this *Journal*. Not only was it handled with great ability but it was from the first a growing concern, selling here and there in all Central European countries: Germany being, as was but natural, by far its largest market.

Zilahi and Adler welcomed all contributions that dealt with their subject, medical or educational, purely literary or purely scientific. Adler was always particularly happy when independent scientists or thinkers sent him information upon their special subjects, which reinforced from a separate science the findings of Individual Psychology.

Zilahi was the one person Adler knew he could trust never to allow unfair or watering-down statements to creep into the *Journal*, under the guise of sympathetic support.

Nor would Zilahi, who knew Individual Psychology from A to Z, have given any chance whatever to the many plagiarists who haunt the pathways of creative spirits.

Adler wrote for the *Journal* with the utmost faithfulness himself and always instigated his friends to send articles to it, although he was no weak accepter of inferior stuff from whatever high or effective sources it might come.

Zilahi must have had a hard fight for the life of his *Journal*, especially when Adler began his long half-yearly absences from Vienna. For the Freudians were remorseless opponents; some of the Catholics severe critics; and many of Adler's own supporters were neurotics who, endowed by him with a new courage, had not always yet acquired sufficient social interest to use their new quality without danger to themselves or others.

All these types—unwise friends, belligerent enemies, and the critics among his fellow Christians—would have been enough, if taken singly, to pierce the armour of most editors.

Zilahi, however, had not only the courage of a lion; he had balance, and knew what it was wisest to ignore and what must at any cost be fought to a finish.

He feared neither his friends nor his opponents; but he always fought clean; and when he could avoid fighting, no self-love or prestige hunting hindered him from conciliation.

Perhaps wisely, Zilahi confined himself as far as possible to his duties as editor of the *Journal* and took little or no part in the other activities of the Individual Psychological group.

Naturally many Viennese Adlerians were from time to time offended and angry with him, for no editor ever escapes the vanity of discarded contributors.

Had Zilahi been less courageous he could never have endured the difficulties of his position, for if the normal human being is vain, how much more vain is the half-cured neurotic?

An egocentric, *fully* enclosed in his shell of anxiety for his own safety, will not allow himself so much as a public squeal; but release his half-baked ego, setting him on his feet for the first time—and he will for a while at least, until his cure is completed, make himself a ubiquitous nuisance.

Zilahi must have had many of these bruised reeds cropping up against him, whenever he refused to let them air their grievances in the pages of the *Journal*; but he was quite extraordinarily intelligent in avoiding open rows with Adlerian adherents.

Adler no doubt gave him, while he was on the spot, all the support in his power; but Adler himself was by no means an easy colleague for an editor. He was afraid of style, and in a hurry to spread what he could of the spirit, rather than collect any of it into the narrow channel of the letter. He did not like definitions; he loathed 'prescriptions', as he called most moral statements; and although sensitive to public opinion, Adler was never known to defer to it. Unfortunately editors *must* defer to public opinion if they are to sell their magazines; though they may if they are really sincere and intelligent persons, as Zilahi was, cater only in order to lead the public towards something solid as well as attractive.

Adler disliked disagreeing with his friends; he even more disliked interfering with them; therefore having left his adherents to take any path they chose, if he saw it was about to damage his work, he was capable of pulling them up very short.

These two contradictory proclivities must have made matters often extremely hard on Zilahi. On the other hand if he reviewed adversely a book by one of Adler's friends—and being a truthful man as well as an intelligent critic, he often felt called upon to do so—the friend in question would run shrieking with grief and pain to Adler to have the review contradicted or public balm of some sort placed upon his wound. Adler might cave in and place it, without sufficient consideration, and indeed often did so, for it was against all his instincts to discourage a weak person.

On the other hand, through Adler's determination not to interfere with wrong ideas until they became dangerous, two fresh difficulties might arise. The psycho-analysts were always sitting like a cat at a mouse-hole, ready to pounce upon the first Adlerian blunder that showed a whisker; and even supposing that a poor or unsound article *did* get by them, what was to prevent a heresy in the bud from flowering into a fine big tree, beyond the powers of the stoutest woodsman to cut down?

Zilahi, however, had two great assets that pulled the *Journal* through all its emergencies; he was—where he loved—patient; and he was—where he hated—formidable.

Opponents thought twice before they challenged him; and Adler, coming up against the patience of his best friend, found himself disarmed.

In this most difficult of all collaborations between men whose ideas of literature were bound to be different, no unhealable wound was ever made.

They loved each other with confidence and without subterfuge from first to last; not until after Adler's death did Zilahi's patience give out, and a deep and bitter anger take its place; and that was against Adler's friends, for what Zilahi took to be a slight upon their Founder's memory. Zilahi fought them, and fought single-handed, for Adler's sake.

The point at issue was a difficult one, with much to be said upon both sides. Should the psycho-analysts, who had never made—and if they had made, could never have kept—a secret of their hatred for Adler and his psychology, be invited with all his other medical and psychological colleagues to the memorial service after Adler's death?

Zilahi, who knew Adler's mind as well as any man living, especially upon the subject of the psycho-analysts, said 'No'! All the rest of the group and the *Verein* took what to many seemed a larger and more generous view, and one more in line with social interest, and insisted that the psycho-analysts *should* be invited.

Zilahi knew that Adler believed Freud's psychology to be a direct attack upon the moral law of the Universe founded upon the selfish wishes of a pampered child. Therefore he felt that Adler would not desire the presence of such thinkers at a service held in his memory. The psycho-analysts were, however, invited; accepted; and forgot to come.

Zilahi resigned in protest from the Vienna group of Individual Psychologists and refused to retain even a nominal membership. The magazine came to an abrupt end. Zilahi had already in 1934 been offered the permanent editorship, and complete immunity from future persecution, if he would undertake to carry the *Journal* on in Germany under another name; he had only to repudiate Adler, as the Founder of Individual Psychology, for one of Adler's now Nazi-minded, German adherents.

No one who has not had such an offer made to him can know what it cost Zilahi to refuse it. For it not only meant personal security from persecution and possible death, as well as security for his wife and child; it meant the continuation of his life-work. Yet this man, at the prime of his life and at the mercy of its obligations—incontinently refused the Nazi offer. Zilahi preferred to remain true —at all costs—to his principles, and to his friend. Zilahi's subsequent career was that of many exiles. He was hunted—with his life at stake

—into Jugoslavia; and finally at the lowest ebb of his fortunes found a home in England. Here he almost immediately became of invaluable help to his adopted country, and worked throughout the War for the Foreign Office, being one of the first of the war refugees to receive naturalization. He was also awarded the honour of an M.B.E. Dr. Zilahi gave up a further fifteen years of his valuable life to working in Vienna for the Foreign Office; and has finally returned to London to continue his skilled and selfless services to his adopted country.

Adler was not only a *self-made* man; he helped to make his friends; and *these* were the friends that he kept.

XXI

European Conferences and German Colleagues

As Vienna slowly healed and straightened herself in the after-war period of 1918, Adler's work became more and more international.

Visitors came over in larger and larger numbers every summer, and the Educational Conferences became a favourite summer holiday plan for bringing together teachers and educationalists from all over the world. There was a short period when it began to look as if the race of man had waked up to the necessity of self-development, and realized for the first time that a way had been found for him to get rid of his self-destructive playthings and to become a responsible grown-up person. Science was at last prepared to show him that there was no need to sit and weep under a juniper tree because he was no better than his fathers. There were steps to be taken that could make him considerably better.

The first Individual Psychological Conference was held in Vienna in 1924 and was remarkable for many interesting factors, not least the meeting for the first time of Adler and one of his most prominent German adherents, a well-known nerve doctor and former Freudian, Dr. Leonhard Seif of Munich, who had mastered Adlerian psychology and adopted it as a treatment for all his patients.

There were three or four such colleague-adherents in Germany, before the Nazi régime, but on account of the 'race question' they cut themselves free from Adler afterwards—and none of their names could be mentioned in a contemporary life of Adler until now, although it would be impossible to write his life without referring at least indirectly to his most important colleagues.

Two of the most remarkable and courageous of these Individual Psychologists, Alice and Otto Rühle-Gerstel, from Dresden, whose sympathies had always been 'Leftist', departed before Hitler rose to power and went to Vienna, where they rather disastrously brought out a book on Individual Psychology under the Dollfuss régime, which was a binding together of Individual Psychology and Marxism. This book was a fatal error as far as Adler was concerned. It came out at a bad moment and wholly against his will and advice, and was the cause of a final rupture between him and these two prized friends. It is curious how much harm such good and vigorous human beings could do to a cause they would gladly have died for.

They committed what Adler himself considered a cardinal error against common sense. Whatever their private thoughts and hopes may have been, to bring out such a book in Vienna at such a time condemned Individual Psychology to political disaster, and was at least a cruelly stupid thing to have done.

The Rühle-Gerstels then left for Mexico, leaving Individual Psychology to struggle on as best it might in Vienna, under its political cloud.

The first Individual Psychological Conference, however, began in full sunlight, in 1924, under the auspices of the Social Democratic Government.

Adler went to the station to meet Seif, of Munich, with a coloured handkerchief sticking out of his waistcoat pocket to identify him, and with nothing but joy in his heart. From that moment began one of Adler's happiest and deepest intimacies, until the Nazi régime destroyed the link between them.

'I thought', Adler once told the writer, 'that this man Seif, beyond all others, had understood my psychology.'

Between them, in their two countries, they began to build up together a bulwark against human ignorance and selfishness. Between them they must have saved thousands of cramped and broken souls, releasing them into the stream of useful normal life.

They held this, and a later conference, together, side by side, each giving of his best.

From that time onward they reinforced each other's work, and for nine years their fellowship was as complete and faithful as any human friendship could ever have been. Perhaps there is no such deep and happy friendship between human beings as that which has the same aim, and moves towards the same goal.

Every individual psychologist in Vienna accepted, loved and respected Seif and everyone in the Munich circle loved, respected and accepted Adler.

This friendship could but have ripened with the years and accompanied each to his grave, except for the one harmless fact, unrecog-

181

nized by either at their first meeting, that Seif had happened to be born an Aryan, while Adler had happened to descend from the Jewish race. What a joke this would have seemed to these two intelligent men, had it been suggested as an obstacle to their friendship in 1924; and what a cruel tragedy this simple little fact had become in 1933, when Adler was cut off from the fellowship of four of his best and most important adherents, and saw his work for *Gemeinschaftsgefühl* go down under a sea of persecution.

What wonder that one of these famous colleagues, although no doubt tortured by his acute and faithful conscience, declared himself to be the discoverer of some of the main truths of his friend's work, and repudiating all that he had learned from Adler, in his own mind, constituted himself the German founder of Individual Psychology? Have we not learned that under the Nazi regime Heine did not write the *Lorelei*?

This is the real tragedy of mankind, that until now the spirit of man has not been able to free itself, even along the path of its own development, from the tentacles of self-deception.

The 'unmasking' that Adler so believed in, upon any and every subject, upon any and every person, had not yet gone deep enough.

It was perhaps little wonder that Adler would allow no step to be taken in his psychology that went beyond the concrete fact.

When any one of his adherents made a statement which he was unable to substantiate by such a fact, Adler would say with sharpness, and as a reproach, 'But that is an *opinion*!'

For well he knew to what use 'opinion' can be turned in the expert hands of a self-deceiver.

The next Individual Psychological Conference took place in Berlin, and brought to Adler the unchanging support of his two great Viennese teachers, Ferdinand Birnbaum and Oskar Spiel. A conference at Düsseldorf followed, spreading and cementing Individual Psychology over many new parts of Germany.

The final Individual Psychological Conference to be held in Germany was at Munich. This was perhaps the most fruitful of all the conferences, since in Munich there was already a highly trained circle of Individual Psychologists, specially fortunate both in their leadership under Dr. Leonhard Seif, and in its adherents.

Munich had always stood for German culture at its best, and was the leader of German genius both in art and science—a town as enchanting and creative in German life as Oxford has been for the life of the mind in England.

EUROPEAN CONFERENCES

This Conference took place at the last free moment in the life of Munich. She could still hear the greatest artists in the world sing in her opera or act upon her stage. She could still enjoy the freest modern art and attend lectures given by the greatest minds among international thinkers.

The door of Life swung wide open, and all races came freely into this beautiful sane city, and left it with regret.

Adler loved Munich. There were many homes open to him in it, and hearts that had learned how to live by his creative words.

When the door was closed to him, it must have been a tragedy only less great than the darkening down and closing up of his beloved *Wien*. Mercifully the actual end of his own beloved city came after his life on earth had closed; but on his last visit to Vienna in 1935, he foresaw it.

'I do not think *Wien* is alive any more,' he said to a friend. 'I shall be glad to leave it. We must let the Dead bury their Dead.'

183

XXII

Adler's Country Home

Adler had watched the deflation melt his savings to nothing. He was in the prime of his life; these were his best earning years. He had all the patients he could take, and at whatever fees he cared to ask. Now he began to save again; but this time he determined he would put his savings into a more solid form than money.

Against the advice of all his business friends and relatives, Adler bought a big house and garden, an hour's run from the Stephan's Platz, at Salmannsdorf, a little village in the Wienerwald. Once more Adler founded his home upon the exact spot that marked a decisive victory for European culture, over the barbaric hordes that attacked Vienna under Suleiman the Turk.

Salmannsdorf was Adler's dream, but like many other dreams, it bore very little practical relation to the facts of his daily life. It was too far out from Vienna; it was too large a house; it was too lonely; and when hordes of visitors descended upon him—not lonely enough. 'Herr Doktor,' Sophie the cook told him, 'this house is too far away from town for working people like ourselves. It is nothing but a beauty spot for tourists!' 'But, Sophie,' Adler objected, 'in this world are we not all tourists?'

The Villa at Salmannsdorf was a large, high, many-roomed house with a big garden.

From its windows, and from the garden itself, the country stretched away in a series of wooded foothills to the distant blue mountains, while Vienna rose from the shadowy plain, slashed and encircled by the pale Danube.

The roof and spire of the Stephansdom stood out above the plain—as St. Peter's silver bubble towers over Rome.

From Salmannsdorf Adler could always see the two places on this 'poor earth's crust' that he loved best—Vienna and the mountains.

Perhaps no home has ever been more enjoyed, and less lived in, than the Villa at Salmannsdorf.

Endless streams of visitors came there; sat in the garden; played and sang in the big music room; and roamed the nearer hills.

Raissa too loved Salmannsdorf; perhaps it was the nearest she ever came in her married life to the wide vision of Russian cornfields and open sky that haunted all her dreams. Perhaps she believed that here she and Adler could make a real home for themselves and their children, with Sophie to take from her the dread burdens of domesticity. But the flood of Adler's unceasing work pursued Raissa, even to the woods and fields. Those waves of troubled human beings who carried him away from her beat upon every shore.

She could not thrust them from her, nor could she adjust her impatient human spirit to their intruding problems.

One of Adler's American friends tells of a visit to Salmannsdorf that always lived in her memory. Adler led her into a sun parlour on tiptoe, to where he had arranged a shelf full of cactus that he had brought back from one of his American visits. He laid his finger upon his lips and whispered, 'Hush! They think to be in Texas!'

For two years Adler gave up the Salmannsdorf Villa to his son Kurt, to enable him to marry and set up a home of his own.

Adler was much criticized for this act; very few parents would have dared the risk of starting an only son upon a marriage, who was not yet upon his own feet or able to support a wife.

But this was not an act of weak self-indulgence as many of Adler's friends thought. It was a considered gift. Adler believed in the developing powers of married happiness, and expected the tremendous trust he placed in his young son would bear fruit. Adler was often anxious as to the path his children chose to take, but I doubt if he was ever disappointed with any one of them. He did not look for the same results that most parents look for. He wanted his children to be fearless, active and happy in their own way, not in his or in anyone else's way.

The home at Salmannsdorf gave Adler the space he wanted, and he did not trouble very much as to what filled it. He had very simple tastes and never required anything like ceremony. Adler was always prepared to share anything he had with his friends, and never considered people dropping in at all hours, or for any meal, in the light of entertainment.

There were generally fifteen to twenty people to tea on Sundays, and sometimes as many as fifty turned up unexpectedly. Once a hundred American students came out to tea in the garden. However many there were, they were always made welcome. 'The Herr Doktor

185

always offered to help me himself,' Sophie exclaimed, 'when there were many people; and that set the others off!'

Adler had a series of dog friends at Salmannsdorf, all leading the freest possible open-air lives; and whenever Adler was there, he made the same careful and considerate study of their tastes and characters that he did of every human being. A slight confusion was once caused by a new puppy being called 'Nelly', the name of his youngest daughter, and another whose name was 'Ali', the name of the second daughter, so that there were often two 'Nellys' and two 'Alis' being called for simultaneously, but for wholly different purposes.

Salmannsdorf was, however, a practical error; it was definitely too far away from Vienna, and Adler had to recognize the threat to his work of the Dollfuss regime (when liberty of thought was already menaced, and children pushed back once more under the old harrow of unreasoning authority). Before long, Adler had to face the thought of giving up Salmannsdorf altogether.

The property was sold before Adler's death, and the money, unfortunately, left in Vienna.

But as a dream, Salmannsdorf was no failure; looking back upon Adler's life and ahead into the lives of his children, that garden with its visions, that clear air, and those filled and friendly hours may well have been the best in Adler's, and the happiest in his children's, lives. The world was open then, and not caught tight into nationalistic pigeon-holes; and the future seemed freer, and promised peace.

One of his daughters said to me after her father's death, 'If you could have my father back again, what would you most feel?' 'Safe,' the author said, thinking of the impending political storms. 'I shouldn't,' replied his daughter, 'I should feel enriched.' Perhaps Adler, too, who never built for security, was sufficiently enriched by his dream of Salmannsdorf.

Often in those lonely New York years, in his hotel sitting-room, close to that great hurricane of Broadway, the silent hills and the blue and silver Danubian plain must have flashed upon Adler's 'inward eye which is the bliss of solitude'.

My husband and I, at his request, spent his last day at Salmannsdorf with him.

Adler never *shared* his sadness with his friends; still I think he liked to have them with him when he *was* unhappy.

It was summer time, and the mountains were close and clear; Vienna shone like a handful of jewels flung carelessly out upon the smooth green plain.

We spent most of the day in the garden. A spoilt little boy of five years old, who was staying in the house, clung to us, although Adler took very little apparent notice of him.

There were many things that Adler had to settle up, and give away, but the sunny hours seemed long.

To my husband Adler gave his most treasured book of collected songs; and to the writer the last of his roses.

When we left, the little boy ran after us down the road, crying out to Adler: 'Come back—and stay for ever!'

Adler's dog walked stiffly with him to the gate, as if he knew this was the end. It was the only time that the author ever heard Adler sigh. He patted the dog's head, and explained apologetically: 'He is staying on with kind people that he likes very well, but I am afraid that they may forget to brush him—and he likes so much to be brushed.'

After the Nazis took possession of Vienna, Salmannsdorf was left empty. That house and garden—once the most populated, the most prized, thought of and planned for, visited and used for giving, in or about Vienna—stands now 'like a forsaken bird's nest filled with snow.'

Adler, after he had left it, never again possessed a home nor did he return to Vienna.

From this time on, he had no 'continuing city' until his far-flung pilgrimage came to its abrupt and peaceful close.

XXIII

Adler on Criminals

T here was no branch of psychiatry in which Adler was more deeply interested than crime. Wherever he made his headquarters for any length of time, he got in touch with prisons, and in the course of his life examined many hundreds of cases for prison authorities.

Adler always made a very strong distinction between delinquency and neurosis. 'Neurotics', he would say, 'are people who acknowledge social interest. Their aim is in harmony with society, however far they may be from training themselves to accomplish it. Theirs is an "if—but" attitude. "I would do my duty if——" then follow the excuses. The delinquent, on the other hand, is an enemy of society. He is a person whose aim is to get what he wants at someone else's expense. Like the psychotic, he has no social interest. It is, therefore, very much harder to cure a criminal than it is to cure a neurotic person. It must also be remembered that you very rarely come on a criminal at the moment of his first crime. By the time he is arrested, he will probably have already committed many undiscovered crimes. He has, therefore, had success upon those lines and upon no others, and, as a rule, the mere fact of arrest or imprisonment does nothing to lessen his sense of self-importance. He is seldom sorry for his crimes, whatever he may say to the contrary. He is merely saying to himself, "It would have been all right if I had not left my spectacles behind me!" or, "I didn't give myself quite enough time for my get-away."

'The criminal's only purpose, when he is set free, is "next time I must be more careful not to be caught!" The blind spot in him is lack of social interest. He has activity without good will, whereas the neurotic has good will (but not enough of it) without activity.

'A delinquent child is very easy to detect. He is a child who tries to get his own way by hurting others. The neurotic child, on the other

188

hand, though equally anxious to get his own way, does it by crying
or making himself a burden for others to bear, not by wilfully attacking or doing them an injury. A criminal has a logic of his own, a
"private intelligence" unshared by normal people. I once asked a
murderer why he had killed a man, and he replied, "I wanted the
trousers he had on and he wouldn't give them to me!" This seemed
to him a perfectly good reason, and in a sense it was so, since it *is*
very unlikely that a man *would* give up the trousers he is wearing
without violence. Still,there are other ways of obtaining trousers than
by murder. Another murderer said to me, "I killed my brother because there was not room enough in the world to contain this man
and myself!" We all have this feeling at times, but the normal solution is to leave the neighbourhood of the person who is aggravating
us.'

Adler loved drawing attention to Dostoevski's description of a
murderer's motives in *Crime and Punishment*. Raskolnikoff wants to
kill an old woman for her money, but has to reason himself out of the
remains of his social interest before he can make up his mind to
murder her. He lies on his bed for a month trying to work himself up
to the pitch of his crime. He tells himself that he has to do it for the
sake of a dearly loved sister, who has had to go on the streets to win
bread for her family, but this motive proves insufficient. At last he
cries out in despair: 'Am I Napoleon or a louse?' and this final probe
to his vanity enables him to cross the passage and batter the old
woman to death. The creation of a false situation instead of the real
one is often the most important part of the criminal's mental outfit.
He has, as it were, to break with the logic of life before he can give
himself up to his crime.

'Why should this man have everything and I nothing?' is a typical
criminal's excuse for kidnapping, murder or robbery. The cosmic
injustice has to be shown up to excuse his own little break in the
moral law before his conscience lets him get away with his crime.

Adler believed that criminals, except certain types of expert burglars or forgerers, are all of a very low mental calibre. Of the many
hundreds he had examined, more than sixty per cent were unskilled
labourers. This seemed to Adler another reason for the difficulty in
breaking them of crime. They were untrained for any other career,
and so had nothing out of which he could help them to make a
success.

Burglars, Adler believed, were very much easier to cure than other
types of criminals, and the more intelligent the burglar, the easier

was his cure. In fact Adler believed that many burglars between thirty and forty, if not found out, voluntarily gave up burglary and took to other careers, such as cabinet-making, watchmaking, or a locksmith's profession. The fact that they were experts enabled them to slip back easily into the community. At this time of their lives their physical agility began to leave them, and, if they had the cares of a household devolving upon them, they no longer desired to take the big risks they had taken in youth. Such men are comparatively ready to take up normal life, especially if anyone gives them a good opportunity of earning their living honestly. Adler once cured an inveterate watch-stealer by getting him started as a jeweller who sold watches. This man never again attempted to steal, but his was a special case with a definite psychotic twist, requiring an Adlerian analysis before he could have been safely trusted in this situation.

Adler had many ex-burglar friends who were doing well, but he thought blackmailers, or those who made physical attacks upon others, very much harder to cure, because such criminals were both cowards *and* haters of their fellow men. Adler believed that all criminals were beneath the normal in courage and he often pointed out, as against the current idea of their heroic quality, that they did their evil deeds generally by night, prepared them in advance, and were well armed; whereas the persons they attacked were always defenceless, without having had the advantage of a plan, and were, therefore, taken by surprise and easily overcome. All criminals are people who have not been able to stand up to the demands of normal living. They have a minus, therefore, rather than a plus of natural courage. Adler believed that the proper treatment for criminals was a retraining in social interest, but he thought very few if any modern prisons had sufficient understanding of psychology to act in a remedial manner. In fact, he thought that prisons could be looked upon as universities for the spread of crime in which young criminals can study the methods of their elders, and older criminals get time to resteep themselves in criminology by making fresh plans and meeting new confederates.

The worst treatment for criminals, Adler stated, was any form of brutality on the part of those looking after them; or solitary confinement. Both these methods, Adler declared, must inevitably lower the criminal's small share of social interest, the lack of which is the cause of his crime. On the other hand, any form of training that gives the criminal a feeling of usefulness or success is to be encouraged, since it is bound to act beneficially upon him. Adler also hoped that some form of earning money while in prison might be made universal, so that men or women returning to their families or their former community could do so as assets rather than as burdens. Adler believed that any form of developing 'trust' and co-operation in prison life was highly beneficial, but he was always a common-sense man, with a high regard for the community itself, and would never have supported any scheme of temporary 'pardons' that released dangerous criminals upon society for longer or shorter periods. Adler would, however, have welcomed any scheme of after-care that could strengthen a criminal's self-respect and co-operative ability, but nothing inquisitorial which could interfere with his new freedom. 'If honesty is not made worth his while, we cannot expect him to give up crime,' Adler used to say. 'After all, criminals are not idiots! I always set out to prove to them that their success was not worth much and that a success of a higher order is well within their power if they give up crime, but I have hitherto been handicapped by the fact that I could not count upon the good-will and co-operation of the community to which the criminal returns.'

For many years, Adler had an ex-convict friend as his own gardener. This man had been considered a highly dangerous criminal when Adler had first come across him. Robbery with violence was his crime, and he was sentenced to eight years imprisonment. As the convict neared the end of his sentence, a prison missioner suggested his appealing for help, when he left the prison, and gave him a list of philanthropic persons, among whom he found Adler's name. The convict wrote to twenty of these persons, but only received one answer. 'Dear so-and-so,' Adler wrote, 'I believe that you could be of great help to me in my work,' and he enclosed his home address.

On his release, the burglar went to see Adler and they took a great fancy to each other. Adler had just brought Salmannsdorf and he suggested that the ex-convict, who was fond of flowers and country life, should become his gardener. All went well and the ex-convict remained in charge of the Salmannsdorf garden until after Adler's death. Nor during these years was there ever a relapse beyond one very small offence in the early stage of the experiment.

Adler had sent his burglar friend to buy some raspberry canes, and he returned with far more canes than the money Adler had given him could account for. Adler saw that this was a situation which could not be overlooked but must be met once and for all, in spite of the difficulties that it presented. Adler was naturally anxious to check this first attempt at dishonesty, and, on the other hand, to do nothing to penalize or injure the new self-respect he was helping the gardener to build up. He therefore praised the plants very highly, saying, 'I see you have made a most excellent selection,' but counted them over carefully at the same time, so that the gardener, who was watching him a little anxiously, should see that he had missed nothing. 'When you take these back to-morrow,' Adler then observed quietly, setting to one side the stolen canes, 'you might say that I had decided to buy ten more. I will give you the money to buy the extra canes, before you take these back.' The gardener carried out Adler's instructions implicitly and without comment, and there was never again the slightest lapse into dishonesty.

Once Adler built a tool shed and asked his gardener what sort of lock it would be safest for them to put on it. 'The easiest to unfasten,' the gardener promptly replied. 'If you put on a difficult lock, it will only make a mess of the door when it is broken into.'

The gardener had a passionate temper and so, at times, had Adler. They had many fights together on the subject of what plants or flowers were suitable for the garden. Adler always brought back new plants or flowers from any country he had been visiting, sometimes wholly out of place or impossible for the Salmannsdorf soil; but he always insisted on having them planted and trying them out. The gardener, on the other hand, would insist with equal passion upon *not* trying them out. It is unlikely that Adler ever used authority to gain his end. It was often astonishing to his visitors to notice the absolute equality and freedom between Adler and all his dependants. Things that had to be done got done; and things that Adler thought *ought* to be done were generally accomplished, but Adler did nothing to *make* people do them.

The gardener had known Adolf Hitler in his childhood and told Adler the following story: 'Hitler', the gardener said, 'never played with the rest of us. He was an unfriendly fellow and always stood off in some corner by himself, watching us. Once we built a snowman. As usual, Adolf had done nothing to help us, but when we had finished, he suddenly ran forward and jumped on the snowman's back—sticking his own hat on the snowman's head, as if it belonged to him!'

After the occupation of Austria, the gardener wrote a farewell letter to Dr. Lydia Sicher,who was one of his stoutest friends and had promised, when Adler left Austria for good, always to keep an eye on him. 'I have no money', the gardener wrote, 'and now no prospects of work, but I don't want to burden you; only to thank you for the good friend you've always been to me and to tell you that I shall always say to myself whatever circumstances I find myself in, "What would Adler have thought that you should do about this?" and when I have thought this out, I shall do it, so please have no uneasiness!'

However, in spite of the German avalanche and the shipwreck of her own life and home, Lydia Sicher made persistent inquiries until she came in touch with someone who could tell her where this friend was.

She told the writer that she had meant to help him and sent him twenty shillings which meant a great deal to her at the time, but the Germans opened the package and took the money. The burglar, however, *did* turn up; but far from requiring help, he gave it, and became, in this her darkest hour, one of the heroes of Vienna.

When the ex-burglar heard that some of Adler's best friends were forced to sell their charming flat with all its furniture for three hundred *Schillinge* and that on the morning of their compulsory departure the Nazi buyers still further reduced the price to a hundred and twenty *Schillinge*, he was filled with righteous indignation. 'I was determined', he told a friend, 'that they should not enjoy their stolen property, so I collected a quantity of lively bed bugs and, finding occasion to enter the flat before the Nazis arrived, I introduced the bugs into the furniture.'

Adler's gardener did, however, a great deal more for the victims of the Nazi terror than provide them with jokes. He acted as a go-between for Lydia and her friends and patients; took messages; faced any and every risk; and worked tirelessly to help and serve all those who were in danger or distress. 'I always admired him for a decent fellow,' Lydia Sicher told the writer, 'but I hadn't expected to find a hero in him. Probably Adler, though, had always guessed what he was really like.'

XXIV

The Nature and Spread of Individual Psychology

The years 1919 to 1931 were the years of the world-wide spread of Adler's psychology. During this time he started and made a habit of his visits to foreign countries, on lecture tours. The Latin countries were closed to him, except for a few short visits to Paris, one directly after the war, one in 1937, and one equally short visit to Brussels, also in May 1937, since he never mastered their languages; but all the German-speaking countries, as well as England and America, were open to his new psychology.

Before this period, patients who needed advice about their souls or characters went either to priests or fortune-tellers, and received advice sometimes good and sometimes bad, but on an unscientific basis. Now every human being who finds himself at odds with life knows he can find a psychologist who can give him help of a scientific nature. There is no secret about it, and even academic scientists have learned how to make themselves understandable and how to use common sense in their advice to their patients. This advance is due not only to Adler, since these years were equally the best and freest for the whole school of Viennese psychologists and their European colleagues, but there is very little doubt that Adler's clarifying common sense method and widespread appeals over the heads of the scientists to the general public, did more to bring psychology into the open, and towards making it a practical science, than any other single factor.

It must not be overlooked that in point of time, Freud and Adler, followed by Jung, were the pioneers of modern psychology and were responsible for many discoveries developed by younger men and no longer called by their names.

Freud, because of his enforced and prolonged training for all psycho-analysts, has been far less plagiarized than Adler; but 'eclectic psychology' is but a dubious way of taking the feathers from all of

INDIVIDUAL PSYCHOLOGY

these three great creative birds—Freud, Adler, Jung—and insisting that a fresh bird has been made out of them.

There has been a good deal of bad feeling and worse practice on these taxidermist lines, especially to be found in countries where there has been no creative psychiatry. A stop to this dishonest practice may well have been found in a lately published book compiled and chronologically correct, "*The Individual Psychology of Alfred Adler*", by Ansbacher, published in America.

The subject of human personality was never a wholly closed field to the artist. Even before the little group of Viennese psychologists had started to batter on the door of consciousness, writers had always studied character and how to depict it.

Shakespeare, the greatest of them all, never wrote a play that did not wind to its end, through all the twists and turns of the human heart. Stendhal, Dostoevski, Flaubert, Thackeray, Dickens, Jane Austen, the Brontës, Turgenev, the Spanish Romantics, and the sterner Scandinavians have all flung character against the background of Fate.

Not what happens to people, but how people take what happens to them has always been the chief part of the novelist's task to reveal, and when he is a genius, he has been able to make his discoveries in the human heart ineffaceable and haunting. We are lucky if we have never discovered the hero of *Crime and Punishment* in our own souls; or failed to recognize a father's grief in *Le Père Goriot*; or if we have not stumbled over our own vanity in *Madame Bovary*. There is a fellow feeling in all our hearts as we watch that arch-deceiver, Becky, tilting against the proud world she coveted, with its own false weapons. In our own day, Gertrude Atherton, Strachey, Virginia Woolf, Maurois and Ludwig have taken the thrill of fiction into biography so that the dry bones of dead celebrities live again, though it depends upon the freedom of some of these modern authors from their own favourite ideas, how accurately the voices of the past reproduce themselves.

Philologists need more than the mere understanding of old lettering. They must learn to unveil, through dead words, the ancient personalities who once wrote them. Those who study the Pyramids of Cheops must first have felt drawn to the Egyptian soul. Theologians do not only cling to dogmas and to doctrines; the saints sparkle out through their writings into the centuries.

The Fathers of the Church built themselves into her pillars; the deserts would be dry stones if it were not for the anchorites.

195

The whole Bible is a literature of personalities: bloody, defiant, erring, loving, lying persons. Are not Joseph's dreams and Jacob's blessings, Saul's evil spirit and his love of music, David's treachery and his cry of 'Absalom, my son! My son! My son Absalom!' more real to us than any of their laws or their precepts? Moses, with his stormy courage, withstanding Pharaoh to the face, striking the rock, hearing the voice of God, rebuking Aaron and dying before he reached the Promised Land, is more alive to us than the tables of stone upon which he wrote—as he asserted from divine dictation—the ten commandments.

Theology is almost more art than pedagogy. It presupposes an interest in human nature and a wisdom in the handling of it. It is not surprising that Adler turned more and more towards educational and religious teachers as his science of Individual Psychology developed.

The doctors left Adler when they found that he would not shut his psychology into the closed box of their profession, but insisted upon making every man responsible for the making of his own soul; but the teachers began to flock to him, for they saw, and were soon able to prove, what Adler's psychology could do for the child. Perhaps it is one of the greatest tragedies of the human race that religion first persecuted science; and that then when science grew strong, through the value of its discoveries, the scientists, in their turn, took every opportunity to hit back at the flaws in religion, instead of both learning to be natural allies and carrying out on parallel lines, but in a co-operative spirit, their great common task—the development of mankind.

The Chinese doctor of the fifteenth century who said to a patient suffering from pneumonia, 'Brother, what has put you into this great passion?' may have had more understanding of his patient than a hurried specialist of to-day dashing at his particular organ, with no time or training to reach the suffering human being whose diseased organ is but one instrument out of the whole orchestra of his being.

The old and still used custom of Austria was for each family to have his *Hausarzt*, a doctor responsible for the family's general health, who guessed usually very well indeed when to call in a specialist, or when to advise a prolonged absence from home (without relatives!) by lake or mountain.

In so far as a good general practitioner understands his patients, he is a good doctor; the unfortunate part, however, of being good as a specialist is the failure of the expert sometimes to understand how to handle the whole human being. Adler loved to tell the story of a

INDIVIDUAL PSYCHOLOGY

doctor whose patient had experienced some doubt of his diagnosis. 'My dear fellow,' the doctor replied impatiently, 'I assure you, you've *not* got a liver complaint. When *I* treat a patient for liver complaint, he *dies* of liver complaint.'

It is from a doctor's own personality, as well as from his understanding of a patient's personality, that the patient gains confidence to help him overcome his illness. A doctor may long to help his suffering patient, to bring him not only physical relief, but a relief that includes the possible psychological cause as well as the physical symptoms of his illness, but unless he is a student of the human soul he does not know how to do it. The patient himself, suffering, but with some knowledge of what he has on his own mind, is the better psychologist of the two. A poet or a philosopher might understand the whole case of such a patient, although he would be ignorant of how to treat his physical symptoms. But how much better could a doctor understand, had he the full training of a psychiatrist instead of the optional smattering placed at his disposal for a medical degree?

It is to the eternal credit of many modern doctors that they make a determined attempt to grasp what psychology they can, in addition to all their other compulsory studies. They know well enough how hopeless the treatment of a sick human being must be without the knowledge of his personality. Adler used to say, 'If a patient suffering from a bad mother-in-law went to an academically minded doctor, he could only say to such a patient, "So have I!" '

A tramp at a coffee stall is probably a better psychologist than most professors of medicine, for his life must often depend upon his understanding of faces. A dog has more mastery of the human motives that concern him, and the way in which the people he depends on manifest them; and yet to hear the frightened outcry of the medical profession the moment it is proposed to teach a little practical psychology to the layman, one would suppose that they had been robbed of a pearl they valued more than the world they get a living by—with almost every other means.

Adler definitely lost the support of most psychiatrists and the bulk of the medical profession for his psychology when he insisted that a truth is not a truth unless it is capable of being explained to every human being and is true for all time. Adler insisted on the importance of teaching every person as openly as possible how to be responsible for his own actions and how not to interfere with other people's responsibility for theirs. In spite of his education of the general public, Adler always treated the science of medicine with the greatest

197

respect, and insisted on every lay psycho-therapist of Individual Psychology having his cases covered by proper medical supervision.

He thought the question of ordinary difficulties in human life well within the scope of a trained lay psycho-therapist but he considered actual neurosis a disease only to be adequately and safely handled by a psychiatrist. Nevertheless, the doctors continued to resent Adler's unauthoritative and undogmatic treatment; they felt it derogatory to their own standing that a layman should carry about his own psychology in his waistcoat pocket.

They did not, *en masse*—though many individual doctors grasped it—see that Adler was attempting to bridge a gulf not yet crossed by science; so that those in trouble should not have to choose between an intelligent layman, ignorant of science, or an accredited scientist, ignorant of human nature.

Hitherto only the religious had understood the cruelty of the soul's dilemma. 'Either I believe in God, or I go to a scientist. If I go to a scientist, he robs me of my faith—but I *must* believe!'

No bridge had hitherto been thrown across this gulf, either by faith alone or by science alone. Pascal attempted to put science into faith. Kant tried to force the whole of knowledge into the human conscience; but neither had the simplicity needed to succeed in reaching humanity at large. Kierkegaard of Denmark was the first to attempt a bridge across this gulf between science and religion by paradox; and there were theologians such as Bauer in Germany, the Jesuit father Przyhwara in Munich, Heidegger and others who, from their different standpoints, saw the need for such an alliance and worked upon its approaches; but no one before Adler accepted life itself, and the movements of life, as the basis for the development of man. Alfred Adler was the first founder of an 'Existence Psychology'. Other thinkers took parts of the mind, or disassociated flesh and spirit into drives, nerves, glands, etc. or at a further remove from legends and archetypes; but they did not treat the whole human being as involved in one main purpose or aim, a being subject to his own opinion of himself, as well as affected by his environment or heredity, and capable of using and governing both environment and heredity by his self-created life-plan. All the psychologists of our day, including Freud, were seekers for the idea, 'a being *as*—so and so'. Adler alone insisted upon reaching out towards a science of the spirit. Through the use of dialectics, he revealed the personality of each patient as the centre where the individual is free, and since free, wholly responsible. If man had no freedom, he would not be responsible. His responsibility is the price he pays, and should be willing to pay, for his freedom.

It was precisely because Adler saw that the field of responsibility was being restricted by the Totalitarian States that he fought most ardently for intellectual liberty wherever he saw it threatened. This was his objection to Communism as it is now practised. Adler did not believe in the freedom of 'licence' or a liberty uncombined with social interest and a radical consideration for the rights of others. It was Nietzsche's solemn goal that Adler defended: 'Liberty is the freedom to do right.'

Adler often said: 'Each man says to himself, "I am the author of my deeds; I am answerable for them; but as I am a weak hound, I often fly from my responsibility. Neurosis is the flight from responsibility. If I deform myself, if I am ill, over-anxious, or have compulsions, then I am not responsible. I make a pretext of my weakness; but a free man can be deformed and yet be free in spite of his deformity." ' Here we return to the Master Paradox that has not yet been grasped by most thinkers. A scientist, unless he is free himself as a personality, does not really know his own science. He is reading into it what he wishes, for he has not yet freed himself into the full responsibility of thinking without wishes. A thinker, attending one of Adler's lectures in German, asked him the interpretation of a word meaning 'misty' or 'unclear' in English. He had caught the word *dampf* for 'steam' or 'vapour', and something in himself had been roused by the sense in which this word was used by Adler. That night this patient dreamed that he was in great physical danger, since his whole being was invaded by live fish, each fish in a separate cloud; in his dream, a doctor pointed out that he could make no recovery until, by a system of injections, all these fish were destroyed. The patient himself explained his dream to Adler. 'It occurred to me that these were not fishes but wishes,' he said, 'and I remembered that you had once told me, "A person cannot be a good Individual Psychologist until he has no wishes." I suppose that I must get rid of my wishes before I can trust my own thoughts?' 'I suppose so, too,' Adler agreed without further comment.

The neurotic and the delinquent were to Adler simply discouraged men who wanted to get rid of their freedom. Adler taught his patients that whatever they did, all their activities must belong to them; and in their control and contribution of their gifts to life, he drew out their courage and built up their usefulness.

He was never blind to the great underlying paradox of life—that *without* freedom, art cannot live; while science must depend on laws. Adler saw, as it were, across this paradox, and taught his patients how to possess both points of view, as he himself undeniably possessed both—the creative openness of art with unfailing obedience to the laws of science.

Adler belonged to the race of the heroic optimists, not to those with rose-tinted spectacles who see only what they wish to look at. He was a Columbus of the soul who knew that to discover new lands, he must sail forth upon uncharted seas.

Adler believed that social interest—the love of man for his brother-man—is a creative force, having the full stream of life behind it; whereas hate is a direct negation of life itself, a turning back into the complete isolation of death. If some one praised a neurotic or delinquent person for going far, Adler would say, 'Yes, I see that he goes far—but the direction in which he is going is towards the nearest lunatic asylum.'

Adler thought all love of power over others was a form of insanity and in the nature of a retreat from the more difficult task of complete self-control. It was interesting to see that he used his own powers only to free, never to control, a human being. One of the psychiatrists who worked in a mental hospital visited by Adler said: 'It was incredible to see how much more *life* Adler brought out in our patients, even in the most inaccessible cases. His actual contact with psychotics or neurotics was instantaneous. He seemed hardly to say anything before they began to reveal themselves to him, as if they had been waiting for him all their lives.'

It was another of the barriers between Adler and his fellow doctors, that he never had any free time to devote to his own confrères. They had always to share him with his ex-patients. After their recovery—or during their treatment—his patients were embarrassingly and permanently a part of Adler's free time. They insisted upon being his friends, nor would Adler ever do anything to break this tie. He never spoke harshly or woundingly to a person, unless they were themselves causing unpleasantness for others; even then, his usual method was to say a quick, unnoticeable word that only the offender himself understood. Often these words of correction were more like the sudden confidence of an equal than the rebuke of a teacher. 'Never say "quick" to him!' he would say in an undertone to a wife who was impatiently hurrying her husband; and once to a very interfering woman, who constantly drew attention to herself by correcting what other people were saying or doing until she succeeded in spoiling the pleasure of the whole party, he said, 'You will never do your own business well, if you are always attending to the business of others.'

It was interesting to notice how easily Adler managed to reassure, without drawing attention to, weak or discouraged people. He never allowed any form of fault-finding to take place in his company without somehow or other, often very indulgently to the fault-finder, coming to the rescue of the victim.

Adler never liked people who complained of others, although he often asked trusted friends if he would do right to put confidence in a person they were in a position to know better than he did.

Once in speaking of a group of psychologists who had rather markedly failed over a long period of time to co-operate with one another or to produce any form of helpful activity, Adler said: 'We are all a little sick; but we do not need to be as sick as all that!'

Adler's final judgment upon any human being was inherent in his favourite question: 'Is he a co-operator or an isolationist?'

XXV

First American Visits and Adler's attitude towards Publicity

Adler's boyhood's dream was to go to America. He never told anyone of it, nor did he make it a conscious goal, since it did not seem practicable; but the dream remained in his heart, ready to materialize at the faintest hint of opportunity. He had actually received in 1925 only three lecture invitations, through an ordinary agent, but any possibility for work or expansion was to Adler like an invitation from a favourite hostess. He knew already that he liked the taste of life, and he never refused the smallest of her invitations. He made his first visit to the United States in 1926, and remained until the spring of 1927. He lectured at the Community Church, New York City; at the New School for Social Research; and at Harvard and Columbia Universities.

Adler knew, at this time, very little English. He could read enough upon his own subjects to follow the sense, but he found it difficult to put even a few English words together correctly. However, in the few intervening weeks before he sailed for America, Adler learned enough English to use it successfully for his trip and even to lecture in it. How severe a task this must have been any lecturer can well imagine, but Adler never showed that he found it difficult. He put his meaning into words as a good hunter takes his fences, without rushing them, but with a fixed determination to get over.

He never really mastered the English language in any scholar's sense, but he so saturated himself with it that after a very short period he could not only speak it fluently and intelligently, but he constantly used words and images beyond those of an ordinary person's vocabulary. Anyone who listened to Adler lecturing in English after 1927 found no difficulty whatever in understanding him, but they had to listen; and those unaccustomed to this exercise or hostile to the sense of what he said, could make it an excuse (in these early years

202

of his Anglo-Saxon visits) that his English was a hardship. Nevertheless, it was good enough for Adler never to mistake a patient's meaning and to answer in public, at a moment's notice, questions that might well have tripped up a speaker in his own language.

Adler had already formed many American ties. One of his Viennese disciples, Dr. Greta Simpson of Vienna, had married an American and lived in New York; Dr. Dey and Miss Dey, the principal of the Mary C. Wheeler School in Providence, were among Adler's special friends; and all of them were prepared to help him and to make his first visit to America a happy and successful one. Hundreds of teachers, known and unknown, who had attended his European conferences, looked forward to his coming. His books were already known and widely read in psychiatric circles; and his name, as one of the three great giants of Viennese psychiatry, was upon all their lips.

Freud had already paid his famous visit to America and in his wake, the psycho-analyst school flourished. Antagonism to Adler's ideas was therefore ready-made. But Adler was never on the look-out for enemies; and his friends were always in the majority.

There are not many great men who would have crossed an ocean and given up months of highly profitable work on the strength of these few lectures; but Adler was justified by his faith in his American dream; and, as Columbus discovered America, so, in its turn, did America discover its Columbus of the human soul, and set to work to keep him. But it was not until 1934, eight years later, that Adler finally gave up his home in Austria and decided to make his permanent abode in America. The political situation in his own country was a constant source of anxiety to him, and, although he did not make up his mind until 1934, his fears for Europe had been slowly accumulating ever since the war, until he felt that if there were to be any hope for humanity at all, it must lie in intensive educational work in the Anglo-Saxon countries. A new human being was required to match the mechanistic and militaristic robot of the Totalitarian plan, with his emptied mind and amoral goose-step activities; and Adler knew that he had the means of helping to develop this new human being.

To quote the words of Philip Mairet, editor of *The New English Weekly* and one of Adler's most understanding English followers, 'In his realistic grasp of the social nature of the individual's problem and his inexorable demonstration of the unity of health and harmonious behaviour, Adler resembles no one so much as the great Chinese thinkers. If Europe is not too far gone to make use of his services, he may very well come to be known as the Confucius of the West.' Yet it was with no great idea of his own powers that Adler set out upon his voyage of discovery into Anglo-Saxon lands.

He never allowed any of his family, except occasionally his son Kurt, to accompany him to the station, nor did he even take a taxi. His heavy luggage—what there was of it, for Adler always travelled light—was sent ahead to the station, and Adler set out with a grip in his hand, and without turning his head to look back at the clustered heads anxiously watching him from the window of No. 10 Dominikanerbastei.

Adler kept on this home in Austria until 1934, as it seemed best for his family to finish their education in their own country, but he urged them all to study English thoroughly, since he had a growing doubt of their futures in their own land.

The night before he sailed on his first voyage to America, Adler had a dream that he was fond of recalling. He dreamed that he was on a ship, travelling to an unknown destination with all that he had acquired in the way of treasures during his lifetime. A collision took place and the boat sank; everything he possessed was lost; but he himself, after a long struggle, succeeded in reaching shore.

Adler had never accepted the psycho-analysts' sexual interpretation of dreams, even in its less exclusive days before 1910, when Dr. Alexander Neuer asserts that Freud for the first time closed the issue to any other instinct. Adler had believed that dreams reveal, with a heightened sense of imagination, the person's own accepted aim or life-plan, and, as it were, egg him on towards its goal. Nightmares or frightening dreams are the self-inflicted warnings of an individual anxious to evade some more or less necessary task; whereas happier dreams are the 'wish dreams' of the individual, prompting him to more successful methods or to more hopeful results of methods already in use.

Adler's shipwreck dream showed that he did not under-estimate the task he had set himself or the sacrifices that he knew he might be called upon to make, but that he believed in his power to surmount them. To those who had studied his character, this dream revealed both his deep underlying pessimism and his indomitable courage. He *was* to lose all he possessed—his fortune and his country; but he reached his goal.

Adler brought this message for America—and for the world, which was, as he knew as early as 1916, moving in a wrong direction.

FIRST AMERICAN VISITS

*Die Gemeinschaft ist richtendes Ziel, ideale Gegebenheit, ewig uner-
reichbar aber ewig anrufend, aufrufend und Wegweisend.* It is difficult
to translate this sentence of Adler's with precision, but as near as
possible its English meaning is: 'The goal of the community is a
guiding aim, eternally ideal and unattainable, yet for ever calling to
us, and pointing out the way which humanity should follow.'

It was Adler's belief, scientifically practised, that a child should be
educated from its earliest years with this aim of bettering its community, rather than the egocentric aim of its own private pleasures
or success. He believed that the child could always be developed into
a 'giver' rather than a 'taker', and that when this aim of contribution
towards a common good is used as the goal of each individual's education, we shall produce a human being whose social instinct or 'love
of his neighbour' is as natural to him as 'breathing or the upright
gait'. Neither wars nor dictatorships would stand a chance in this
common-sense and yet altruistic world. Adler did not believe that
politics alone, science alone, or economics alone would bring about
any improvement in the race of man; but he believed that man himself might bring about these improvements if he practised a scientifically ethical education open to all, from their earliest years. Politics, economics and science would then be used to further this aim,
rather than to exploit the present egocentric goal which, should it
become universal, would inevitably bring the race of man to a violent
and self-destructive end.

Adler did not take America by storm upon his first visit, but he
made a deep and favourable impression, which his subsequent visits
did even more to increase.

In the spring of 1928, Adler lectured at the New School for Social
Research, New York City, and in 1929 he returned to give forty
lectures and to hold forty clinics.

In the autumn of 1929, Adler was attached to the College of
Physicians and Surgeons at the Medical Centre of Columbia University as visiting Professor, and during the winters of 1929 and
1930 he was invited by the Twenty Million Michigan Children's
Fund to tour the State during the month of January, and delivered
four to five lectures daily, conducting clinics and taking private
patients. The effect he produced in the child-guidance life of Detroit
was miraculously great; and so deep was the interest taken in his
teaching by the fully qualified teachers and experts who heard him
that perhaps his most permanently important work for America was
done in this brief time. It was in Detroit ten years later during the

winter of 1938 that one of Adler's students, who was lecturing all through America, found that the most practical and constructive use had been made of his teaching. It happened that she was asked to give a lecture at Dearborn to the Michigan Teachers' Conference—a lecture on 'The Art of Living', founded upon the teaching of Alfred Adler. The audience of a thousand teachers was obviously entirely in sympathy with Adler's work, and responded in the deepest and most thrilling way for a lecturer to the subject. This could not have happened in the same way, if at all, to any but a most thoroughly understanding audience. In Michigan and among its teachers Adler had found the response he needed.

During the winter and spring of 1930, Adler not only conducted his clinic at the Medical Centre of Columbia University every day in the week except Sunday, but he also lectured on this clinical work for two hours every afternoon in amphitheatre A at the College of Physicians and Surgeons, between 4 and 6 p.m. The audience often filled this great amphitheatre to the brim. Adler also gave a series of thirty lectures to the graduate students in psychology at Columbia University, and in addition he gave a course of seven morning lectures and fourteen in the afternoon at the Macmillan Theatre, Columbia University, under the auspices of the Institute of Arts and Sciences. He added to these a series of special lectures open to the public on the subjects of 'Crime' and 'Love and Marriage'. His friend, Mr. Charles Davis, who followed every step of his American career and to whom the writer is indebted for the history of these engagements, relates that Macmillan's was filled to capacity during Adler's lectures, and that the authorities testified all previous records of large audiences in the history of Columbia University were exceeded.

This was not surprising, since Adler had always had an effortless power of drawing large audiences in any and every country when he lectured. It was this faculty—if faculty it should be called—that caused such consternation in the hearts of many of his colleagues who had never been afflicted by any such response to their own public appearances. The purity of science, they felt, must be poisoned at its source when one of its exponents could be so comprehensible and attractive to the general public.

What was no doubt an immense help to Adler as a lecturer in a foreign tongue was his power of instantaneous and friendly contact. He entered lecture halls without the slightest change in his demeanour. He was not nervous; he was perfectly sure of what he had to say; and he treated his audience with a friendly respect that they were quick to sense and return. Adler never talked 'down' to a child or to an audience; and he always talked straight. Those who do not like straight speaking either actively disliked, or asserted that they did not understand, Adler's lectures; or that the lectures consisted of platitudes which the hearer had known all his life. Sometimes the listener gave all three reasons, without observing that they were somewhat self-contradictory.

The writer attended between thirty and forty of Adler's lectures, many of which were on the same subjects, but she has never heard one which did not contain some creative, freshly minted thought, difficult to evade or to forget. 'Thoughts', Adler once said, 'should be like burrs—they should irritate.'

His indomitable presence of mind, and the quick flashing wit of Adler's answers to hecklers, brought him a special welcome from his American audiences; nor did Adler ever use his wits unfairly or to evade issues as many witty people do. He answered both question and questioner to the best of his ability. No question was too silly for him to give a sensible answer to it. It was only when he thought the questioner was dishonest or trying to be purely obstructive that Adler's answers became formidable.

On one occasion, when lecturing in Washington to psychiatrists of other schools, Adler had stated that we were approaching an age which would lead to a universally increasing leisure, as life becomes better and better organized and science more and more productive. 'But what', a hostile psychiatrist demanded, 'use will that be, if what you say is true? How will people be able to employ all this leisure time you speak of?' 'There are, I think,' Adler observed benevolently, 'many ways in which leisure time can be employed quite usefully. For instance psychiatrists might even study a little more psychiatry.'

On another occasion, a member of an audience in Boston, afterwards discovered to be a press correspondent, demanded, 'Does not Professor Adler think the present King of England, Edward the Eighth, will never grow up?' (at the time of the King's abdication). Adler immediately answered, with obvious indignation, 'I have always found it a useful rule never to talk about matters where all the factors cannot be publicly known · and I should strongly advise you to do the same.'

XXVI

Adler's American Life

'With merit and even greater modesty,' Montaigne points out, 'one can remain unknown for a long time.'

Adler certainly bore out the truth of this epigram in his new country, for he knew nothing about American publicity methods; and, although some of his academic colleagues complained acidly of Adler's 'bid for popularity', it was evident that popularity —in the sense of the lay person—did all the bidding there was to be done for Adler. He himself had neither the time nor the inclination to seek for fresh opportunities of work. They came to him.

William Beecher, of the Dalton School in New York, writes of his first meeting with Adler as follows: 'Dr. Adler had no publicity, and it was only by chance that I discovered that he was working in New York. When I learned the fact, I went directly to find out when and where he was teaching. I made several trips to the hotel to contact Dr. Adler, but no one answered the house phone. My intention was to inquire from his secretary about classes, for I did not feel justified in taking up his time. On my fourth trip he answered the phone in person and asked me to his room. I went up and protested against invading his privacy and time for a matter that could be settled by his secretary. Adler waved aside my objections, insisted on placing me in the best chair in the room, offered me a cigar, sat himself on a straight chair near me and gave me his undivided attention. This was a great shock to me, for I have met many busy and "important" people. They never lost an opportunity to impress their importance on me at the beginning of the interview. I believe that this was the only time in my life (before or since) when I met anyone who did not do this. I felt perfectly "at home" in spite of myself. There was not the least trace of a superiority attitude on his part.

'The interview acted as a tonic, though we spoke of nothing but the lectures I proposed to attend. . . . I have never seen Adler in any other light except when someone tried to take an unfair advantage of a situation. At such times he would stiffen a bit and end the exploitation with a few words so devastating that there was no comeback. I have never known him to try to dominate a person or a situation, but I have seen him thwart the attempts of others who tried to do it in his presence.

'Dr. Adler taught impartial justice as against special privilege. He was as near the perfect example of his teaching as any human being could hope to be in this world of injustice and inequality. Adler's lectures were not advertised and he had no ways of being known to the public at large. . . . I urged him to broadcast but he would not do it because of "medical ethics". This was the greatest tragedy of all time! He was dominated by a tradition which serves a special group. He never was able to master it and serve the larger group by defying the tyranny of the smaller. It goes without saying that when he *was* able to contact the outer world, he had a profound influence.'

Adler, however, was as usual trying to safeguard the rights of his profession while appealing for the equal rights of laymen to understand the laws of their own being and to become more and more responsible for their actions. He might have won far wider support temporarily had he overlooked the rights of either party, but it is doubtful if his contribution to mankind would have been as valuable. Adler's personal integrity was the final seal upon his work, as it is upon every man's.

It is an interesting fact that in Vienna, where Adler was naturally most thoroughly known and understood, the medical profession was by no means antagonistic to his teachings. Most of the heads of his profession, with the exception of the psycho-analysts, who tried in ways that were both unfair and unscientific—since to be open-minded and disinterested is the glory of science—to check the spread of Adler's psychology, spoke of Adler with the greatest affection and esteem. Professor Julius Bauer, for instance, the gland specialist, could hardly praise him highly enough, and many of his other most famous medical colleagues were outspokenly grateful for the knowledge of human nature Adler had instilled into them. A general practitioner of high standing said to the author, 'The whole approach of the Viennese School of Medicine to their patients was altered, and favourably altered, by Adler's teaching. I do not believe a single doctor of any standing in Vienna failed to attend, at one time or another, Adler's lectures and to profit by them.' The head of a well-known hospital asserted: 'Adler not only taught us how to treat our patients. That was a great advantage; but he also taught us, and this perhaps was an even greater advantage, how to estimate ourselves as human beings.'

Naturally Adler was not known and could not be known in foreign countries from this point of view. He did not begin to visit England and America until he had given up his medical practice and confined himself wholly to psychiatry.

Dr. Erwin Wexberg, one of Adler's ablest followers, now attached to Louisiana University in New Orleans, the well-known author of one of the best text-books written on 'Individual Psychology', writes as follows: 'Adler's influence on American psychiatry is not very evident, though much larger than people generally are aware of. His ideas are being used to a very large extent, particularly in child psychiatry, without quotation. As a lecturer and philosopher, his success was considerable in the broad public; and, more than all child-guidance has been directly influenced by him.'

There were two main reasons for Adler's partial failure to co-operate with the American schools of psychiatry.

The first was his unfortunate experience at Columbia University, for which no one was actually to blame, but which was largely due to the over-enthusiasm of a devoted colleague. Columbia University had been prompt to invite Adler to lecture on psychiatry and he was for a considerable period attached to the university for this purpose, although rival schools of psychiatry were already represented there.

All went well, and Adler had, as usual, a growing band of devoted students to attend his lectures. He was, however, invited on an important mission to Detroit, and during his absence, his great friend and colleague, the late Dr. Tilney, without consulting Adler, suggested that a permanent chair of psychology should be offered to him, and put this suggestion to a large meeting of the various schools of psychology represented at the university.

The plan was premature, and his adversaries fought it hard and succeeded in out-voting Adler's supporters. When Adler returned, and found out what had occurred in his absence, he promptly resigned, to the deep distress of everyone concerned except his gleeful opponents.

Adler seldom spoke of this rebuff if he could help it, so that it is difficult to understand quite what was his point of view in resigning. There was no question that his lectures were increasingly popular, and that had he carried on his work for only a few months longer, the opposition would probably have been overcome, and a majority

ADLER'S AMERICAN LIFE

vote would have been cast in his favour. Dr. Tilney's action had been premature, but as Adler had known nothing about it, no harm would have been done to his reputation by its failure, or to his eventual chance of obtaining the chair, which even his adversaries considered to be good. Nobody was to blame for what happened, but it was a great misfortune for Adler's career in America, and perhaps a still greater misfortune for America.

Probably Adler was unduly sensitive, after his Viennese university experience, to any academic slights. He seems to have consulted no one and to have acted upon the spur of the moment. He wrote to one of his daughters a simple statement of the facts, but made no comment upon them. No one can blame Dr. Tilney for his whole-hearted enthusiasm; had the step he took succeeded, it would not only have redounded to his credit, but would have been highly acceptable to Adler, who could not have had a better sponsorship than Columbia University for his American career.

The second and most characteristic reason for Adler's failure to win professional support for his psychology in America was, as Dr. Wexberg points out, 'Adler's disinclination to use some of the generally accepted methods of research, such as statistics, extensive case records, etc., which made it easy for his critics among medical scientists to disregard his findings.'

This criticism of Adler was brought up later in the *British Medical Journal* by a former English disciple of Adler's, who had studied Individual Psychology for many years without being at all impeded by this lack of statistics, and did not bring up the point until after Adler's death.

Adler's objections to a rigid dependence on statistics in psychiatry were twofold. He did not think that they could be wholly trusted to represent the truth, and, as such cases are usually highly confidential and of a most private nature, he feared that extensive case notes might lead to the blackmail of his patients, should they ever be inadvertently accessible after his death, or through some accident during his lifetime. It was not true to say that Adler took *no* case notes, for in Vienna such notes had been (over a space of years) most methodically taken and kept by his chief child-guidance experts and are now in existence, though on account of the war they have not yet been published; and case notes were also kept by his assistants at the hospital. *Problems in Neurosis*, skilfully put together for Adler by Philip Mairet, was taken from such case notes as Adler thought successfully evaded any personal application, or which the patients themselves

211

had given him permission to use. Adler kept many others, but only those which his infallible memory and discretion allowed him to feel freed his patients from any danger of exposure.

There was another reason that should not be forgotten, why it was unnecessary for Adler to keep intensive notes of his cases. Almost all his patients, cured or partially cured, remained his friends; and he was in a position where he could not fail to keep check upon their improvement or their cure.

When Adler failed to satisfy his medical colleagues it was generally because he was refusing excessive reliance upon intelligence tests or claims that he felt brought him into conflict with ethics. Common sense ethics were the core of Adler's psychology. He had no 'medical etiquette' that was not human 'etiquette'. Dr. Leonhard Seif of Munich once said to the author, 'If there was any way of being a good Individual Psychologist without being a good man, be sure I would have taken it, but there is no such way!'

Adler was an exceedingly shrewd human being. He must very well have recognized what publicity could do for him, and what it could do against him. If he did not take advantage of its usual methods in America, it must have been for a purpose. He was equally aware of how important for any scientist is the support of his own colleagues, and where he sacrificed this support, it is probable that he did so consciously and for the same purpose that he disregarded publicity.

The results of Adler's self-limitations were that much credit which should have gone to him personally was snapped up by lesser colleagues. As Wexberg neatly puts it, 'Adler's ideas are used without quotation', so that what might have been accepted during his lifetime superficially over a wider area, has had to sink deeply and over a narrower surface into posterity. Nevertheless, there were many avenues, even during his lifetime, down which his teaching made its way. His lectures were always largely attended and highly memorable. For over five years he trained the third-year men of his own profession at the Long Island College of Medicine in Individual Psychology.

He had a clinic for adults which roused great interest and was increasingly successful. Schools, mental hospitals, prisons and reformatories constantly asked for Adler's advice and services, and never asked in vain. He had a daily string of patients that would have daunted most psychiatrists. He edited with great success and devotion a quarterly on Individual Psychology, founded and run by an indefatigable group of Individual Psychologists in Chicago. In addition to these activities somehow or other Adler continued to write his books. He was in constant contact with his fellow human beings, and he understood contact as few people have ever understood it.

There is a passage in the New Testament which records that: 'They knew from their faces that they had been with Jesus.'

It is perhaps not impious to say of Adler that those who were his real adherents had in their faces a good will and reliability, an absence of tension, and a cheerful courage which were more helpful in spreading Adler's theories than any other single factor.

XXVII

Adler's Main American Difficulties and their Compensations

At least six of Adler's friends claim that they were his path-finders to American life; but it was always difficult to determine what influenced Adler's plans or who, if anybody, contributed to his carrying them out.

Probably the American friends who did most to assist Adler's American career, and certainly the most to make him feel at home in this new country, were Charles Davis and his family. Their home in New York gave Adler, until his own family joined him, the focus for his private life. His face always lit up with joy whenever the name of this great friend was mentioned: 'What that man has done for me', Adler would say, 'is simply marvellous! It is unbelievable!' The late Mrs. Bernheim was also a great and loyal friend of Adler's, and Individual Psychology owes much to her memory.

Dr. and Mrs. Dey were young and stimulating friends, and of great assistance to Adler, since they gave fortnightly meetings at their house to whomever they felt Adler would most like to meet. Miss Dey, of the Mary C. Wheeler School at Providence, gave him the opportunity he valued most of regular work among children; and, as she kept careful case notes of his patients for him, her friendship and co-operation had a quite special value, apart from his deep respect and affection for her. He spoke of this school often to his friends in Europe, with admiration for its mixture of freedom and good sense. It maintained the job of natural discipline in which Adler believed, drawing the children unconsciously towards work with, and consideration for, each other.

Adler was well served by many of his American friends, though in most cases he gave more than he received, and in some cases he gave without return. His open-handed fellowship to all who came to him was often taken advantage of, and even where the harm done him

214

ADLER'S DIFFICULTIES IN AMERICA

was through ignorance or misadventure, the flamboyant enterprises of grateful patients were seldom beneficial to his reputation or his opportunities.

There can be no question that several of these over-enthusiastic and excitable patients made Adler's introduction to American life far less fruitful than it would otherwise have been.

America has specially guarded her academic life from the eruption of charlatans, and no doubt experience has taught her that distinguished strangers with wild disciples are as dangerous as charlatans.

Adler's European reputation was certain to ensure his being treated with respect and consideration by his American colleagues, though it would undoubtedly have made his path easier and their welcome still more generous had he been a Professor of his own University of Vienna; but they very rightly refused to open their doors to an influx of excited and semi-neurotic disciples, trying to force the pace of their psychology as if they were selling a patent medicine.

Adler was, for the first year or two, at a great personal disadvantage, owing to his inadequate knowledge of English and also of the habits and customs of his American colleagues. He always followed a usage, when he knew what it was, since he would have considered it an anti-social act not to have fallen in with any harmless general practice; but in a foreign country he was naturally at the mercy of his friends and advisers; and he was most unfortunate in some of his advisers.

Genius needs a caretaker. Adler was without the defence of his own family, nor did he even employ what would probably have added ten years to his life, a thoroughly trained professional secretary.

He liked to keep this office open, so that he could give it in turn to difficult patients who needed employment and were dependent on his wisdom and kindness. These part-time amateurs often caused a great deal of confusion and hindered rather than helped the work they were supposed to perform. No doubt they gained much as patients, but what they gained as patients Adler lost in methodical care and attention to important details. He did a great deal of this secretarial work himself, and was meticulously careful to keep all his appointments and to appear on time; but articles for his *Journal* were sometimes lost, and many letters left unanswered or answered hurriedly, which should have received care and attention.

215

There is no doubt that opportunities slipped past him which might have led to the kind of work Adler most desired. Even more dangerous were the pushing and inexpert efforts of some of Adler's disciples, which prevented the efficient co-operation of really friendly colleagues.

Adler was aware of these difficulties to some extent, but he was probably less conscious of their importance than many of his more worldly wise friends who understood the value of a right approach in a foreign country. To Adler, the presentation of a truth was nothing; the truth in itself was all.

Even if he had realized how much harm was being done to the cause of Individual Psychology by some of its adherents, it is doubtful if he would have tried to restrain them; and he certainly would have refused to protect himself by limiting his open fellowship.

He probably felt for his anti-social patients the same amused tenderness that he had for his cactus plants. Here were creatures, cut off from the normal source of life—social interest—just as the cactus were cut off from their normal source of supply—water—and yet what brave, even if prickly and ugly, efforts they were making to overcome their starved interests!

Adler never looked for gratitude from his patients and where he met with ingratitude he rarely suffered from disappointment.

· There were some patients, and among them some of the most distinguished and notorious, who betrayed his trust and went over to his opponents in order to spite him for refusing them a specially privileged affection; others acted in public against his teachings; or, having learned all they could of his methods and discoveries, went off and practised them elsewhere as their own.

Dr. Ira Wile, of Mount Sinai Hospital, New York, a loyal and friendly colleague whose relationship with Adler throughout his American period was particularly friendly and helpful, drew one of these cases to Adler's notice. A prominent disciple of Adler's, who had worked with him over a space of years, and indeed owed to Adler's teaching and philosophy his own subsequent celebrity, sent out and published notices that he was authorized to take over all Adler's work and engagements, and gave the public the impression that Adler had left the country for good, though he well knew that Adler had merely gone to Chicago for a few weeks' lectures.

When Dr. Ira Wile, indignant with what he knew to be a rank betrayal, called the matter to Adler's attention in order to warn and protect him, Adler wrote in reply: 'I agree with you in the matter of

216

Dr. W. I have written to him, when I heard about his activities. He damages himself if he continues.'

Two prominent women psychiatrists, both doctors, also left Adler for self-interested motives. One became a Freudian because, as she explained, Adler refused her 'a transference' and she was dissatisfied with a public friendship which all shared equally; the second, in a less spectacular manner, took all she had learned from Adler to a distant city and practised it as her own invention.

These explosions of fellowship were hard for outsiders to understand; but the claims of a psychology that is re-educating the whole personality are greater and more arduous than those which merely teach a fresh branch of intellectual psychology involving nothing beyond concentration and intelligence, so that it is not surprising if a few of these semi-cured Individual Psychologists broke down and revolted from the self-discipline involved.

Adler's cures were many, silent, and unadvertised; his failures, on the other hand, were few, spectacular and self-advertised. Adler's cures depended upon the co-operation of his patients. They were not miracles, and had quite as much to do with practice as they had with faith. 'The Doctor', as he used always to say to his new patients, 'sits in your chair.'

'Experience', Adler was fond of saying, 'is like a low door in a wall. It is necessary for most people to bow their heads in order to go through it. The neurotic does not wish to bow his head, but I show him that if he does not, he is obliged to strike it against the wall and that it will not be the wall that suffers. All I can do is to point this out to him. I have no further responsibility.'

Adler's main difficulty in America, however, did not arise from his patients, or from those who betrayed him by accident or on purpose; it arose from the attitude of his fellow psychiatrists. Those belonging to the Freudian school were his natural opponents, and continued to act in America as they had always acted in Vienna. It was unfortunate that many most open-minded and skilled American psychiatrists resented bitterly what appeared to them the exclusive type of Adler's psychiatry. Many of them had been trained in different schools and branches of psychology, and were quite willing to accept Adler as one patch in a variegated patchwork quilt, even as a particularly large and important patch; but they were by no means willing to give up all their learning and practical experience on eclectic lines and to adopt instead the whole-coloured quilt of Individual Psychology. They asked and expected Adler to 'mix' his psychology with theirs, but this, to Adler, was to 'divide' the individual. He could not mix a psychology that he believed to be the basis of the development of human personality. It would have seemed as reasonable to Saint Paul to join the teachings of Christ with those of the prophets of Baal.

This was the core of Adler's American difficulties, as it proved to be the core of his English ones. His psychology could not be used as part of a club sandwich; and it was as part of a club sandwich that the eclectics wanted to use it. Why could he not act *with* them, and as one of themselves? Why should he ask them to accept a psychology that demanded a moral restraint that they neither desired nor, as some of them thought, deserved? 'Physician heal thyself' has never been a popular doctrine in medical circles.

Adler was a psychiatrist by profession, and many of his American colleagues were willing to admit that he was probably the greatest practising psychiatrist of his day; but they were *not* willing to admit his ethical claims as a philosopher.

Adler made attempt after attempt to co-operate with his American colleagues without throwing away the gist of his life work; but he was never able to adapt his psychology to the demands of the eclectic school, and they were never able to make the sacrifice Individual Psychology required of them and be 'born again of the spirit'.

After a time, Adler settled down into an intellectual loneliness tempered by friendships without professional understanding, or professional understanding without friendship; very rarely indeed did he find in New York a friend who combined both. Until 1934, this solitude did not weigh too heavily upon Adler, because he still had his home in Vienna to which he returned every half year. These half-yearly visits kept Adler in constant touch with Europe and all his old activities.

He would leave New York in April and remain in Europe until the end of August. Vienna was his headquarters, and there he immediately took up his lectures, classes, work at the Franz-Josef Ambulatorium and child demonstration clinics; and best of all, his home life and his old friendships.

Later in the summer he took lecture engagements, conferences or short summer schools in the surrounding European countries, and went back to New York in the early autumn like a giant refreshed.

Adler's working power was incredible and appeared to be unshaken by the years. He loved the idea of a holiday, but never, in any real sense, took one. Whenever he agreed to go to mountains, sea, or countryside, a string of patients followed him, appearing shortly after breakfast and taking up, in turn, most of the day.

Two of Adler's children were now married, his eldest daughter, Vali, and his youngest daughter, Nelly. Adler was always on good terms with his sons-in-law, though he complained once to an intimate friend, 'These fellows are too cold for me—it is hard to give my daughters up to them. I know that I am merely jealous, but I can't help wanting to have my girls back under my own wing!'

He took a great joy in watching the opening career of Alexandra, his second daughter. She had become a neurologist of brilliance and distinction, and her work in Vienna was being most favourably commented upon; indeed, had it not been for political interference, she would have obtained an important appointment in Austria, for which her former Professor Pötzl and fellow specialists considered that her work as a neurologist had specially entitled her.

Adler's chief longing was to see his only son settled in a career that promised success. Kurt had qualified himself as a physicist, but there seemed to be no opportunities open to his endeavours.

Adler saw that the times were largely accountable for Kurt's difficulties, and urged him to master his English as soon as possible so as to join his father in America.

Adler's great respect and affection for his only son held firm against all discouragements, though both father and son must often have felt discouraged. 'Anxiety?' Adler at one time exclaimed to one of his greatest friends who had complained of suffering from it. 'But is that not high treason against the Holy Ghost?'

Adler had many occasions, and was to have still more dire ones, when the necessity to overcome anxiety was vital to his existence, but this desire to see his son succeed was perhaps his chief private wish. Father and son had many differences of opinion, but a deep underlying confidence bound them to each other, and they were better friends than many men of the same age. This quality of agelessness entered into all Adler's relationships, and constituted one of his greatest charms.

With Adler's great genius for friendship, those who had once been admitted into his circle of intimacy learned for the first time how deep and free an impersonal and unsentimental relationship can be. He loved best friendships that spread to whole families; perhaps the two most intimate friendships of his later years were with Anglo-Saxons. Neither race, class, age nor sex ever made any real difference to Adler's enjoyment of human beings; and these two men, one

English and one American, brought their families to Adler with them. The wives soon became equally devoted to him, and owed Adler as much as, if not more than, their husbands owed him. Still, it was the husbands in both cases who came nearest to Adler's heart, and to whom he gave any personal confidences that he wanted to make.

The scope of these confidences was never great, for probably no one ever spoke less of himself that Adler, but in later years I think it was easier for him to speak of himself to his men friends than to women. He was essentially a man's man; he could be certain, too, of how far a very little will go with a fellow man, and that no more than he chose to give would ever be asked of him.

His friendship with his daughters was an exception to this rule. He loved them with a depth of pleasure and confidence that could not perhaps have been either so deep or so refreshing had they not been daughters. They, in their turn, found in their father's comradeship an ideal relation—protection without authority; confidence without weight; a fiery, straightforward tenderness that gave all and exacted nothing. They were his greatest joy; and they knew it. 'We always had the feeling', one of his daughters told the writer, 'that however many failures or mistakes we might make as persons, or even suffer in our family life, still ours *was* the finest family in the world—one in which we were free to do whatever we had it in us to do—and could count on all the others helping us to carry it out!'

As the quick, vital years slipped past, driving Europe nearer and nearer the rocks of the dictatorships, Adler grew more and more depressed with the European outlook and gradually transferred all his hopes and roots to America.

In spite of the limitations and discouragements that his work in America had entailed, it had succeeded, and succeeded beyond the bounds of most men's capacities. Nor had Adler's faith in his old dream once faltered. There, if anywhere, he believed, lay the hope for humanity at large: there liberty could be preserved and a reasonable freedom practised. Man could become a 'whole human being' in America better than anywhere else. He could learn to direct his aim and form his life-plan upon social interest rather than upon egocentricity; and for this hope Adler worked on, alone—encumbered—misunderstood—with the fiery zeal of youth and with the patient wisdom of maturity.

XXVIII

Adler's Long Island Appointment; Illness, and Reconciliation with Raissa; his last visit to Vienna

As soon as Adler had resigned from his visiting post at Columbia University, Charles Davis, who had been following Adler's work in America with the greatest interest and confidence for several years, set to work to establish a position for him in connection with the Long Island College of Medicine.

This was the first chair of 'Medical Psychology' to be established by any medical school in the world, and it was pre-eminently suitable for a man of Adler's European reputation, as well as for carrying out the spread of Individual Psychology in America.

In the late spring of 1932, Charles Davis conferred with Dr. James C. Egbert, the director of the extension work at Columbia University, regarding opportunities for Dr. Adler to lecture. Dr. Egbert is the Trustee of the Long Island College of Medicine and was its former President. The possibility of Dr. Adler's joining the staff was discussed throughout the summer, and final arrangements were made in August. Adler assumed his duties in 1932 as Visiting Professor of Medical Psychology. This gave him a seat on the Executive Faculty.

At first, Adler organized his clinic in connection with the Medical College, an institution with which the Long Island Hospital is in intimate contact, rather than with the hospital itself. Adler delivered a series of lectures to undergraduate students of medicine throughout the winter months, and in the late autumn of 1932 he also gave a series of talks to the medical profession through the auspices of the Medical Society of Kings County.

Adler's adult clinic grew steadily and later was moved from the college to a private house a few doors away from the college. Throughout his whole connection with the Long Island College of Medicine, starting in 1932 and closing with his sudden death in 1937, Adler enjoyed the full support and friendship of Dr. Babbott, its

221

President. It was always a pleasure to see the devoted loyalty and confidence with which Adler spoke of his American chief.

The Faculty, however, were not wholehearted in their welcome of this distinguished stranger. Some of them were already strongly influenced by the Freudian School of Psychology, others were unable to separate what they knew of Freud from what they suspected of Adler, and were out of sympathy with the psychological view of medicine altogether. There was, however, one group, which started with a small number but steadily grew larger, of men who were deeply aware of Adler's knowledge and sympathetic to his point of view. This was invariably the case with all Adler's work. Time and the support of his personal character were always on the side of his creative spirit. The opposition he met with was Janus-headed, since it was composed of those who did not understand him, as well as those who did not *want* to understand him. There was something in Adler which threatened their position, not only as thinkers, but as human beings.

Adler never mentioned any difficulties in his work at the Long Island College of Medicine, beyond that he had been hitherto unable to establish an open child-guidance clinic where he could give demonstrations and lectures based upon them, such as had been the core of his work in Vienna. Adler considered such a clinic the best way of spreading Individual Psychology, and it was his hope that either in England or in America a permanent institution of this nature could eventually be started. Otherwise, his work at the hospital was of the kind that best suited Adler. He was free for six months of the year to continue his lecturing in Europe; he was working with colleagues of his own profession, for their future interests; and he was at liberty to carry on his private practice or to give lectures elsewhere in America from time to time.

There was one drawback which Adler's work never suffered from and that was ill health. He died at sixty-seven in a minute, without any previous signs of illness; and during his lifetime he had had only one minor operation and one dangerous illness. In his youth he had suffered from a slight lung infection, *Lungenspitzen Catarrh*, very prevalent in Vienna, but a few weeks in the high mountains had put this trouble right, nor did he ever have any return of lung trouble. From the time he was six years old till he was sixty-four, he had the untroubled health of an athlete. It is difficult to put this down to any material cause. He had good physical habits and used common sense; he did not take precautions, and was always interested in other people and their problems rather than his own. Until he went to America, he had taken a good deal of exercise, at any rate in the summer, both mountain climbing and swimming.

In New York he was deprived even of his walks, and probably in the long run this told upon him. He had no home in America, and during the last four months of his life, an absorbing personal anxiety and grief. His eldest daughter was held in prison as a hostage in Russia. His work hours were uninterrupted and sedentary. To meet this last difficulty, he ate very sparingly and was careful in his diet.

After his evening meal, unless there was any real emergency that he had to meet, or he was giving an evening lecture, he would say, with a charming smile, 'I fear I have an important engagement.' His friends knew very well what this meant, since they were often chosen to accompany him; he was going to hurry off to his only recreation, the cinema. The pictures had several tremendous advantages for Adler: he did not have to talk and so could spare his over-worked voice; they kept him amused but free, and yet never for a moment out of touch with the humanity he loved. His chief favourites were Charlie Chaplin and the Marx Brothers; he considered them to be geniuses of the first water; nothing ever entertained Adler so much as people behaving in an unexpected manner.

He believed also that physical habits and appearances were directly symptomatic of the inner man. He went far more by how a patient looked, how he came into a room, shook hands, laughed or moved, than by a man's words or a description of his feelings. 'When patients come to see me,' Adler would observe with a twinkle, 'they have already made up their minds how to put their case in a presentable form, but they haven't made up their minds not to fall over a footstool. This tells me something; it also tells me something which chair they take and how they sit down on it. If they sit very far away from me and talk in a way which is difficult for me to understand, I know that they have no strong desire to co-operate in their case. If they push themselves upon me, so as to inconvenience me, I also know something. Bodies do not lie so easily as the minds behind them, and what is in one part of a man, you will find in all the rest of him.'

In 1934 Adler suffered from his first and last severe illness. It would not have been anything like so dangerous had he gone in time to have it attended to, or even had he consented sooner, when in the hospital, to an operation. He had a carbuncle on the back of his neck; and he was determined, if possible, to let it heal by itself. This it did not do, and he had finally to go to the hospital, where he remained for seven weeks and where he very nearly died from general sepsis. It would have given Adler great joy to have known that the obscure youth who looked after him with such consideration and intelligence was to become one of the foremost writers of his day. A nephew of my husband postponed his return to England in order to look after Adler, as he knew we should wish. Nigel Forbes Dennis devoted himself to Adler and took as much of Adler's work off his shoulders as possible. He was with him almost every day throughout his illness. It was soon realized how ill Adler was, and his wife was sent for, from Vienna. She joined her daughter Alexandra, who was already setting out on her way to America, in order to take up her Boston appointment. From the moment that Nigel told Adler they were on the way, he began to recover. When they arrived, and Nigel found them sitting one on each side of his bed, Adler said, his face beaming with satisfaction, 'Here are my two Prides, come to look after me. You will see now how quickly I shall get better!'

When the surgeon had decided, after very severe fights with Adler, that the carbuncle must be opened, the nurse brought a stretcher on wheels to Adler's bedside to take him to the theatre. Adler, though terribly weak at the time, tried to jump upon it by himself. His first jump failed, and he sank back on to his bed, very crestfallen and with tears in his eyes. The wise young nurse said, 'Never mind—try jumping again, Dr. Adler. I will move it a little nearer and I believe you could do it like a two-year-old!' Adler flushed with pleasure, tried to jump again, and, to his great delight, succeeded.

His illness and Raissa's instant response to his need of her changed both their lives. For the first time, Adler realized how deep his wife's devotion to him really was; and his whole nature responded to it, and to her care for him.

They were restored to each other in the truest sense of the word, and no serious misunderstanding ever again separated them. For the remaining years, all too few, of Adler's life on earth, the harmony he had always longed for in his married life took place, the task for two was fulfilled and fulfilled admirably by each. No miracle had occurred, the pin-pricks remained, and some of the incompatibility, but these two strong spirits were joined together, not to be put asunder, until death parted them.

Adler made an unprecedentedly quick recovery, and in a few weeks' time resumed his normal life. When we met again in Vienna in the summer of 1935, Adler looked older and weaker than when we had parted from him in New York a few months before; but in a fortnight this look had vanished and he was his old buoyant self again, capable of twice as much work as most men of forty could shoulder.

This was his last summer in Vienna, and I believe that he knew it to be his last. Salmannsdorf was to be sold and the big, roomy flat at No. 10 Dominikanerbastei, where Individual Psychology was first defined and christened, had already been given up by Raissa when she had joined Adler in New York. In 1934 the Individual Psychological clinics attached to the State schools had been closed for political reasons. Adler's friends and followers were either dispersed, or their lives and activities so curtailed as to wring his heart. His *Journal* was in danger. Vienna was slowly creeping towards that state of apathy and paralysis which heralded her doom. Schuschnigg's position depended entirely upon outside influence. There was a cleavage in the heart of the Austrian people. The working classes could neither forget nor forgive the guilt of Dollfuss, shared by Schuschnigg, for the Vienna massacre. They could not trust Schuschnigg again, and they had no other leader. Austria was safe so long as Mussolini's troops held the Brenner and not an instant longer. Adler foresaw what the bankrupt democracies of Europe—bankrupt in sincerity and faith, though still rich in everything else—would *not* see—that Hitler and Mussolini would soon form a natural alliance, and that when this happened, there would be no more real democracy possible in Europe.

Adler's *Wien* had been already taken away from him. 'It is not alive,' he told the writer. 'I want very much to get away from it. Our duty is always towards the living.' And yet his memories and his friendships tore his very heart out. They were the friendships of a lifetime—deep, unshakable alliances of the spirit, tested through years of successful growth, through controversies fairly hammered out, through decisions won by courage and cemented in an indomitable hopefulness.

Adler realized that he was leaving the wreck of his home, but that his friends were still alive among the ruins. There was his gallant band of teachers, who could no longer act publicly upon the psychology that had formed their whole careers; there were his fellow psychiatrists—trained in his methods and permeated by his spirit—never again would he have such pupils, so rooted and grounded in his creative thoughts; and there were his patients—the cured, and those who still clung to him for guidance. For his work's sake, he must desert them, and leave them crushed and heading, with their country, towards an ultimate and irretrievable catastrophe.

Adler did not live to see the disaster take place; but he foresaw it. It was impossible for those who loved him and lived near him not to realize the crucifixion of his spirit. On the surface, Adler was just the same—each patient's individual problems seemed more important to him than his own. After the day's work was over, we would talk in one of his favourite cafés, while the long summer evening turned into night. Sometimes Adler would come out to us at Grinzing where we had taken a flat for the summer, among the vineyards on the slopes of the Wienerwald, close to Adler's old home. Once a teacher friend from England brought out a group of girls from her training college to meet Adler; we invited them all after his lecture to a big garden restaurant, surrounded by its own vineyards.

We sat round a great table under the trellised vines, drinking the sparkling yellow wine and eating *belegtes Brot*. On one side of the table sat a group of English girls, and opposite was a group of German and Viennese students. Turn by turn they sang, first English folk-songs and then German *Lieder*—song after song. Adler was a little saddened by the fact that the Viennese students had forgotten many of their old songs. 'It is a bad sign,' he said to us, 'when a country forgets its songs!' The honours of the occasion were easily won by two Welsh girls with beautiful voices. One of them was extraordinarily pretty and sang with a perfect dignity and unselfconsciousness which delighted Adler. 'Why cannot people always live like that!' Adler said next day. 'It was such a perfect evening—two races in such accord, a little moonlight, a little wine, a little music. I saw no one take too much. I saw no one show off. We all *enjoyed* each other!'

Adler was giving two series of lectures in Vienna this last summer, one to medical students in the university, and one to his own group of Individual Psychologists, joined by many summer visitors drawn from Europe and America, in a large upper room of the Café Siller. These latter were informal lectures upon early memories and the significance of dreams. The audience would place anonymous slips of paper by Adler's place, with their first recollection, or a dream, and he would take them in turn and show their significance and how the person's life-plan was likely to have formed itself from these indications.

Neither Adler nor his audience knew to whom each paper belonged, but several people afterwards expressed their astonishment and even awe at the singular appositeness of Adler's inspired guesses.

Adler was full of humour in these informal talks among his own psychological children, not only in his treatment of the case histories, but in his reaction to any incident that took place.

A long table ran down the centre of the room, a group of us sat round it, while rows of chairs were placed behind. On one occasion a lady, sitting exactly opposite Adler, asked the writer (who sat on Adler's left) to open one of the windows as she felt faint. The writer did not wish to get up and perhaps disturb Adler while he was lecturing; however, as the lady demanded it again in a still louder voice, she thought she had better satisfy her, so she got up, opened the window as she thought, and returned to her seat. The lady opposite looked much relieved and no disaster took place. Adler made no comment till afterwards, when he pointed out in a low voice to the writer that the window was still shut—she had merely opened an inside pane. 'Still it seemed to have the desired effect!' Adler added with a twinkle.

On the next occasion, the lady repeated her tactics. This time Adler stopped the lecture and asked her what was the matter. 'I am fainting from lack of air!' the lady told him. 'I *must* have a window open!' 'But of *course* you must,' Adler replied. 'Air is good for all of us; why should we not indeed have *all* the windows open!' He bounded from his place and flung open window after window, down the large room. The windows all faced one way, upon the busy waterfront of the Danube Canal; the result was that the lecture was inaudible to the greater part of the audience. For a few moments the lady looked enchanted with the success of her appeal, and then very slowly it dawned upon her that by her selfish act she had spoiled the whole lecture. She blushed to her forehead and we heard no more about open windows for the rest of the series.

On another occasion, a lady moved the heap of papers by Adler's seat, on which the early memories of dreams had been written, in order to place her own, which had been covered by later arrivals, upon the top. 'What are you doing with those papers?' Adler asked her. 'I was afraid', she explained, 'that as there are now so many I might have to wait for my turn, so I put mine on the top of the pile.' 'And you were perfectly right,' Adler replied, taking hers from the top and putting it into his pocket. 'There do seem to be a good many, and we may not have time to finish with them this evening. I will, therefore, keep yours over till next week.'

Adler's last evening in Vienna seemed the same as all the other

227

evenings. He had first taken his final lecture at the university, and I was told afterwards it was a singularly fine and moving one. He ended with the words, *'Kinder, macht etwas, und macht's gut.'* ('Children, do something—and do it well.') In his last talk at the café to his group, he made no farewell. The writer remembers only the quiet joy on Ida Löwy's face and the sparkle of humour in her eyes as she followed his every word. Afterwards, his youngest daughter, Nelly, and her young husband, Heinz Sternberg, came up to Adler, and Nelly said, 'Father, you promised to spend your last evening with us alone.' Adler said, 'Yes, and I will!' and moved away from the group round him with them to another café on the opposite side of the street. He was to leave at eight o'clock next morning, and we asked Ida Löwy, who knew him and his likes and dislikes better than anyone else, 'Do you think he would like us to see him off at the station?' 'I think he would not like it very much,' she told us, 'but perhaps you had better ask him yourselves and then there will be no mistake.' We ran over to the other café to ask him. Nelly, looking quite lovely in a beautiful blue fox fur cape her father had given her as a parting present, was clinging to his arm, as if she could never let it go. 'As *you* like!' Adler answered our question; but when we persisted that we only wanted to come if he wished it, he replied, 'Well, then, you had better *not.* I always whine at railway stations when I have to say good-bye to my friends.' He gave us his quick warm handclasp, and when last we saw him, he was being led firmly away from his group of friends, Heinz holding him by one elbow and Nelly by the other.

It is good to think that Nelly had his last evening, for she never saw her father alive again. The next summer he spent in England, and the summer following, just as Nelly was about to join him in Paris, came his sudden death. Perhaps, of all his children, this beautiful youngest needed him the most.

XXIX

Adler's Dutch and English Visits

C hronologically, Holland and England discovered Adler before his American period.

Adler had already paid two visits to England, one in 1923 and one in 1926, before his first visit to America; and he had also started an annual lecture tour in Holland dating from 1924. The writer, however, thought it clearer to give the whole effect of Adler's teaching upon each country in turn, rather than split up the different lecture periods according to their dates.

During his visits to Holland, Adler had the good fortune to form two friendships with women already famous for their altruistic activities. Mevrouw Allmeyer and Mevrouw Frohnknecht were friends before they met Adler, and became still greater friends, as well as co-workers, after their acceptance of Individual Psychology. Mevrouw Allmeyer was the first to go to a lecture of Adler's upon Family Constellation and its effect upon character. She was astonished and even thunderstruck at hearing what sounded like an actual description of her own childhood and its special difficulties and disadvantages, stated and made clear to her by a perfect stranger in a public lecture.

She immediately sought Adler's advice and worked with him steadily until she had mastered both the science and the art of living, which is the core of Individual Psychology.

Mevrouw Allmeyer became and remained one of Adler's best friends, and worked tirelessly in spreading his teaching in Holland. She and her whole family were murdered by the Gestapo during the War. Visas to England had been procured for them, and they were on their way to escape, when their supposedly devoted chauffeur drove them to the door of the Gestapo, to whom he had betrayed them for a bribe.

Mevrouw Frohnknecht, the wife of a well-known banker at Amsterdam, first heard Adler lecture in Holland in 1924 upon backward children. She was so much interested in his ideas that she brought him a problem child for treatment, and his success with this patient convinced her of the truth of his teachings. The whole Frohnknecht family entered into this friendship, which continued without a shadow until his death.

Mevrouw Frohnknecht supported Mevrouw Allmeyer's efforts to spread Individual Psychology throughout Holland. Together they arranged yearly courses of lectures for Adler from 1924 to 1933. Groups of Individual Psychologists were formed in The Hague, Amsterdam and Utrecht, and are still flourishing. Mevrouw Allmeyer, trained by Adler, began, and ran successfully, a child clinic at Amsterdam. Both these courageous and intelligent women made Adler's teaching their life-work.

It is interesting to notice how very easily Adler's psychology penetrated and developed in this enlightened and common-sense atmosphere, and how straightforwardly and without friction these two women patients worked together. They had accepted the more difficult entry into Individual Psychology, that of being themselves trained as human beings before teaching it, although they had never been neurotic sufferers in the accepted sense of the term.

They profited, as many teaching Individual Psychologists with more expert knowledge fail to profit, by that training in social interest which made them morally 'whole human beings'. These were no 'cactus plants' to prick and gall the hands that tended them, but faithful students who spread their teacher's discoveries by example as well as precept. Adler always spoke of these two Dutch ladies with a special pleasure and respect.

Mevrouw Allmeyer told a story characteristic of both Adler and herself. While walking with Adler to a lecture, they were nearly run down by a careless boy on a bicycle. 'How awful', Mevrouw Allmeyer exclaimed, 'it would have been had that boy knocked you down!' 'Terrible if I had upset that poor boy!' Adler exclaimed simultaneously with equal concern.

Of all the countries in which Adler worked, Holland is probably the one where his teaching is most deeply and permanently accepted, and where its growth has been less impeded by explosive neurotics, or by colleagues who ran away with his ideas and claimed them for their own.

The intellectual tie between Vienna and Holland was a closer one, closer than to any other country except perhaps to Germany under the old regime; even up to the last days of Austria's independence,

Dutch students were attending the Individual Psychology lectures held in Vienna by Adler's pupils, and returning to spread his science in their own country.

Adler's first visit to England, in 1923, was to attend the Psychiatric Conference at Oxford, where he spoke upon Individual Psychology. At this time he knew practically no English, so that his visit was without general significance, though several of his English colleagues who knew German were deeply interested in his theories.

His second visit in 1926 was of far greater importance.

There was living in Bloomsbury at this time a Serbian philosopher —Mr. D. Mitrinovic—who had a school of thinkers already interested in theories which they felt had much in common with Adler's Individual Psychology. Adler came to London at the instance of one or two medical and psychological societies towards the end of 1926, before his first visit to America had taken place. Miss Lillian Slade, a great supporter of Mitrinovic, went to Adler's lectures and was so impressed that she persuaded Mitrinovic to attend one. After this, the two men met and had several long and intimate talks.

The Editor of the *New English Weekly*, Philip Mairet, was one of Mitrinovic's most ardent supporters, and the following quotations, dealing with the founding of the Gower Street Club of Individual Psychology, are taken from his account: 'The large cost of equipping the Gower Street rooms, etc., was all borne by Mr. Mitrinovic's interested supporters, of whom I was then, and for long have been, one of the most enthusiastic. We worked immensely hard with meetings and lectures nearly every night. One of the men who did most to get Individual Psychology started, especially in the month or two just after the opening, when Mitrinovic was away in Vienna, was Alan Porter . . . subsequently Professor of Literature at Vassar College in the United States. That was early, very early in 1927. Adler had been in London at the end of 1926 and lectured in the studio of Miss Valerie Cooper, another great Mitrinovic supporter, on Dostoevski and Nietzsche, with considerable repercussions among the intelligentzia. . . . I believe Adler prolonged his visit a little in order to cultivate these new friendships. Alan Porter was a marvel. He had no time, I believe, to read much of Adler at the start; but he knew *all* the opening of the *Neurotic Constitution* which, though very obscure, is a mine of *concepts* out of which you can construct a system. On this impulse, Porter held forth extempore at least two evenings a week for all the spring and summer; and by the time he had done, there was probably as much "head-knowledge" of

Individual Psychology about the quarter of Bloomsbury as in half Vienna! There was a fine, sacrificial enthusiasm about all this period and, throughout, quite a large circle of "workers".'

The writer feels obliged at this point to say that it was probably due to the fact that this sudden knowledge of Individual Psychology *was* only 'head knowledge' that the eventual disruption of the club took place. Individual Psychology is averse from dividing up the individual. Its basis is a discipline of the whole personality, a practical and scientific training away from egocentricity towards the love of our neighbour. The 'goal' of Individual Psychology *is* 'social interest'. Mr. Mairet believes that Adler took his name away from the Gower Street club in 1931 largely, if not wholly, upon the grounds that it was politically tainted; there is every reason to believe that he is partially right, for Adler was determined to keep his psychology free from any form of political bias; but there was a further objection, still more serious from Adler's point of view.

Adler was not satisfied that the Gower Street group had grasped or was intending to follow the open morality of Individual Psychology, or that it was functioning upon common-sense lines. This was his fundamental reason for dissociating himself from it. Where his leading Viennese friends and students always differed from those of a later period—unless they had been also successfully subject to an Adlerian analysis—was that they were the growth of Adler's whole system—they grew up *in* it and *with* it, fully realizing that the 'head knowledge', by however brilliant and expert a mind, was no substitute for a trained and disciplined life.

'The Adler Society', Mr. Mairet goes on to say, 'at its height was a brilliant show, with an enormous number of brilliant people occasionally appearing in it. At one time, John Strachey came a good deal, and his sister, Mrs. Clough Williams-Ellis, was also for a long time a keen supporter. After the "excommunication", which was not really that either but a sort of disbanding by Adler of Fascist, Marxist and other groups (we, of course, had a strong sociological wing which was out for a sort of pan-European socialism), Dr. Crookshank founded another Adler society in Torrington Square; but his personal tragedy badly compromised it. . . . It was the eloquence, personal magnetism and tremendous intellectual brilliance of Mitrinovic that turned Alfred Adler into a sort of "movement" in London. Otherwise, Adler would have been a more or less disorganized influence upon a few doctors; with here and there an educationalist interested through correspondence, or by occasional meetings.'

This last paragraph is not quite convincing since, subsequently, a way *was* found by one of Adler's most devoted friends, Captain Forbes Dennis, to introduce Adler to many of the most prominent people in the religious, political and social life of England, and this gave Adler the opportunity to present his teaching in a manner that has taken deep root and is still actively developing. Even during this earlier period, Adler had made many valuable friendships among members of his own profession; such names as Drs. H. C. Squires, Cuthbert Dukes, O. H. Woodcock, Sir Walter Langdon Brown, and others will always be remembered for their generosity and the steadiness of their friendly support, and the open-minded interest which they took in Adler's psychology.

The tragedy of Dr. Crookshank (the most intellectually convinced of Adler's English adherents) was that, while accepting the discoveries of Individual Psychology from an intellectual point of view, he had not accepted its moral discipline. Crookshank refused what might have released him from all his difficulties—a personal training by Adler or Seif, whose influence was deservedly great among English people, and who had urged his need for such a treatment. 'Seif', Crookshank said with ironic emphasis, 'seems only able to speak to us of "Caritas—Caritas—Caritas".' Crookshank had not the moral discernment to realize that Seif did not only speak of 'love of the neighbour'; he practised it so faithfully and with such a depth of courage and understanding as to be equally able to train others along the path he had himself followed. Crookshank, however, could not submit to a retraining in social interest by men whom he believed to be no more than his equals, if not his intellectual inferiors. He took his own life; and with him died the most convinced and the clearest exponent of Adler's psychology in England.

Of Adler's other medical and psychiatric English colleagues, each in his own way was deeply interested in Individual Psychology, but all had careers of their own to follow and minds which had been moulded and fixed upon their own lines. Each adopted what he found most useful in Adler's teaching or was influenced by his personal friendship with Adler himself, but none of them could be called fully trained or equipped exponents of Individual Psychology. Nevertheless, they had sufficient interest in Adler's theories to form an Individual Psychological Medical Society which still flourishes under that name, although its teaching has gradually edged away from the name it bears and has become—as indeed the whole English School of Psychiatry has more and more tended to become—'eclectic'.

As the political trend of the Gower Street club increased, Dr. James Moore publicly protested against Individual Psychology being mixed up with politics; and Adler congratulated him for his good sense and courage in having brought the matter into light. Mitrinovic then proposed that they should form a medical society of Individual Psychology, using the Gower Street premises whenever available. Dr. O. H. Woodcock was eventually appointed chairman of this group; Dr. James Moore, vice-chairman; and Dr. Redfern, secretary. In the early days, no medical student or other than a registered medical practitioner was accepted as a member. A few months later, Dr. Crookshank joined as a new member, and soon became the predominant influence of the society.

It was a misfortune, from an Adlerian point of view, that Groddeck was invited to lecture to the club. In European circles of psychiatry, Groddeck was not taken very seriously. The Viennese laughed at his theories; and his German colleagues were shocked at the unscientific exaggerations of his views. A neurotic follower of Freud's, Groddeck had repudiated a good deal of his master's philosophy, supplementing it by some of Adler's which he grossly exaggerated or misinterpreted; and finally weaved round himself and his patients a strange web of his own.

His book *Das Buch vom Es* (*The Book of the It*) has been translated into English and is very amusing, if hardly convincing reading. Adler considered Groddeck a dangerous character as well as a highly unsafe doctor. Groddeck had, however, some brilliant successes among his patients. What Adler mainly objected to about him was his lack of common sense, manifested by the exaggeration of his views and their distance from reality.

It was not enough for Groddeck to believe that illnesses *can* be used as moral alibis by the patient; he asserted that *all* disease had such a basis. He was, in fact, an 'all or nothing' man; and Adler believed that such persons are fundamentally neurotic and unreliable.

It was curious that Anglo-Saxon medical men should have evinced so strong a taste for Groddeck's doctrines, since their main tendency as a school of medicine was to set neurology higher than psychiatry precisely on account of its more material proofs. But it appeared from their subsequent behaviour that if they were interested in psychiatry at all, they infinitely preferred to be hanged for a sheep rather than a lamb.

Groddeck's psychology had this advantage over Adler's, for a medical man, that it led back to the complete control of the patient by the doctor. If *all* disease had a psychological origin, or if *no* disease had such an origin, the medical man was equally necessary. He was the deciding factor, not the patient. No longer was the patient led to rely on his own common sense to judge if he were ill or well; the doctor must be called in to cure either his mind or his body.

Adler had already discovered that those human beings who increased their common sense, and became more responsible for their thoughts and actions, were greatly benefited physically and seldom suffered from other than occasional brief illnesses which confute or render doubtful a neurotic origin. Adler held that each case has to be judged on its own merits. If it is necessary to call in a doctor, he must put himself to the trouble of weighing every possible physical or psychological cause for the illness. He cannot take for granted that he must be in the right and the patient must be in the wrong. He has, as it were, his own character to deal with, as well as his patient's, before he can be relied upon as a true physician.

In fact, doctors found themselves—as Individual Psychologists—in a very troublesome and far less powerful position. Groddeck's theories released them automatically from this uncomfortable predicament.

Neither the English nor the American psychiatrists were prepared to submit themselves to the moral retraining necessary before they could become 'whole human beings', and only by such retraining could they free themselves from tendentious thinking. They were honestly unaware how convenient to themselves and to their livelihood the more complicated forms of psychiatry were. Naturally, the more complicated the psychiatry, the more need of a psychiatrist and the longer and more financially advantageous the treatment; on the other hand, general medical practitioners and particularly surgeons were often most willing to accept and to use a simpler psychology, since this helped them in their approach to all their patients alike, and jumped to meet both their common sense and their experience. To such men, Adler's psychology made a predominant appeal.

The comparative shortness of the Adlerian analysis persuaded some of his colleagues to believe it more superficial than their own, though it is difficult to see, except from a financial standpoint, why a longer cure should be considered more successful than a shorter one; and it is certainly *not* more advantageous to the patient, or to his pocket. Perhaps such men forgot that simplifying, for the greater understanding of the common man, had also been one of the charges brought against Socrates, and was used as one of the chief factors against him at his trial.

ADLER'S DUTCH AND ENGLISH VISITS

There were two as cogent and more disinterested reasons given to the author by sympathetic English colleagues as to why Adler's psychology failed to inspire more practical enthusiasm on the part of his fellow psychiatrists. One suggested that psychiatrists generally see very little of children, from whom the quickest and most convincing results of Individual Psychology can be obtained. 'It is the teacher, not the doctor', this friend explained, 'who profits most by Adler's psychology; he has the same child under his eyes for a space of years, whereas most ill children get well or die far more rapidly than grown people, so that their medical adviser has neither the need nor the opportunity to tackle them from a psychiatric point of view.'

The superintendent of a large mental hospital gave the following reason for not using Adlerian therapy in the hospital under his care: 'I am convinced', he told the writer, 'of the truth of Adler's theories; but I was not brought up on them, and I have no time to change the system that I was trained in, even for a better one, which I fully believe Adler's to be. I modify the whole spirit of control by what I have learned from Adler, but I cannot adopt individually a new form of therapy. I have no staff competent or sufficient in numbers to apply his teachings, and as superintendent, I am equally unable to do so myself. The administration work and the guidance of the policy of the hospital is all that I can manage.'

The writer, who considered this hospital even as it was, under the care of this enlightened and good human being, the best she had ever seen, still ventured to suggest that psycho-therapy should not be denied to the patients and might be obtained by admitting trained lay psycho-therapists from outside. 'Impossible,' said the superintendent firmly. 'The moment you get outside workers in psychiatry, you halve your own control over the patients, and risk jealousy and mischief; besides, I do not believe in the use of lay psycho-therapists.' I repeated this explanation to Adler, who quietly replied, 'They also run another risk if they use no psycho-therapy upon individual cases —that of not curing their patients.'

The obstacles placed before Adler's final visit by the envy and prejudice of the English school of psychiatry were almost unbelievable, and it would be pleasanter not to have to drag them into the light of day. But as such obstacles still remain between the common sense of the general public and these self-seeking pedants, there is an obligation on the part of the writer to let the public know all the facts. At the same time, it should be understood that none of the following incidents are meant to cast any aspersions upon the English

236

school of medicine as a whole. From far the greater part of the profession, including several of its heads, Adler received generous recognition and a warm welcome. Nevertheless, that such acts and manners could obtain in the twentieth-century school of psychiatry shows very plainly in what a condition of illiberal and uncontrolled temper many of these psychiatrists exist, and in what need they stand of the very character-training they so much resented as the basis of Adler's psychology.

At one of the best-known universities of Great Britain, a newly made professor of small private means had been for years a convinced Individual Psychologist. He promptly gave the weight of his name to an open committee which was arranging lectures for one of Adler's summer schools. His university colleagues immediately threatened that if he did not withdraw his name, his new opportunity for research would be denied him. Feeling that his life-work was at stake, Professor X. withdrew his name and begged the writer to explain the situation personally to Adler. 'He did right,' Adler said earnestly. 'It *was* his life-work; but it is a pity that those who threatened him should be called scientists.'

At lunch in honour of Adler given by an equally famous university, at which all the Faculty were present to do him honour, two of the professors were so full of spite and malice that they could not refrain from attacking their guest behind his back. They were indiscreet enough to make the writer their confidante. They accused Adler of 'being gaga', 'so simple as to be almost a charlatan'; and finally one of them declared: 'At the demonstration given for Adler by Dr. M. the other day, Adler completely exposed himself. There never was such a public fiasco!' Neither of these gentlemen had been to the child-guidance clinic in question, but the writer had; and had been amazed (as the whole audience appeared to be) at the way in which Adler reached the core of this unknown child's difficulty. He threw a new light upon the child's whole situation. No one who had studied the reactions of a child to a skilled psychiatrist could fail to have seen that Adler had put into the boy's mind a new weapon against the dangers of his discouraged spirit.

On another occasion, my husband went to call upon the Secretary of the Royal Medical Society, armed with an introduction from Lord Dawson of Penn, whose secretary had kindly rung up on the morning of my husband's visit to smooth the way for an interview.

The Secretary of the Royal Medical Society, however, received my husband with studied discourtesy. The moment my husband mentioned the cause of his visit, he burst into an explosion of denunciation against Adler and all his works, declaring that he was against the whole idea of such a visit or of any scientist lecturing on psychiatry to a lay public; that Adler's psychology was without the least significance; that *should* anyone want to know *anything* at all about it, the Society had one of the best libraries in the world and there was a book of Adler's in it that would tell one more than enough.

After listening to a sharp scolding rather than a criticism of Adler, my husband withdrew, more startled and amused than angry at the sight of such an unscientific exhibition.

One of the acting professors of psychiatry at a well-known university was then approached, and evinced great interest on hearing of Adler's visit. 'I am particularly glad to hear of it,' he told the writer with great cordiality. 'Since Adler's is the psychology I consider most valuable—indeed, Individual Psychology is what I am teaching my students at present—I shall certainly miss no opportunity of hearing Adler while he is in this country.' But when it was suggested that this professor should strengthen such an opportunity by helping to arrange for a lecture from Adler at his own university, he appeared appalled at such a responsibility and made no attempt whatever to bring such an event to pass.

A great society, very well backed financially, and boasting Adler as its vice-president, was unable to see its way to offering him a lecture upon the subject of the Prevention of Delinquency—the aim of the society—although Adler was the greatest living authority upon the subject. Several of the society's lay patrons were most anxious to invite their vice-president to give such a lecture, but the sharp negative reaction from the psychiatrists of other schools, whose services were engaged by the society, prevented the invitation from being forthcoming. One of Adler's friends suggested that after such a slight he should withdraw his name as vice-president, but Adler shook his head. 'My name cannot do them any harm,' he said with a twinkle. 'It might even do them some good, and after what you tell me they have decided upon, I think that they need all the help my name can give them!'

Time and Adler's death have softened this bitter antagonism to some extent and have brought Adler's work into a truer perspective. Professor John MacMurray made an after-dinner speech at the Individual Psychological Medical Society in the early spring of 1939, at which a friend of Adler's was present, who wrote the following account:

'The after-dinner speech was given by Professor MacMurray, and he was very good indeed. He was the only one who mentioned Adler. He said that we should think of Adler as one whose work is greater than that of any other psychologist, because he has given more than just a new scientific outlook. Adler has pointed out that every important thing is the act of an individual, and his psychology is really a social psychology. All the other psychologists must realize more and more that there is only *one* psychology, and must unify in the attempt to work on the right principle. Adler even tended to a general philosophy for the whole world, he was not limited in the narrow conception of a science. We can only understand his importance when we try to see that everything *is* due to the psychical behaviour of human beings. There is no such thing as economic circumstances, because the economical situation is made by persons, and is therefore a psychological problem. The greatness of Adler lies in his new outlook, and the religious aim for the improvement of all our actions. He is the greatest of all the new psychologists.

'Professor MacMurray made some amusing as well as true remarks. He said that Adler had discovered the inferiority feeling, and when he found himself giving an after-dinner speech, he realized the truth of Adler's discovery. "If there are doctors who treat my body, and if there are doctors who treat my mind, who is going to treat *me*?" "There *must* be something the matter with a person who goes to a doctor when nothing is the matter with him."

'I spoke to him afterwards (I fear it was bad manners, but I was so interested in what he had said that I could not help it). And he told me something very interesting. "If Freud's theory is right, his practice must be wrong; if his practice is right, his theory must be wrong." "Yes," I said, "because if there is a success in the psycho-analytical treatment, it is always due to encouragement. Adler, however, has made encouragement the centre of his practice." '

Individual Psychology made no rapid headway in England until the closing years of Adler's life, when sufficient interest was aroused to admit of a prolonged visit by Adler. Adler was always his own best producer, and as soon as he was introduced by people of sufficient standing and importance to reassure the general public, Individual Psychology took root and developed with increasing activity and success.

A fresh Individual Psychological group of Adler's English friends and patients had been started in London, when Adler resigned his presidency of the Tavistock club, and Adler became this group's president just before his death; later, his daughter Dr. Alexandra Adler consented to become the President of this group, but unfortunately it was broken up by war activities.

The group, however, has again been reconstituted with Dr. Alexandra Adler still as its President, calling itself 'The Adlerian Society of Great Britain'. It is held at Friends' House under the chairmanship of Neil R. Beattie, M.D.B., N.Y., D.P.H., Senior Medical Officer, Ministry of Health. A Child Guidance Clinic has been started under its auspices with Dr. Weissmann in charge, assisted by Mrs. N. R. Beattie; and an *Individual Psychology News Letter* is edited by Paul Rom, and run as an organ of the International Individual Psychology Society. Dr. James Moore, 45, Wimpole Street, W.1., is the President of the Individual Psychological Medical Society, which is of long standing, and with which the London group is affiliated. The new Child Clinic is a great step forward for the Society to have taken.

Adler set great store by this co-operation of teacher, parent, child, and audience. He liked his students to be present, both for their own sakes and for the child's. He believed that it encouraged the child to be told that grown-up people shared his difficulties and that what could help him could also be of use to them. Many grown people and students could not afford private treatments, but by watching the training of the child by a good psychiatrist, they could recognize their own difficulties and profit by the child's treatment. The child clinics always afforded an invaluable activity and field for observation for students of Individual Psychology as well as many opportunities for co-operation, should the child's circumstances or the parents' situation need practical assistance. A group without such an activity, Adler had found, was always inclined to eat itself up or get under the control of some domineering member, but when there is an outside interest with a natural growth, the co-operative spirit has far more opportunity for developing itself in a democratic and impersonal manner. 'What do we need in order to found a group?' one of his friends asked Adler on one occasion. 'Good will and a rubber stamp,' Adler promptly replied, and then, after a pause, 'Perhaps even the rubber stamp is not wholly necessary.'

XXX

Personal Impression of Adler: 1935 Visit to England

I n dealing with the last few years of Adler's life, it will be necessary to explain the author's contacts and opportunities for understanding Professor Adler and his work.

In 1926 my husband went to Vienna to make Adler's acquaintance. He was, at that time, deeply interested in language teaching, and took pupils into our home at Kitzbühel in the Austrian Tyrol for this purpose. Boys from sixteen to twenty are not an easy age for a childless couple to tackle, and my husband felt that he would like some light from this great educationalist, who was within our reach.

He therefore went to Vienna on purpose to acquire this new knowledge. 'What is it that you want with me?' Adler asked him.

My husband explained that he had been told that Adler could give a great deal of information upon educational questions. Adler, however, sat there smiling and kind, but shedding no light whatever upon anything. Finally my husband again asked Adler what his theories upon adolescent education actually were. Adler then said, 'There are some books upon the subject, written by me; perhaps you should take them away and read them. You might then come back and we will talk about them together.' 'When may I return?' my husband demanded, expecting to be told in a few weeks or days. 'Oh, in about a year's time, perhaps,' Adler replied vaguely. My husband, however, read Adler's books through with great thoroughness and absorption, returning to see him in a few weeks' time. He had by then realized that what was needed was a complete retraining, not only of the boys, but of those dealing with them.

This was no mean task for a man approaching middle age to set before himself. My husband, nevertheless, returned to Adler, prepared for what lay before him. He held five long and exhaustive conversations with Adler which laid the foundation of a deep and intimate friendship. 'This fellow', Adler said to a mutual friend, 'is a

241

most wonderful companion. We laugh together all the time!' After this period, we never wholly lost touch with Adler, though his work and ours often kept us apart.

My husband attended the Locarno Educational Conference which was opened by Adler; and on his way there, Adler broke his journey to visit us at Kitzbühel, with two doctor friends.

This was my first meeting with Adler. His visit was chiefly memorable to me because of the fact that it felt at the time so little memorable. I had been greatly stirred and interested by my husband's reports of Adler, though less impressed by reading his books, which I had failed to understand. There was something in them that seemed trying to break through into my consciousness, but there was an obstacle in myself that prevented this penetration. I know now that at this time I did not want to understand the meaning of Adler's teaching. However, I looked forward to wonderful psychological discussions with Adler himself and was thrilled at the prospect.

There were no such discussions; nor do I remember during this visit that the subject was ever mentioned. Instead of the stimulating and awe-inspiring psychologist whom I had been looking forward to meeting, I beheld a small, stout, active man, abstemious, unrigid, full of the love of living, his twinkling eyes like those of a Paris gamin. Only, his great brow was the brow of a sage. Adler sat on a high, straight-backed chair, his feet swinging off the floor, as if only a joke could hold him there. Our boys, one and all, delighted in him. I found, after Adler's departure, that no one in our large household had failed to feel drawn to him. He had spoken what seemed like a chance word of encouragement or good fellowship to everyone.

I only once, during this visit, came upon the mind I had been so looking forward to meet. One evening we took Adler down to a café in the little town of Kitzbühel. It was an evening in early summer, and we sat out of doors at a round table under a flowering chestnut tree, looking on the village street. Adler spoke of the war, of the dislocation of the country, and of how unnatural and unwanted it had been to the whole Austrian race. A guest, who was a fellow countrywoman, bitterly resented Adler's speaking before English people of the unpopularity of the war, but he gently waved aside her patriotic indignation. 'We are all fellow men,' he said earnestly. 'Those of common sense in every country felt the same. Organized torture and murder against our brothers—how should it not be unwanted?' He spoke of the artificial humbug that had to be kept alive in order to continue the wholesale slaughter, and the deadly effect of so much falsity and violence upon the human mind. As he talked we seemed to see the naked structure of war, and to understand how so much suffering inflicted by each country upon the other must destroy the standard of living for generations.

It was not only what Adler said which reached his friends and remained with them so unforgettably. Adler was himself a living witness to his theories. His words became flesh. Those who spoke most bitterly of his psychology, if they came into personal contact with him, could seldom avoid loving him. He had a bed-rock sincerity; only those people who expected to be charmed or who relied mainly upon their own charms were startlingly disappointed and disconcerted in Adler's company. He was as bare of all superfluous foliage as a tree in winter.

Our home in Kitzbühel was on the lower slopes of a mountain, at some little distance from the village, surrounded by an orchard, and during spring and summer we always took our meals outdoors under the trees.

Adler liked this open-air life, and said of our dog Luchs, who shared all our activities and outdoor interests, 'If only human beings could live as naturally and happily as your wolf-dog, what a good world we should make of it!'

'If you want to really understand Individual Psychology,' Adler told my husband, 'do not come to me, since I live too far off from you in Vienna, but go to my colleague Seif in Munich. He will give you all you want to know.'

For a time it was impossible to leave our work to undertake this fresh adventure, but a year later we freed ourselves for the purpose and went to Munich. Both of us took a deep Adlerian analysis from Dr. Seif as well as attending all his lectures, child clinics and special classes. We formed a great friendship with him, and felt that Munich would make an ideal spot for continuing our experiment with young people, especially those who needed character training as well as language. Kitzbühel was already becoming too much a haunt for tourists and holiday-makers to be a good educational centre, but Munich was ideal for all our purposes.

We gave up our mountain chalet and took a flat at Munich, prepared to settle down there for life. Our plans and our hopes expanded together until the shadow of the Nazi régime fell upon us. We remained as long as we could after the rise of Hitler, but we soon saw that it was impossible to continue a psychology that taught individual freedom and love of our neighbour, under a régime which

turned its citizens into State slaves and tortured its minorities—
Jewish, Catholic or Liberal. We realized the falsity of the Jewish red
herring, since no one could possibly prove what his exact racial
origin may have been, and we guessed that behind it lurked the
necessity of choosing a scapegoat with sufficient possessions to make
wholesale robbery worth while.

Adler, we knew, had already established himself in America, where
we soon joined him. 'What do you find the chief difference between
Seif and myself?' Adler once asked me. 'You are a Viennese and Dr.
Seif is a German,' I replied. 'You make jokes all the time. Dr. Seif
was much more serious, otherwise your treatment is the same.' 'Perhaps you are right,' Adler replied. 'But I am sometimes very serious
myself when I joke.'

Seif was a man of infinite patience, courage and kindness. He was
a great moral teacher and filled his patients with deep affection and
awe. A word of reproach from him had a terrible finality. Adler was
not, in the accepted sense of the word, a teacher at all. He was a
creative thinker bent only—as all true artists are—upon understanding the meaning of life. Seif wanted to save that which was lost or in
danger of being lost; Adler wanted to find out why the patient
needed saving.

From Seif one learned psychology; from Adler, one found it out.
Nor was there any awe-inspiring quality in Adler. He was, to his
friends and patients, more like what an expert cracksman is to fellow
burglars with less professional skill.

Adler knew how to open the most secret and complicated safes of
the mind; and there he sat, twiddling away with his burglar's tools
and his tremendous wits, finding out the exact combination that
would swing back those fast-closed doors. First and last, Adler was a
workman; he made no sacerdotal claims, and this was the secret of
the deep malice roused by him in certain types of psychiatrists. Adler
was out not to control his patients at all, but to set them free, if they
wanted to be set free, from their difficulties; and if not, he left them
alone until they found they *did* want freedom or had finally decided
to do without it. 'A patient is like a person in a dark room,' Adler
would explain. 'He complains to me, "I cannot get out." I switch on
the light and point out the door-handle. If he still says that he cannot get out—I know that he does not wish to get out!' There was only
one type of patient upon whom Adler had no apparent mercy—one
who pretended to be interested in psychology and asked for treatment as an alibi for not giving up his neurosis. Adler felt that such

patients were out to wreck his psychology, not only by wasting his time and theirs, but by a secret enmity. They wanted to be able to say, 'I have tried all this time and *yet* this man has not cured me. His psychiatry must be a fraud!'

To such a patient Adler might say, 'I do not set out to cure people. I show you how to cure yourself. If you do not intend to cure yourself, it is you who are the fraud. Why come to me?' Or, since he was seldom angry with human beings, he might shrug his shoulders and simply say, 'You are too strong for me!'

During this visit to America, our contact with Adler was again as frequent as we could make it, and we arranged to spend the following summer with him in Vienna. My husband began to work out a plan for introducing Adler to England upon a larger scale than had hitherto appeared practicable; and, after seeing Adler off for Vienna in the early autumn of 1934, we went to London to see what lay within our power. This was the first time for twenty years that we had had a home in England. We were, therefore, rather at sea as to how the interest of so set and traditional a country could be roused to accept a new form of human education.

At first we went to Adler's accepted friends to gain their co-operation. The Torrington Square group had already financed and run a visit of Adler's to England which had been a difficult and expensive attempt, nor were they prepared to risk any further financial experiment. They were, however, willing to co-operate without too great a responsibility, and, we, therefore, arranged a guarantee to cover the preliminary expenses, and agreed to share the dates Adler was prepared to give us by filling in what engagements we could arrange for him.

My husband met Adler at Southampton in 1934, and started by taking him to Plymouth. Lady Astor, who had always been greatly interested in the educational problems of her own constituency, gave us valuable assistance. The mayor and corporation of Plymouth gave a luncheon in Adler's honour. He lectured for the University College of the South-West, and the Medical Circle gave him a real welcome and were present at the child demonstration which Adler gave for the Plymouth Child-Guidance Clinic, who provided him with cases and their notes upon them. The interest shown in this demonstration was extreme, the doctors being particularly struck with the thoroughness and tender patience Adler showed towards the child. 'It is his whole life we are trying to set right,' Adler explained to them. Adler was accompanied upon his English visit by Frau Adler and

Miss Frin Davis, the youngest daughter of his great friend, Charles Davis, as well as by Mrs. Roth, who acted for a time as his secretary. 'I was constantly with him for six months,' Miss Davis told the writer. 'I wanted to see if he was *really* as consistent in his daily life as in his teaching. Well, I have to admit he *is*! He only made one break —he *did* get excited when his train was an hour late and he thought he had missed his lecture and let your husband down. It is the only time I ever saw him lose his poise.'

My husband then took Adler to Dartington Hall for a lecture. Adler always enjoyed lecturing to young people, but he was by no means wholly in sympathy with the free school ideas. It was not that he objected to freedom, but that he thought it was not always guided towards the aim of social interest. The individual should be free in order to serve others, never free in order to act like a spoilt child— at the expense of others. Nor did Adler believe in having things made too easy for children; he believed in having them made interesting enough for the child to want to overcome difficulties inherent in the subject.

A lecture had been arranged at the University of Cardiff, and Adler was deeply interested in this keen and wide-awake city. Adler had landed with a very severe cold on his chest, and neither his Plymouth nor his Dartington Hall visits—nor a run back to London for a public dinner between them—had improved his condition. 'If this goes on,' Adler admitted at the door of the hotel where we left him, 'I shall have to be careful. Perhaps I will take an aspirin before I go to bed!'

We rang him up the next morning, fearing we might have to cancel the whole tour, only to hear his cheerful voice declaring that he was greatly better and thoroughly rested. His cold hung about him for the whole of his tour, but he seemed gradually to lecture himself out of it and refused to allow it to interfere with any of his engagements.

Professor Cyril Burt, of London University, arranged a lecture for Adler in the big hall of University College which drew a splendid audience. The Torrington Square Club gave three most successful public lectures at the Conway Hall, having to turn away part of the audience at each lecture. They also arranged a three-day conference at Liverpool in conjunction with the Home and School Council which proved a specially vital piece of work. The Catholic Archbishop Downey of Liverpool was chairman at one of Adler's lectures, and his interest and understanding were a great pleasure to Adler, who always liked to find himself co-operating with religion. 'These people', he used to say, 'I sometimes believe will be the best to spread my psychology because their profession is already one of good will.'

The two ancient universities, Oxford and Cambridge, were diffi-cult to break open, but the introduction given us by Lady Isabel Margesson, Lady Cushendunn, and Sir Alfred Beit were of great value to us. At last Sir William Brown, whose interests were in a different school of psychology from Adler's, although he was on friendly terms with him, decided to invite Adler to give two lectures at Christ Church, Oxford, one to his own students and one to the public under his auspices as chairman. He also gave both a tea and dinner to Adler and Frau Adler, so that we were able to show Oxford to Adler in a way that he had never known it before. We were parti-cularly glad of this welcome for him, both for his sake and even more for England's, since we believed that in the far future his place in the eyes of man and in the history of human thought would be far greater than during his lifetime.

Sir William Brown gave an unfortunate impression as chairman since he was unable to refrain from a somewhat petulant outburst against Adler's psychology. He was, however, quite unable to shake Adler's equilibrium. Adler gave his lecture without commenting on his chairman's adverse criticisms, and, when he had finished, laugh-ingly patted him on the shoulder.

Cambridge University refused point blank to invite Adler to speak for it; but a society of undergraduates, in collaboration with the Home and School Council, collected a large audience for him, at which Professor Ernest Barker of Peterhouse consented to act as chairman.

We had been warned that as it was examination week, we should probably only obtain a very small audience, instead of which the hall was packed; not only was every seat taken, the aisles crowded with men standing and the platform filled with undergraduates sitting on the steps round the speaker, but more than fifty had to be turned away at the door. Professor Barker said in his speech as chairman that he had never, in his seven years' experience, seen such an audi-ence at such a time. It was a lovely May evening. Adler had been enjoying a walk round the Backs. He asked us, 'What should I speak to these boys about to-night?' One of us suggested a lecture on Delin-quency, believing that Adler's ideas upon crime were perhaps the most original and easy to grasp of all his psychology. Adler agreed; but when he saw the white, strained faces of his young audience facing their great ordeal, he gave them instead, on the spur of the moment, a most touching and encouraging lecture upon how best to meet the emergencies of life.

The president of the society said to us afterwards, 'How *could* he know that was *exactly* what we wanted?—it was simply *grand*! None of us will ever forget it.'

We had also been advised to warn Adler that his audience might heckle him, but we had not thought it necessary to give this warning to Adler; and, as a matter of fact, the whole audience was breathlessly still from first to last. No one made a sound until the lecture was over, when Adler received an acclamation of applause that brought the colour to his cheeks.

The British Medical Association invited Adler to lecture, with his great friend, Sir Walter Langdon Brown, in the chair. Eight hundred doctors were present, as well as many of their invited guests. It was a great audience and Adler felt inspired by it and gave one of his best lectures.

Adler always enjoyed a challenge; on another occasion, when his chairman, a fellow psychiatrist (astonished and perhaps not wholly pleased by the size of the audience), spoke slightingly of Adler's psychology as 'popular', Adler gave a particularly fine lecture in clearer and more correct English than usual. 'He made me angry,' Adler explained to a friend afterwards. 'You should always arrange to have a chairman insult me before I begin!'

The London Society of Teachers invited Adler to speak in Essex Hall, but on account of the small size of the hall, more than half of his audience had to be turned away. The Goldsmiths Hall; which Adler spoke at, and which holds 1,600 people, was really about the right size for Adler's lectures. The public seemed to know by a kind of instinct that Adler and Adler alone had something for everybody to understand, and something that everybody needed to understand.

One of Adler's most important London engagements this summer was an 'At Home', given for him by Lady Beit at 49 Belgrave Square; to this practically all London of that particular type of London was invited. Lady Isabel Margesson and Lady Cushendunn, who had already been of great assistance to us in arranging for the Plymouth reception, as well as in obtaining for us several representative chairmen, on this occasion added to their kindness by procuring Mr. Oliver Stanley, the then Minister of Education, to act as chairman for the reception. The Earl of Lytton consented to return thanks to Lady Beit for her hospitality. Mr. Oliver Stanley asked us in advance to forgive him if he left before the lecture was over, since there was an important debate on at the House which he was expected to attend, but much to our delight, he not only remained till the end of the lecture, but actually stayed on another half-hour, listening to Adler answering questions.

It was unfortunate that on the same day Adler had been invited to a lunch held in his honour at the House of Commons, where he had met leading representatives of three Ministries especially anxious to discuss his theories with him. It was a most interesting occasion. My husband, who accompanied Adler, was delighted to find how at home Adler was, and how eager and friendly was the ministers' reception of his ideas.

The lunch lasted a long time on this account, and Adler, who had not thrown off the effects of his heavy cold, was tired and husky when it came to his four o'clock lecture. This 'At Home' was perhaps the first time that Adler had had to face a wholly fashionable audience; in spite of his fatigue, it was very interesting to watch his effect upon this new kind of audience. A great number of those present were frankly bored; they had obviously expected something exciting about sex, or mysterious about dreams, or anyhow entertaining upon lines where they were accustomed to seek entertainment. But part of the audience were the picked intelligence of England, and these knew at once that they were listening to the first-hand theories of a genius. Neither Adler's hoarseness nor his simplicity put them off. English people of a class accustomed to meet and control emergencies, which need both courage and wit, were delighted to find Adler's psychology composed of both these qualities. Here was a man who loved and understood the common sense that was their heritage; and was prepared to show them where to find it, and how to cultivate it in their young.

Adler, and this particular type of English person, whom he now met for the first time, were bound to get on together. 'I think the English a powerful and benevolent people,' Adler told a friend. 'I should like to live among them, for I do not think that they will readily yield to dictatorship.'

Adler was given another occasion on this visit which he specially valued, through the introduction of Miss Anne Talbot to Canon Percy Dearmer of Westminster Abbey. Canon Dearmer gave, at his beautiful old house in Amen Court, a yearly meeting to about fifty of the clergy of the Church of England. These were usually specially advanced and intellectual members of the Anglican Church, and it was his custom to ask some special celebrity, with whom they might find a common meeting-ground, to give them a talk followed by general discussion. Adler gave this talk in the summer of 1936, the last Canon Dearmer lived to preside over, for he died of sudden heart failure a few days later. The clergy gave Adler a most earnest and interested reception, and, owing to their responsiveness to his psychology, my husband found it possible to arrange with Archbishop Temple of York, later Archbishop of Canterbury, for Adler to speak before a thousand of his clergy at his annual diocesan meeting in the following June. There was no question that those most alive to the need of changing and developing human nature realized that Adler could put the means of doing so into their hands.

Adler wound up this extensive programme with a very happy evening at Mr. Evans's preparatory school at Betteshanger near Dover, where he lectured to a group of teachers and greatly enjoyed the beauty and freedom of this lovely place. The next day he left Dover with his family party and my husband for a fresh series of lectures in Holland.

Before he left, he said to the writer, 'No one has ever done for me what your husband has done, in the arrangement and carrying out of this great programme. Would you think it a good plan if from now on he acted as my European representative?'

It was characteristic of Adler that he should ask a wife for her agreement before even putting his plan before the husband. 'Do not think I shall take him away from you,' he added with great earnestness. 'I know very well what he does for you and how successfully he shares all your interests; he will do the same for us both. He will be a sort of double Guardian Angel!'

XXXI

Adler's Last Days

M y husband spent the intervening months arranging a much
longer and more ambitious programme for Adler's following summer. Adler objected strongly to giving single lectures upon Individual Psychology to different audiences. He knew
that he could only make a superficial impression in trying to crowd
the knowledge of a lifetime into a single hour, although this never
prevented him from accepting such lectures, if no other form of contact with the people could be provided for him.

What he chiefly wanted was a course of fourteen lectures, with all
the opportunities for private discussion and explanation possible
over such a space of time. Eventually he hoped an Institution might
be founded, with a permanent child-guidance clinic and regular lectures for teachers such as he had held in the Pedagogic Institute in
Vienna. He believed this to be the best—and indeed only practicable
—way of spreading his psychology, in the shortest possible space of
time and with the widest human results.

It was not within our power financially to start such an institute.
My husband therefore in addition to a few special lectures, such as
the one at the Archbishop of York's Conference of a thousand clergy
drawn from all over the British Isles, and the City of London vacation
course for teachers, concentrated his efforts upon preparing three
summer schools of fourteen lectures each; one in Edinburgh run by
a general committee; one at the University of the South-West at
Exeter, and one in Liverpool at University Hall, as well as a full
week in Manchester among teachers and doctors prepared for him
by Mrs. Nagelschmidt.

The summer programme began with what pleased Adler most of
all, a course of lectures held at Aberdeen University specially for
medical students.

This was the only part of the programme that Fate permitted him
to fulfil.

251

ADLER'S LAST DAYS

He gave these lectures at Aberdeen University the last three days in May 1937 and the first days of June. He died in the early morning of the day on which he was to have finished his course.

There had been no sign of this impending doom when Adler arrived in London on May 22nd and gave a Press meeting, presided over by his new friend, the Duchess of Hamilton, whom he was to have visited later in the summer at Dungavel.

Stationers' Hall, now damaged by bombing, set in its quiet courtyard in the very heart of London, off Ludgate Hill and close to St. Paul's Cathedral, was a fitting place to greet and to part from a timeless philosopher.

In spite of the fact that Adler had given over forty lectures in Holland between the last of April and May 24th, he seemed more full of his deep vitality than ever. He sat perched on a high chair, his legs swinging, and with that gnomish expression on his face which always made one think of him as a little boy about to play truant and hoping that he would succeed in slipping away unobserved; but we who shared his jokes and profited by his wisdom little thought that it was from life itself that Adler was about to effect his final truancy.

The writer had met Adler early that morning on his arrival from France. He came fresh from an experience in Paris that had deeply pleased him. For the first time in his life he had been publicly recognized, and more than recognized, by his French colleagues.

My husband, with the invaluable assistance of Dr. James Moore, who was French on his mother's side and practically bilingual, had prepared this meeting. Père Ricquet, the Jesuit head of the hospital Laennec, had put the Salle Laennec at Adler's disposal for a lecture. Père Ricquet, Professor Dr. L'Ermite and Professor and Frau Adler dined with my husband, to make all the final arrangements. Dr. Moore co-operated in this plan, and, indeed, made it possible to carry out, by reading a paper in French on Individual Psychology at the meeting. This he was, apart from Adler's active co-operation, fully qualified to do, since he had followed Individual Psychology from the foundation of the Gower Street group, and subsequently by constant attendance at the Medical Individual Psychological Society. A member of the French Government was present at the Salle Laennec to welcome Adler in the name of the French Republic, and after his lecture was over, the distinguished audience, almost entirely composed of fellow psychiatrists, held an animated discussion upon Adler's theories.

ADLER'S LAST DAYS

Some of these psychiatrists (including a Chinese Professor of Psychiatry from Peking) told Dr. Moore that they had been unable to accept Freud's or Jung's theories, since they had found their psychologies too complicated and illogical for practical purposes. Adler's theories appealed more to the clear common sense and logic of the French mind, and they now felt completely justified in their preference for Individual Psychology. Adler and Dr. Moore travelled together to England, and arrived early on the morning of May 22nd. To the writer it seemed that Adler looked in some strange way different. He was heavier; and his face had lost its firm outline, and sagged.

Nevertheless, he showed all his old energy and peacefulness. When the writer objected to the very heavy programme he had already carried out in Holland before even starting the tremendous one he knew awaited him in England, he said, with his reassuring smile, 'But it was altogether easy!'

Half of this last year of Adler's life had been a particularly happy one. A long visit to California, where he taught at a summer school in connection with the Williams Institute near San Francisco, had been a surprisingly gay and successful piece of work. It was not Adler's first visit to California, for he had already given a course on Psychology at Mills College for Dr. Aurelia Rheinhardt, but it was his first prolonged stay, and it was on this last American tour that he fell in love with California.

A most energetic and delightful band of people worked with him; and still work for his ideas. It was the only personal wish the writer ever heard Adler express—to return to California every summer and perhaps to let it take the place of his own beloved Vienna.

That autumn Adler went back to his Long Island College of Medicine immensely refreshed and invigorated, and it was only in the early spring that the blow fell on him which darkened his life and hastened, if it did not cause, his end.

His eldest daughter was suddenly and without pretext imprisoned in Russia as a hostage for her Russian husband. It was known that Vali was alive in March 1938, when she was officially 'pardoned'; but she was never heard from again. All that could be done privately and through the efforts of those in authority, both in America and other lands, was done, and done in vain. 'We know that she is alive,' Adler said to the writer, 'and for the moment we must satisfy ourselves with this.' That was all the writer ever heard him say upon this subject. He had asked for our help and we had given it, on both

253

sides of the Atlantic, without avail. Adler never heard any further
news of this, his 'most intimate child'; but her mother finally received,
after years of suspense and agonizing conjectures, a notification from
the Russian Government that her death had taken place some years
previously.

Two reporters appeared shortly after Adler's arrival in London at
his hotel on his last visit and requested interviews. One, who had
obviously not very much knowledge of his subject or how to approach it, asked nervously, 'Dr. Adler, do you mind if I ask you
rather a peculiar question. Are you specially fond of sex?' 'In my
psychology', Adler replied promptly and with all the respect due
from one serious thinker to another, 'we do not pick our parts.
We look on a human being as a whole. Since sex is a function
belonging to the life of man and natural to it, we accept it as such
—but perhaps I should not call it my *favourite* function!'

The second reporter was more anxious to prove to himself that he
was not less intelligent than his son, who had menaced his intellectual
supremacy by beating him at chess, than to find out Adler's psychological views. 'Do you think my son's beating me at chess means he's
really got a better brain than I have?' he asked anxiously. 'It might
not be so,' Adler replied with soothing benevolence. 'I myself have
frequently been beaten at chess by men who I do not suppose were
any more intelligent than myself. I have even known quite stupid
people who played chess remarkably well.'

After they had left him, Adler turned to the writer with a smile
and asked, 'What do you suppose those fellows made of all we tried
to tell them?'

We travelled up to Aberdeen with Adler on the following day. It
was a long day's journey and Adler talked a great deal of the new
group we were helping to form in London. He was pleased that it
was heterogeneous and composed of equal numbers of both sexes, as
well as members drawn from entirely differing professions and tastes.
'They'll quarrel less', he explained, 'if they all have different professions. Besides, such a group is wider in its interests. It is good you
have some doctors, since they can help to explain physical limitations and reactions, but they should not be predominant. In an Individual Psychology group, no one should be predominant, though it
is by no means easy to prevent this. I have several times myself had
to ask a member to resign from a group because he was succeeding
in holding up all co-operation by his obstructive tactics. I always do
this in public before the whole group if I can, so that they may all

understand why it is done and support me with their approval if they think it is fair, or give me their criticisms if they do not. Such an expulsion may often help the person himself very much.'

It had already been arranged that the writer should write Adler's life, and he had promised every assistance; he took occasion on this journey to talk much of his early memories and his first relationships. The writer took down a few of his sentences so as to keep his actual words intact. In talking of his psychology, he said: 'The science of the mind can only have for its proper goal the understanding of human nature by every human being; and by its use, brings peace to every human soul.'

He asked my husband and myself to describe each member of this new group personally to him; he listened closely to our descriptions, and, when we had finished, said, 'I will be your President, and I believe, after what you have both told me, that I could build up my psychology in England upon the foundation of this group.'

After his death, his daughter Alexandra took his place as our President, and we were able to count upon the active presence and co-operation of Franz Plewa from Vienna, who had worked for five years as Adler's assistant at the Franz Josef Ambulatorium Hospital and had been chosen, after Adler's death, as the President of the Viennese group.

Adler disliked long journeys, and we were glad when we could leave him safely to rest at the Caledonia Hotel in Aberdeen. We were invited to stay at Fintray House by Lady Sempill and her daughter, but it was more restful for Adler, with such a programme in hand, to have his time solely at his own disposal, but my husband joined him after one night at Fintray, so that Adler should not feel lonely.

The lectures at Aberdeen University were a particular pride and joy to Adler, for he was asked to take a course mainly for medical students and those who were to become teachers. He had splendid audiences, and several of his colleagues from the Faculty of the University were there at every lecture. He particularly enjoyed making the acquaintance of Professor Stanley Davidson and Professor Rex Knight, who were largely responsible for his having been asked to give the course at the university.

The lectures were all well attended, and the last two crowded. The writer remembers in particular two sayings from these last lectures: 'All form of criticism of other human beings is a camouflage behind which we seek to hide our own weaknesses—never very successfully,' and, 'We must not bagatelle-ize our emotions. Emotion can be very useful when it is taken seriously. It is like the gasoline; when you tread on it you accelerate the whole machine.'

My husband had tried to make this first week of Adler's programme an easy one, and had made as few social engagements as possible for him. He gave his daily lecture at the university between five and six, and this was no real task to Adler, though he always went out promptly and with an air of relief, once it was over. He made himself responsible for every word he uttered in a more complete way than most people dream of doing, and a word from Adler always had the full weight of a deed.

Our hostess gave us all a treat which we greatly valued. She took us for a picnic on the moors. It was a bright, cool, Scottish summer day, with a wind full of life and fragrance. Light, silvery clouds scudded above the hills, their shadows moving upon the heather beneath as swiftly as flying swallows.

'Let us find three flowers,' Adler said to the writer in an undertone. 'They must be three—one for us each to keep in memory of this day.' 'If we cannot find three violets,' he said, 'we will throw the other two away.' Nor would he rest until he had found and gathered the third violet. We drove on, after a magnificent luncheon in the car, to Corgarff, a small village close to my husband's old home, where the Rev. John Linton lived, who was translating Adler's *Social Interest: A Challenge to Mankind*.

Mr. Linton was in bad health at this time, and it would have been difficult for him to meet Adler in any other way.

Adler sat with him in his manse for two hours, talking out the few difficulties in sense and language that Mr. Linton had been unable to solve to his own satisfaction. The two men were delighted with each other, and it was a special pleasure to Adler to find that translating this book had converted Mr. Linton, who had been a former translator of Freud, to Individual Psychology. This was not a personal or spiteful triumph on Adler's part, for he always gave his old friend and colleague credit for his great discoveries, especially that of free association, which Adler believed threw a light upon the whole field of psychology; but Adler had long felt that the Freudian form of psychiatry was without moral safeguards and must result in anti-social types of human beings. 'It is a spoilt child psychology,' he complained, 'but what can be expected from a man who asks, "Why should I love my neighbour?"'

On our way back from Corgarff, we stopped at the beautiful old half-French, half-Scottish castle of the Forbes-Sempills, called Craigievar. Adler was enchanted with it, and insisted on climbing to the battlements so that he could see all the surrounding country, nor did he seem at all out of breath or fatigued by his climb.

Adler gave one last lecture at Aberdeen for the City Child-Guidance Society. The mayor was in the chair, and most of the city corporation were present. Adler gave them a most clear and closely reasoned lecture upon child psychology, and this—one of the last acts of his life—was destined to bear the fruit he would most have valued. The city decided to help the university to found a chair of psychiatry, each paying three hundred a year, so that they might have the right to send delinquent children from Aberdeen to the university for this special treatment. Professor Rex Knight was the first to occupy the chair.

'What form of punishment', one of Adler's audience demanded after the lecture, 'does Dr. Adler think most suitable for the child?' 'I believe that *no* form of punishment is suitable for the child,' was Adler's swift response. It is interesting to observe that the Esquimaux in their original condition have the most happy and well behaved children; and these are never given any form of punishment. The children have, during much of the year, the continuous example and presence of their parents and are allowed a full share in the work and play of communal life, and they behave exactly as they see their elders behave.

Two days later, at Adler's special request, it had been arranged for him to give a Demonstration Clinic before a specially chosen doctor, clergyman and teacher from Aberdeen. He spoke to my husband of this project and of the talk he was giving to the Archbishop of York's clergy on June 2nd, with eager anticipation. 'It seems to me', Adler said, 'that it will probably be the clergy—of all denominations—who will do most to spread my psychology in the future. This would be very beneficial in two ways: i.e., the clergy *are* the chief practitioners of social interest already by profession; and also—which specially appeals to me—they need not take money from their patients. I have always felt this to be a real disadvantage to psychiatrists who practise character training. It would be far better not to have a question of money between them and their patients. The clergy would gain their living by looking after their parish and church, so that they could treat their patients' psychological difficulties without any question of personal interest arising between them.'

At a luncheon party given to Adler by the superintendent of a mental hospital in the neighbourhood of Aberdeen to meet several noted Scottish psychiatrists, Adler spoke very little; but afterwards he wandered out into the garden with great enjoyment. He specially admired a small, but very charming, rock garden. 'I have an idea', he said to the friend with him, 'that the *husband* thought out this garden. I think he has that sort of mind.' The friend spoke somewhat impatiently about the hostilities and jealousies which had been Adler's lifelong hindrance among his own colleagues. 'My enemies have always blessed me,' Adler replied quietly. 'It is true that when they do not resent my ideas, they very often run off with them and call them their own; but they will spread them all the more readily on that account! I believe that I have made some discoveries, and whether they are called "Adler's" or not does not concern me. I believe, however, that those discoveries are true and that, therefore, they will be of lasting use to mankind; and this makes me happy.'

A few minutes later, the same friend commented upon the joy and relief it was to have him again in England, and spoke of the gain it was to his friends to share his activities. Adler answered with a strange seriousness that almost amounted to severity: 'You and your husband should remember that what is disagreeable has just as much value for us as what is agreeable.'

We *were* soon to remember these words, and in our bitter grief at his loss, we found them a support.

Adler took special pleasure in a treatment he was giving at this time to a young girl who had already made a deep and serious study of his psychology. She was no neurotic patient, but a very honest, courageous and gifted being, who felt her responsibilities and the part she must play in life demanded from her a full acceptance of these claims. Adler rejoiced in talking over with her what he thought were her main difficulties, and in showing her how he believed she might increase her strength and capacity for dealing with them.

It has always been a comfort to remember that this young creature, full of hope and promise, was the last patient Adler ever saw. The day before he died, he spent part of the morning with the writer at a typist's—a most intelligent and valuable worker—to whom he dictated the notes for his final lecture on sex. He was a little concerned as to whether he ought to dictate an article to so young a girl upon such a subject, and asked her if she would not prefer his finding someone older. 'No,' she said firmly, 'I should like to type whatever you have written, and I could not object to any subject you wrote about.'

Adler was a splendid giver or recipient of criticism. He himself
never made a captious or hypocritical objection; in fact, he was often
too lenient, if anything, to what he thought the rights of another
person to express himself exactly as he chose; but Adler never let
pass the slightest slip in fact or verbal accuracy. 'How do you *know*
that this is so?' he would ask with anxious seriousness. 'Can you
prove it?' On the same morning, he was reading through an article,
by the writer, on the four types of his special enemies. 'Do not say',
he begged urgently '*what* psychiatrists have been my enemies. We
need not single them out—or make it a personal matter that they
have attacked me. They may be *my* enemies—that I cannot help—
but I will not be theirs!'

The writer had suggested four special types of enemies: Adler's
psychiatric opponents; the Nicodemus type of disciple, who never
had the courage to acknowledge what they had learned from him;
the plagiarists, who stole his ideas and called them theirs; and the
determined neurotics, who either consciously or unconsciously called
themselves Individual Psychologists merely in order to wreck the
psychology they preached but never intended to practise.

'The Nicodemuses have done me very little harm,' Adler suggested
gently. 'It is only that they are afraid. Do not be too stern with them;
in time, they may even become brave!'

That last night Adler suggested going with my husband to a
cinema, but there was still a great deal of work to do upon the lecture
programme and my husband said he ought to stay in and write
letters. 'It will be wholly easy,' Adler insisted with his most seduc-
tively cheerful smile. 'We will go together to the cinema, and then,
when we return, *I* will help you to write the letters.' They went off
together arm in arm, Adler's last words ringing in my ears as I drove
off with our cousin, 'it will be wholly easy!'

The picture they saw together was 'The Great Barrier'. It was the
story of a magnificent feat of engineering, the tunnelling of the
Rocky Mountains. Adler was greatly impressed by it, and delighted
that after a whole series of accidents and disasters the engineers
should achieve their purpose and the last barrier fall.

Adler and my husband came back and wrote their letters for a
couple of hours; then Adler went to bed, leaving my husband to go
on writing for another hour. They never met again. Adler got up
early as usual and went for a short walk after breakfast. A young girl
on her way to work told us afterwards, 'I was just saying to myself,
"What a vigorous old boy that is! He steps out like an athlete," when

259

he seemed to slip; and fell. At first I thought it was just an accident; but he never moved again.' A young theological student who was attending Adler's lectures recognized that it was Adler, and dashed across the street to apply first aid. As he was unfastening his collar, he heard Adler murmur the word 'Kurt', which was his son's name; but although the student massaged his heart immediately, Adler never recovered consciousness. When he was lifted up and placed on a stretcher, one of the bystanders said, 'It looked as if he were trying to help them arrange him, so that it would be easier to carry him.'

They took his body to the police station, where my husband was called to identify him. By a most singular coincidence, the Fiscal was passing in a tram; he saw Adler fall, and immediately stopped the tram and satisfied himself that the sudden death was natural so that he was prepared to sign the death certificate. It was thought best, however, to have an autopsy upon so eminent a foreigner in case of any questions being raised later on. The autopsy took place and disclosed (what the Fiscal had already told us he was sure was the cause of Adler's death) a condition of degeneration of the heart muscle.

Adler had suffered no pain, his expression was one of the most perfect repose; he looked, in fact, many years younger, and the strength and firmness had come back to the contour of his face and features.

Only the day before he had told us he was feeling extremely well. 'I woke smiling,' he said to us, 'so I knew my dreams were good, although I had forgotten them.'

XXXII

The Death of Adler

Within an hour of Alfred Adler's sudden collapse in Union Street, Aberdeen, between nine-thirty and ten o'clock of a beautiful May morning, the news was telephoned to Raissa Adler in Paris. There was no real way of breaking the shock to her, though fortunately Mrs. Roth of the Chicago group was with her and showed a common sense, energy and kindness for which all Adler's family and friends must be grateful to her.

Raissa was struck to the heart. They had been very happy together for those few days in Paris, between the Dutch tour and the English one. Raissa was only waiting in Paris for Adler to return from his Scottish lectures in order to join him, with their youngest child, Nelly, in London for the remainder of the English tour.

It did not seem credible that just as Raissa had learned how to found once more her whole happiness upon their life together, it should, without a hint or a warning, be shattered under her feet. Her children were grown children with loves and interests of their own. Her life in Russia was like a half-forgotten dream. Her second life in Austria, with its new language and its new friends, was closed behind her. Her life in America—once more in a new country with an unknown language—had only just begun. All her friends there were Adler's friends. She had had no time to make any of her own. She had, in fact, now nothing of her own, except her grief.

On the day of Adler's death, she flew from Paris to Croydon, travelling all through the night up to Scotland, and arriving in Aberdeen before noon next day. Heinz and Nelly Sternberg arrived only a day later, also by air, from Vienna. They were in time to see Adler's strong, untroubled face. Alexandra Adler, who was to have shared her father's work at the three summer schools in England and Scotland, cabled that she would still carry out her part of the programme. Kurt Adler, who was at work in the Long Island College of Medicine, hastened to join his mother.

261

THE DEATH OF ADLER

In a few hours after Adler's death, the whole of Aberdeen was mourning for its distinguished and already loved visitor.

It was extraordinary how quickly this small, single-minded and deep-hearted city accepted Adler, as if he were part of itself.

No honour, no kindness, no consideration within the power of the city of Aberdeen to confer was denied to Adler in death, or to his family and friends after his death. From the Lord Provost to the smallest lift boy at the Caledonia Hotel, each person with whom we came in contact showed the same humane and considerate respect.

Messages poured in from all over the world, and, in spite of the distance and difficulty of the long journey from the Continent to the north of Scotland, representatives from Holland, from the former Berlin group, from Belgium and London, as well as Mrs. Roth who was a member of the Chicago group, attended his funeral.

Wreaths and flowers buried his coffin; cables and telegrams poured in from high and low. 'How is your work getting on in America?' one of his friends had asked Adler only the day before. 'Marvellously,' Adler had replied, his face shining with joy and enthusiasm. 'I have such wonderful friends!'

One of the most devoted of his younger friends, Frin Davis, was at a party a few days later in New York when she saw a young girl, whom she did not know, crying in a corner of the room. She hastened across to her and asked if she could be of any service, and if she would tell her what her trouble was. 'I have just heard of the death of a friend,' the girl said between her sobs. 'You must have loved him very much!' Frin Davis said with real sympathy, thinking of her own deep loss. 'Oh, I *did*,' cried the girl, 'but I haven't ever *seen* him. It was something that he wrote that made a difference to my whole life. I knew he was my friend, and that as long as he was alive there was someone who really understood my difficulties. Have you never heard of him? His name was Alfred Adler.'

Adler died known and honoured—as many great men have died known and honoured; but he also died loved—as few great men have ever been loved.

A memorial service was held for him in King's College Chapel, Aberdeen, where the coffin stood before the altar, at two o'clock on Tuesday, 1st June 1937. The service was conducted jointly by Bishop Deane and Professor A. Fyfe Findlay, the Dean of the University. The whole Faculty, in their robes, attended. The Lord Provost was present, and a representative from the child clinic, where he was to have given the demonstration on the morning of his death. Raissa

Adler, Nelly and Heinz Sternberg, the representatives of the groups of Individual Psychologists from Holland, Germany, Belgium, Chicago and London, our cousins from Fintray House, the Rev. Mr. Linton, his translator, and ourselves, made up the remaining congregation in the strange city that had so quickly ceased to be strange.

It was a very beautiful service. Adler's favourite Bach Chorale, 'Jesu, Joy of Man's Desiring', was played upon the organ, and the choir sang exquisitely 'Abide with me'.

It had been suggested that Adler should be buried at Springbank Cemetery, Aberdeen, but Raissa wished, and the whole family (except his eldest daughter who could not be reached) agreed to, cremation. It was, therefore, decided to take his body to the Edinburgh Crematorium the day following the funeral service held at Aberdeen. The ashes were afterwards placed in an urn, chosen later by Alexandra Adler, and left at the Edinburgh Crematorium, where there is a very beautiful loggia, above the chapel, specially fitted for such a purpose.

For obvious reasons, the ashes could not be sent to Vienna, and yet the family hesitated to send them permanently elsewhere.

Raissa, Nelly, and Adler's other friends went by train to Edinburgh; Heinz Sternberg, accompanied by my husband and myself, followed the hearse by car to the crematorium.

One of the most memorable things about those heavy hours was the perfect naturalness, courage and common sense of the Adler family. They neither concealed their grief nor inconvenienced anyone by its display. They met every duty, effort, or problem as it came, with complete steadiness and calm, invariably thinking first of the difficulties for others, never of their own. They showed no forced cheerfulness and made no unnecessary efforts, but whatever was advisable or sensible, they found out and achieved. If Adler had been with them, they could have behaved no differently.

Charles Davis and his family sent every possible message of consolation, and flowers that filled the crematorium chapel so that it looked like a spring garden.

The final commitment service at the chapel, on a hillside above the city of Edinburgh, was dignified and touching. Here, too, there was music; the organist played through Schubert's song, *Der Tod und das Mädchen*, a song that Adler loved and sang. The coffin, beneath a pall completely covered by flowers, disappeared into the furnace below, without a sound or sign, during the singing of a hymn.

The end of physical life is always a sad, and, in a sense, an ugly business, but all that could be done to let mortality take its unhampered, natural course, without emphasis or unseemliness, was done for Alfred Adler. His immortality will take care of itself. 'Death', Adler said once to my husband, 'is really a great blessing for humanity. Without it, there could be no real progress. People who lived for ever would not only hamper and discourage the young, but they would themselves lack sufficient stimulus to be creative.'

The following extemporary prayer was given by the clergyman, the Rev. John Bailey:

'O Thou who art the refuge of the living, the rest of the blessèd dead, and the hope of all whom Thou hast made, we praise Thee for all Thy true servants, who have faithfully and diligently served Thee in their several callings, bearing their due also of the world's burdens and going about their daily tasks in all simplicity and uprightness of heart. Especially to-day we thank Thee for him whom Thou hast now taken from our midst. We bless Thee for Thy loving-kindness to him throughout his earthly life, for all that he was by nature and by grace to those around him, for his high devotion to the advancement of knowledge, for his skill in healing, for the help and comfort which, by Thy grace, he was enabled to bring to many troubled spirits, for the guidance he has bequeathed to those who follow after him.

'We praise Thee, O Father of spirits, for the finished life, the burden laid down, the Pilgrim now come to the city of God.'

Dr. Peter Ronge, the Dutch leader of the Utrecht group, gave a touching and beautiful address in German on what Adler stood for, in his friends' love, as well as to the world.

It is impossible and would, indeed, be presumptuous, for the writer, through her own lack of expert knowledge, to make any estimate of Adler's work in psychology. That must be left for someone with greater scientific knowledge.

'We live', Adler himself told us, 'upon the contributions of our ancestors. Nature is a good scavenger. She soon gets rid of her rubbish.'

Those of us who loved Adler upon 'this poor earth's crust' need not be afraid that his work will not last. Wherever childhood is respected, creative living understood, and wherever the human being is prepared to accept the full responsibility of loving his neighbour as himself, Adler's contribution will be remembered. Mankind needs his psychology more to-day than it has ever yet needed it. It is not without interest that now, for the first time, artists, scientists and all those who really believe in God find themselves in the same camp against the retrograde morality of the dictatorships.

These strange bed-fellows find themselves looking out upon the troubled world with the same vision. We know that until we pull down the barriers between countries; accept the responsibility of freedom; practise moral and intellectual honesty and defend, if need be, common fairness for all mankind, we cannot be considered cultured, civilized or even human; nor shall we be so considered by posterity.

A few days after Adler's funeral, Dr. Alexandra Adler, then Research Fellow of Harvard University and assistant to the Boston City Hospital, arrived in England to take up her father's work. She had caught a serious cold on the voyage over and was on the verge of an illness, but she fought through it, as her father would have done, and most ably and nobly fulfilled all the obligations she had accepted.

Edinburgh, Liverpool and the City of London carried through their original invitations, though some of these had to be curtailed in length; only Exeter College cancelled the summer school that had been arranged for Adler. My husband, overwhelmed as he was with grief and work, improvised a fresh summer school at Bishop Otter College, Chichester, to take its place, and with the help and support of the new Individual Psychological London group, it was carried out with very great success. Lady Whitson, the wife of the former Lord Provost of Edinburgh, had, with great skill and energy, formed an open committee in Edinburgh of those already interested in Individual Psychology for Adler's summer school, and this, with the strong and expert backing of Dr. Rushford, against a most discourteous and determined opposition on the part of the university authorities and opposing schools of psychiatry, was a triumphant success. A distinguished list of chairmen had been chosen to preside at Dr. Alexandra Adler's lectures, but it was supposed that though the lectures would have a success of esteem and sympathy, they were hardly likely to arouse any universal public interest. Far otherwise was the result; in spite of the lovely June weather, the hall was packed to the brim for ten long evening lectures, and so clear and sound was Alexandra Adler's exposition of her father's psychology, and so extremely well-chosen and intelligent the reporters, that every day her lectures occupied a column to a column and a half in a prominent position in the two chief daily papers. Alexandra proved herself to be a first-rate lecturer. She had two most exceptional qualities for her

265

task: a beautiful cadenced voice, such as her father's had been in his youth, and a great sense of humour.

Her English was actually clearer and more correct than Adler's, though she had not, of course, his wide range of vocabulary and life-long felicity in choice of diction. She had an extremely good platform presence and was as steady as a rock. From a scientific point of view, her lectures were very clear and simple, and never once off the range of concrete fact. For whatever Alexandra Adler asserted, she always had proof, and gave it in the simplest and most convincing manner. Her answers to questions, which took half an hour to three-quarters after every lecture, showed the same prompt emergency-wit that had always characterized her father's.

She was never provocative, even when dealing with questioners who meant to be provocative, and she never budged from the modesty of nature or of fact.

Her very distinguished chairman was obviously delighted with her, as well as delightful *to* her. On one occasion, half a dozen clergy asked if they might take her off for an afternoon's discussion in private. This conference took place with a calm and good humour seldom achieved by those who should be bound together as natural allies—science and religion.

Edinburgh was a great ordeal for Alexandra. It took place only a few days after her father's death. The Liverpool Summer School was a much easier affair. This, too, had been arranged for by a local committee under the indefatigable guidance of Dr. Clouston, Medical Officer of Health. Dr. Stallybrass, also a medical officer of health, and Mr. Jackson, head of the Social Service Association, were invaluable in the help they gave us. The Liverpool Summer School was a smaller and far more intimate group of people, built upon the usual summer school lines, and carried through with great success and a continually increasing audience from outside. Mrs. Charles Booth and our invaluable and constant friends, the Home and School Council, all did a great deal to increase the interest of Liverpool and its teachers in our meetings. The Warden, Miss Buller, gave us the hospitality of University Hall. She was a true friend of Adler's and did her utmost to help his daughter through her difficult task.

The easiest of the series was, however, the Chichester Summer School, held at Bishop Otter College, for by now Alexandra had grown not only used to her heavy task, but heartened by her success; and physically she was feeling a great deal stronger. Eleven of our small London group were present and our school soon expanded its

THE DEATH OF ADLER

number to fifty. The place was ideal, the weather perfect, and the neighbourhood specially fitted for excursions. Many of our members had brought their own cars and there were always eight or nine available for expeditions. The London group of Individual Psychologists showed a fine and eager loyalty to Adler's memory, and the true spirit of co-operation. It was as if they put all they felt for him into this work for the summer school, and no one who attended it will ever forget its harmony and beauty. We benefited greatly at Chichester, as we had done through all the educational part of Adler's programme, by the real personal interest shown in Adler's psychology by the then Minister of Education, Mr. Oliver Stanley.

One specially delightful feature of this third summer school was the presence of our American friends. Five or six of them had originally intended to go to the South-West University College course at Exeter and transferred themselves to Chichester, an act of faith in itself. They were all teachers and gifted teachers, so that their co-operation was specially valuable to us. We had several especially appreciated members, one a Dutch friend from the Montessori School; the late head of the Theosophical Church of England, Mr. Barker; and Miss Désirée MacEwen who was a particularly prized visitor, since on two occasions she gave us a magnificent piano recital.

Alexandra Adler carried out all the engagements in England that were suitable for her to take in her father's place, including the very important lecture given for the City of London Vacation Course for Teachers at Bedford College. Received and greeted at first for Adler's sake, Alexandra always won her own place and left behind her an ineffaceable memory of courage, good will and personal genius.

Memorial services were held for Adler at Amsterdam, at Brussels and in Vienna, but owing to the strange political situation in the city of Adler's birth, no public honour was shown to his memory, although he had once been given the Freedom of the City and his name was upon the Vienna roll of honour. The authorities were invited to attend ten days before the memorial service took place, but they replied in a letter dated two days earlier than the invitation, curtly refusing. All the known psychiatrists in Vienna, to whatever school they belonged, were invited to attend this service, so that science might hold the torch of tolerance higher than any personal enmity. The Freudians, having accepted, forgot to come. An obituary article was sent to the *Neue Freie Presse* by Adler's leading colleague, but the editor replied that 'it was not a suitable moment to bring out an article upon Alfred Adler'.

267

THE DEATH OF ADLER

The writer feels that posterity should know this lamentable slump in intelligence and courage which marked the approach of the rising dictatorships. Thinkers belong to Time; but the Viennese contemporaries of Alfred Adler felt that they belonged to Hitler.

The writer has put in the appendix to this biography two tributes to Adler which seem most to reveal the scope and value of his work. One of them is by Professor Birnbaum, one of the teachers who carried out, with such courage and success, Adler's work for Viennese education. The second is by Dr. Lydia Sicher, his fellow-worker and the successor whom Adler himself chose to carry on his work at the Ambulatorium when he resigned his position.

When Adler died at sixty-seven years old, he was at the height of his powers. His last published book, *Social Interest: A Challenge to Mankind*, had been particularly happy in its translation.

All Adler's books are of interest and hold creative thought; some, however, are put together from lectures and have no sustained logic. Some are only suitable for fellow psychiatrists, such as his well-known text-book, *Organic Inferiority and Psychic Compensation*, and *Problems of Neurosis*. Some are merely educational, such as that most delightful book, *The Understanding of the Child*. Perhaps Adler's creatively greatest book is *The Nervous Character*, but unfortunately it was badly put together and published in America under auspices that Adler had not chosen. *What Life Should Mean to You*, *The Science of Living*, *Understanding Human Nature* are specially written to meet the needs of the general public, and generally scoffed at by those who wish to keep their psychiatry well above the heads of the laymen who might profit by it.

Dr. Babbott, the President of the Long Island College of Medicine, sums up the last period of Adler's professional life in America in the following words: 'Personally I regarded him with affectionate esteem and had the highest respect for his contributions to science and for his individual application of his philosophy. He stripped things down to first principles with kindliness and with precision, and very helpfully assisted in planning the rebuilding. I regretted exceedingly his untimely death, for he was just working himself into the confidence of the Faculty and I am certain that, had he been spared for another three or five years, he could so securely have established his point of view in the medical thinking of the Institution that it could not be shaken.'

This is a fitting epitaph, written by the person Adler would have chosen above all others to write it, since President Babbott was in the best position to understand the immediate effects, and the potentialities, of all his colleagues' work. Adler had much to contend against in his American life: language; the urgency of speed (which had less hold upon European intellectuals when they were allowed to function freely); the fact that his standing in European thought was ignored or brushed aside by those who had no means of proving it, or who wished, for purposes of their own, to ignore it; his deep, natural modesty which refused to make any personal claims or to lean upon any form of publicity or advancement other than his own powers of exposition. 'I will gargle like a tenor at them if they want me to,' Adler once said to a friend who wanted him only to accept academic lecture invitations and never to lecture in public under any other auspices; but though Adler would brush aside, to reach the men in the street, any artificial barriers set between them, he would never for one instant or for any purpose sacrifice his own integrity of thought.

Adler adjusted himself to every blow and to every difficulty life gave him, but he kept intact against all temptation the inviolability of his soul.

He had his reward in the just appreciation of the few men wise enough to understand him, and good enough not to shrink from the rigour of personal effort such understanding entailed.

Adler lost his *Wien*. He lost a fortune won by severe and continuous hard work. He lost the harvest of his teaching in the schools of Vienna. He lost his eldest child, one of the chief companions of his mind. But he won more hearts and freed more personalities than any of his great contemporaries; and in his own life he gave to the world the truest example of his science. Adler *was* the 'whole human being' he set out to train; and when Death called him, he went 'smiling, from the snare of this great world, uncaught'.

APPENDIX I

1. A Memorial Address by Dr. Lydia Sicher

It is with the deepest devotion and gratitude to our Teacher, Alfred Adler, and with pride in being deemed worthy, that I have undertaken, at the request of my colleagues, to speak some words of remembrance at this place from which the voice of Adler reached us so often.

At the same time, however, I feel profoundly the difficulty of the task assigned to me. With short strokes and in brief words I have to present a living likeness of a man with the greatness and breadth that Adler possessed; and to show his intellectual power and genuine humanity.

Moreover, the task that has been given me consists not only in doing that, but also in making clear what was—to use Adler's own expression—his *contribution to life*, or at least the narrower contribution that he made to the science of medicine.

It is really superfluous to speak of Adler as a man. Those who were acquainted with him know what he was, and know, too, what they have lost in him. Those who were not acquainted with him may see what he was in the *leit-motif* of his life—the answer he gave to the question: What is the meaning of existence to the individual? That was—*to help, encourage and gladden.*

We know that his whole life was devoted to the realization of this ideal. We need not wonder therefore that he chose the profession of medicine since it offered him the widest opportunities of fulfilling the meaning of *his* life, though he grew beyond it and became a *healer—* an encourager, a dispenser of gladness.

Adler began with medicine, and the medical knowledge utilized in Individual Psychology was the foundation on which he raised the structure of his pedagogics and his prophylactic against mental diseases. His early interest was drawn to pathological anatomy and internal diseases. From a slight work of this period concerned with

270

eye-troubles among a special group of workers we may conclude that the 'sphere of the visual'—to use the terms of Individual Psychology —had a notable attraction for him. He also learned to *see*—to see what other people did *not* see—the life behind the façade, the hidden, the veiled, the invisible. But with his great musical gifts he learned also to *hear* what other people did not hear—the thing unspoken or kept secret, the harmony or discord in the note of the soul.

This absolute hearing (as one might call it) of the psychologist made it necessary for him, however, to pass beyond purely organic medicine. He was not satisfied merely with healing disease; for him that did not exhaust the resources of medicine; he longed for another outcome—*the doctor as the educator.*

When Adler's *Studie von der Minderwertigkeit der Organe* appeared in 1907 he was still essentially a natural scientist. Starting with nephritic pathology he began his investigations into the morphological and functional insufficiency of organs. At that time also there emerged the conception of compensation—a revaluation of the organic experience by its transference to the psychical. He wrote: 'The ensemble of the phenomena of organic inferiority colours the psyche in such a fashion that its whole structure receives a special character. The psychical structure thus acquired becomes, as a result, the foundation of neuroses and psychoses.' 'Neuroses and psycho-neuroses', he writes in another part of this study, 'are to be traced back to organic inferiority, to the degree and the nature of the central compensation that has not been completely successful and to interferences with compensation.'

When these facts with regard to the part played by the central compensation were established, the first step was taken towards understanding the connections between bodily and mental experiences. An indication was given here of the view ultimately adopted which afterwards came so prominently into the foreground that it was this conception that distinguished Individual Psychology from all other psychologies. For Adler, while employing this conception, began to see that the external or internal, organic or social situation could no longer be considered the *cause* of the mental structure, but only the impetus used by the individual to compensate himself rightly or wrongly in accordance with the personal goal he had chosen.

This view, which is adumbrated in the *Studie der Minderwertigkeit der Organe*, becomes clearer and clearer in his doctrine of organ dialect—the over-compensation of the individual's feeling of his own insufficiency heightened by organic inferiority—and in his conception of *training*, i.e. of the method the individual employs to overcome his feeling of inferiority. These were the foundation stones on which Adler's great doctrine of neurosis rested.

This conception, which was ultimately adopted, has, strangely enough, again and again become the point of attack against Individual Psychology. The supporters of the theories of heredity and environment, in particular, opposed it on that account. From the medical side, too—largely through a complete misunderstanding of the position of Individual Psychology—it has been maintained that Adler denies causality, and that therefore his views are opposed to all the laws of science as it is universally recognized. This mistaken idea, unfortunately still widely prevalent in the camp of the opponents of Individual Psychology, will only disappear when it becomes better known that not only man can and must be explained as *one* of the many objects of Nature, but also that he has a claim to be understood as a *subject*.

If the individual is in the first place the *passive* object that is to be investigated by exact science—and therefore also by medicine and experimental psychology, which are concerned with his bodily, mental and spiritual *reactions*—he is also the *active* director of his fate, and his path can only be understood when the goal to which this path leads is kept in view.

Adler in his first great work already shows that purely medical considerations no longer suffice. His other medical publications— *Ueber den nervösen Charakter, Studie über der Homosexualität, Praxis und Theorie de Individualpsychologie, Heilen und Bilden*— which appeared in the years from 1911 to 1922, bear witness to the fact that he made the *unity* of the personality the central point of his interest and substituted the standpoint of healing and psychology for that of natural science and medicine. It was no longer a question with him of the individual's organs, but rather of the *whole* individual with his organs.

And here we reach the point which in Adler's teaching was to become central for the understanding of the patient and empathy into his case. If Adler, too, originally had seen the neurotic as a separate individual who attempts to come to terms with his organs and his situation and who compensates himself rightly, or overcompensates himself wrongly, he came more and more to regard everyone—the neurotic also—as a member of a community, as an *in*dividual, as an undivided and indivisible unity, who, as he said, could only be understood in his cosmic relationship. Accordingly he no longer regarded even neurosis as a disease *sui generis*, but unmasked it as a *social deviation*, as the effect of imperfect 'co-operation' with the collective action of humanity. Further the neurotic is no longer to be treated as a sick person who is to be pitied, who by the ordinance of fate has become the victim of heredity, his environment or his instincts, but as a person who has made a mistake, who has not learned to accommodate himself to the rules of the game of life. Perception, feeling, thinking and willing—all the bodily and mental situations of an individual—are actively directed by himself, and are employed unintentionally and unknowingly for the purpose of safeguarding his own personal ideal, which allows him to develop an activity centred solely on himself.

This conception—that the individual (the sick person as well) cannot be considered apart by himself, but only as he is seen in all his relations to his external and internal conditions—is still to-day alien in many respects to medical thought. Doctors still even to-day to a large extent oppose the view that in the case of neurotics and psychotics also, in short in the case of all mentally afflicted persons, it is not the deed—the illness—but the doer—the sick person—that has to be understood. He is to be looked upon as a deserter who flees to his own tiny microcosm from the problems presented by the macrocosm. Starting from the isolated person—the individual in the usual sense of the word—Adler advances to the person who seeks to turn his individuality into uniqueness, and who therefore refuses to give to the world the co-operation, the work in common for the advancement of all, which it is entitled to demand from him; he gets experience not of the world, but merely of himself. He is an individual in a magic circle, as Adler calls it. From the standpoint of Individual Psychology neurosis is not causally conditioned and is therefore not the cause of fresh results, i.e. of morbid symptoms, but is the path which an individual follows who turns aside from the world and rejects its values in order to live for himself and for his own self-valuation.

Adler saw the essential problem of neurosis in the conflict between social feeling, as he calls the consciousness of the homogeneity of human existence immanent in all, and the feeling of personal worth centred on the individual's own Ego. The *whole* person is still at the point where the development of social feeling has been neglected, i.e. where the individual does not fulfil the duty of self-realization that follows from it, even when he only complains of particular symptoms and particular troubles. *Every* symptom, whether it is apparently of a bodily nature, or whether it seems to belong to the sphere of the psychical, is nothing but the smoke that shows there is a fire.

Adler's conception of the freedom of the will, in so far as it means that everyone at every moment of his life has a choice between striving for the welfare of all or merely for his own good, and his firm conviction that every single individual is responsible for his own action and is jointly responsible for the actions of other persons, throw quite a different light on the emergence of a neurosis from that in which it has up till now been regarded. Precisely because he unveiled in every neurotic the creator of his own disease, 'cases' and 'types' did not exist for him, but only the individual's special style of life, which apart from the similarity of the symptoms, was never the same as that of any other person. In numerous lectures and works Adler has shown from hundreds of case-histories how every divergence, whether it manifests itself as neurosis, psychosis, addiction, perversion or criminality, arises from the individual's attempt to be rid of his responsibility and to create, in *opposition* to the meaning of life, the structure of a glittering existence *ad majorem personae gloriam.*

This conception of social deviation, which no longer is seen as an inescapable fate, but as an error in life, is still to-day opposed by many medical men. For us, however, who 'have the responsibility, because we understand'—to recall a recent saying of Adler's—there is optimism implied in this practical view, because it shows us the possibility of correcting mistakes that have been committed; it is the streak of silver that illumines the horizon of the doctrine of neurosis and psychosis. In days to come it will be universally accepted and will result in as great a change in the treatment of mental illnesses as the malaria-therapy in organic medicine has done for paralysis.

Again and again, here in Vienna, on the European continent and in America Adler showed that he was able to 'co-operate'. In 1929 at the Mariahilfer hospital in Vienna the first consultation-hour for the treatment of mental patients by the methods of Individual Psychology was established. The intention was to provide a place where the poor and the workless would find aid in their mental sufferings and learn the courage to prove their worth as human beings despite the heavy burden of their external conditions.

For us as Individual Psychological physicians, who had the good fortune to be among his closest fellow-workers and were able to observe how he dealt with a patient, it was a great experience to watch with humility how the *patient* was transformed into a *human being* under Adler's guiding hand. Raging maniacs became quiet when he spoke to them, fascinated by the fact that they had met a man who understood them and appealed to the human being within them. We were permitted to witness with him how, from behind the symptoms and illness and mental torment, there emerged a human being, who for the first time learned from Adler to see himself, recognize his errors and gain courage to construct another and better life —a life that would make its true worth real.

That was one of the miracles one could see, when one was allowed to work with Adler. But it was just here that Adler was also seen as a real physician—as the helper and friend of his patients. He himself was so ready to get into touch with people and so capable of doing it that even the most unwilling and refractory of his patients were unable to elude him. All that was dark and unintelligible vanished before Adler's personality with its empathy into the patient's inmost being. The most complicated symptoms were dissolved, and on the background of the neurosis there stood out crystal-clear the personality of the individual who created it.

Adler never missed any detail, either organic or mental. Just as he was the first to observe the 'segmental insufficiency' in the stigmata on the skin (e.g. nævi) which represent danger-signals indicating processes of disease in the body that are still unseen or have not yet become manifest, so he recognized also what might be called every 'mental segmental insufficiency' as a danger-signal flashing out in childhood's memories, dreams, movements, apparently insignificant modes of speech, etc., and indicating mental disturbances. Often it had still little meaning for the patient himself, but for Adler it was a sign that the individual was training himself for the retreat from life.

He taught his patients to see—to see not only what they actually were, but also what they were able to become; he taught them courage to follow the path towards the realization of their innate worth as human beings, despite organic handicaps, despite difficulties within them and around them; he taught them to bring themselves into line with other persons and as a result to become complete human beings.

He wished to educate human beings as regards the viewpoint of their cosmic relationships, or rather to re-educate them with these relationships in view. Both in his pedagogics and in his therapeutics he kept steadily before him the ideal of a healthy fellow-worker.

I cannot describe adequately the knowledge, the intuition and the ability with which Adler took his patients in hand. But he not only taught his patients, he also taught us, his scholars and fellow-workers, as doctors to see in our suffering sick folk the human being of whom we are conscious as our other self, demanding and having the right to demand the co-operation of our Ego. He taught us not to judge and not to condemn, not to pity anyone *because* he was ill, but to respect the human being who is hidden behind the illness.

'When a child is beaten somewhere in China,' Adler once said, 'then we are to blame, for that shows we have not worked hard enough; when there are people anywhere who are anti-social and are not fellow-workers, then we are jointly responsible, because we understand how easily mistakes arise in childhood that distort the world for the child and prevent him from bringing himself into line with other persons. Only when we have all done what we can to co-operate in the development of life and worked for the welfare of the whole— only then have we done our duty.'

And now death has torn him away from co-operation—the man who was the vanquisher of so much human suffering. He, who was always unwearied and always active, who gave countless human beings the power to live, had no longer the power to preserve his own invaluable life for us and for a world which will only at a much later time understand what it owes to Adler.

He himself always called the practice of his teaching an art, for it is only the artist who has the gift of empathy that enables him to see in the rough stone the statue that can be made out of it.

He was a genius in the art of healing, a genius in the art of being a complete human being, and like every genuine artist he was so far in front of his age that only future generations will recognize his worth and understand him. That is the lot of every great man, but it did not trouble him in the least, for he achieved his co-operative mission *sub specie aeternitatis*; and this was the attitude he again and again asked those to take whom he had taught to see.

To us, however, who count ourselves among his disciples and whom to our pride and joy he often called his friends, is now given the task of seeing that Adler's work will not perish with his death. On our shoulders now rests the responsibility of carrying on his work according to his intention. To us here in Vienna from which he set out never to return has been entrusted Adler's Individual Psychology. On us rests the obligation of re-asserting his 'heroic optimism', of going on with our work still more strenuously and intensively than before, although he has gone from us, of seeking unceasingly to make

276

ourselves complete human beings, meeting, in the station in which we have been placed, our responsibilities towards those to whom we can bring help, encouragement and happiness.

Adler bequeathed to us his legacy in the last words I heard from his lips, when I took leave of him two years ago. It is a legacy we should all preserve: 'Children, do something—and do it well!'

APPENDIX II

2. Memorial Address by Professor Ferdinand Birnbaum

L adies and Gentlemen,

Death grants to none a time of grace,
Or respite from his sudden menace.
He halts man in the swiftest race,
And drags him hence when life is fullest.

'When life is fullest!' What life could have been fuller than Adler's, when he passed away at the height of his activity, working and striving in a foreign land? Adler's death, in truth, suggests to us a noble variation on the theme of his whole life, which consisted in action and roused it in other persons.

What was Alfred Adler? He was a scientist, the world says. And the world is right. But it sees only the rays that streamed from a hidden light. We, to whom he was like a father, know that for him science was only the path—the means to which his training and genius pointed so that he might become what he had to be—a helper. To lift up other persons, to help and encourage them and restore them to themselves again—that, and that alone, was the mission of this life whose ending we mourn.

And now let us turn to this life itself.

Alfred Adler was born on 7th February 1870 in Penzing, Vienna. He grew up in the narrow streets of Penzing—and the words are to be understood literally. All his life he was proud of his youth spent among the despised urchins of these mean streets, and he recognized that he had learned there respect for courage and comradeship. Two events of his early years deserve mention. One morning, when he awoke, he found one of his brothers lying dead beside him in the bed. To this terrible experience the child reacted with the desire to become a doctor, so that he might have the mastery over death; and this desire grew stronger and stronger. But a long road lay between

278

APPENDIX II

the wish and its fulfilment, and from the very beginning the difficulties seemed almost insurmountable. Alfred failed to pass in the first class of the grammar-school. It was mathematics that stood in the way. Once more the youth reacted in a manner that befitted the future founder of Individual Psychology. He took the bull by the horns and became in the end the best mathematician in his class.

Anyone who wishes can reconstruct from this slight material the theme of his life. It is courage that decides the destiny of the individual. In the days that were to come this was the motif on which the symphony of his life, so rich in contrasts, was to be built. But before this theme was disclosed in splendid clarity, Adler had still to pass through many a stage.

When Alfred Adler finished his medical studies he turned his attention to ophthalmology, and he afterwards became a specialist in internal diseases. The first book that he wrote dealt with hygienic conditions in the tailoring trade. It appealed to the worker and to the general public and pointed out the grave dangers that threatened the health of large masses of the people as the result of their low standard of living.

Then came the decisive period of Adler's life—the years he spent in Sigmund Freud's circle. Looking at these years *sub specie aeternitatis* we may venture to assert that the result of this former friendship was a productive antagonism—productive because Freud and Adler were two great men who came into conflict in the fight for truth. But the work that we owe to this period shows that even then Adler was a man who had his own views. That work is the *Study of Organ Inferiority and its Psychical Compensations* which appeared in 1907, and was to furnish the foundation of the new doctrine. In the region of biology Adler, in the first instance, saw what other investigators before him had seen: viz., that an organism had the power of finding in itself compensations for inferiorities. But in addition to that he saw something new; he discovered that the mind was associated with certain efforts at compensation made by the bodily organs, and that mental difficulties corresponded to a maladjustment to life that had resulted from organic defects. From the struggle with these defects there arise mental attitudes and noticeable traits of character. And along with this still another fact is recognized: the fact of over-compensation is linked with several conditions. One of these conditions, as we have come to know, is—social feeling. On the model of compensation Adler now constructed his own doctrine, which could no longer be contained within the framework of the

Freudian theory although it still had to make use of the terminology inherited from the latter. It was not long, however, before he found an adequate form of expression for his own ideas. At this period Adler wrote his book on *The Nervous Character,* followed by *The Practice and Theory of Individual Psychology* and the pedagogic *Healing and Training*—this last in collaboration with his earliest fellow-workers. In the work on *The Nervous Character* he sought to establish his position. The nineteenth century could make nothing of a psychology that opposed atomistic and physiological theories, and Adler was rejected. This episode may be looked upon as a stroke of good fortune; for Adler now became the founder of a new system of pedagogics. He gave lectures in the Volksheim. People thirsting for knowledge, who worshipped science as a goddess, formed his audience. After the lecture they came to him with their troubles. He advised them and gave his first pedagogic instruction. One of his hearers who was a teacher arranged that Adler should explain his novel pedagogic ideas to a small society of teachers and give them advice as to the management of 'difficult' children. Adler desired to help these children and their parents and teachers; but he wanted to do more than that; he carried on the succession of the great educationalists, Pestalozzi and Fröbel. He became the teacher of the teachers! This fact became widely known. Here was a psychology that enabled one to understand why children grew 'difficult'. The great mass of teachers obtained fresh insight into their profession; they learned that children *made* difficulties because they *had* difficulties. Adler taught us the art of seeing with a child's eyes, hearing with a child's ears, and feeling with a child's heart. We no longer regarded our 'problem' children as disagreeable disturbers of our teaching community. Roused to fresh efforts by this new vision we began to give special attention to those backward pupils and to make an effort on behalf of each individual child. To-day we are able to say that if Adler had done nothing more than give us this impulse to explore to his innermost being every child who was likely to be lost to us, and to try to save him, we should be grateful to him for that reason alone; for by doing this he has given us, in our calling, hours that have been, at once, the most anxious and the finest and most sacred.

It is not Adler's fault that nothing of his teaching has gained currency in the world but the banal couple of expressions—inferiority feeling, and the struggle for appreciation. Naturally man possesses both these qualities and many others besides. And just as naturally will he endeavour to rid himself of his feeling of inferiority, while he struggles to attain greater and greater power and value, or, at the least, to guard against any loss of value by not attempting anything in which he would risk a defeat. But all this forms only the outer court of Individual Psychological knowledge.

This begins with the recognition and understanding of the immense disparity that exists between what man can be and what he actually is. For this reason the nervous character—the life-form of a man who has a wrong idea of his own resources—is the entrance-door to an insight into human character; for in it there is seen the immense distance between the potentialities a man possesses and what he is in reality—between possibility and actuality. The question, therefore, that the Individual Psychologist has always to answer is this: Why has this man not become what he might have been? Why does he not realize his tremendous possibilities? Just as the modern physical scientist sees in a stone a quite unimaginable amount of energy that could be set free by the breaking up of the atom, so the Individual Psychologist always compares man's innate splendour with its pitiful manifestation.

This comparison or contrast forms the viewpoint of Adler's pedagogics. Confining oneself only to what is essential one may state this in five propositions:

The educator must believe in the potential power of his pupil, and he must employ all his art in seeking to bring his pupil to experience this power. This proposition expresses what Adler has made known to the world as the demand for encouragement. It has been misunderstood in many ways and encouragement has been identified with the creation of experiences of success, indeed even with effeminacy. But the man who uttered the words—'If no difficulties exist for a child then one must invent them'—has never at any moment of his life been an advocate of effeminacy; he has rather seen in it the arch-enemy of all education. In his profound wisdom he saw self-pampering where no one else before him had seen it. He saw it when a child, misled by harsh treatment or want of affection, excused himself for everything he did, and fell back on self-pampering as a protest and a compensation. Adler could allow himself to form a lofty idea of the potential power of the human spirit since he found a twofold confirmation of this appraisement. The tricks of the neurotic showed him what the spirit was capable of doing in order to reach its useless goal. And his scrutiny of the factors of capacity and environment gave him proof, always growing clearer, that above all everything depended not on what a person brought from this quarter or that, but on the use he made of it. He set the psychology of use (*Gebrauch*) in opposition to the psychology of possession (*Besitz*).

There are times when reality seems to contradict the belief in the unfettered decision of the spirit; but does it not show in some ways a decided advance when the modern treatment of criminals takes into consideration extenuating circumstances and regards these persons as the victims of inherited inclinations or of their external conditions? Adler also made allowance for extenuating circumstances; he has enriched, as no one else has done, the inventory of these circumstances in his catalogue of environmental conditions.

But for him these circumstances were always enticements, they were never causes. He went right to the root of a mistaken mode of life and recognized that circumstances never directly turned a child into a wrong course, but always exerted an indirect influence by giving the child a mistaken idea of himself and of his life—by misleading the child to look at the world through coloured glasses and to apperceive tendentiously.

The second proposition may be stated as follows: *The educator of a child must get to know his tendentious apperception and remove it.* But this removal comes up against difficulties when the educator overlooks two things.

It so happens that one discouragement draws another in its train. If a person grows by his lofty goal, he becomes weaker and less useful as the result of lower aims. In the course of education, however, two tendentious apperceptions often come into conflict with one another —that of the child and that of the teacher himself. As Adler emphasized again and again, it may happen that the doctor or the teacher becomes the patient. The child will not allow his accustomed orientation to be destroyed without making a struggle for it, because shifting of his long-accustomed orientation makes him uncertain and discouraged. But the teacher himself may become discouraged owing to the fruitlessness of his efforts. In this way a continual sense of discouragement may result for each of the two partners, and in the end the two discouragements may cross one another. Pestalozzi had already drawn attention to this. As soon as one begins to treat a child correctly the difficulties multiply, and they cease immediately when there is a return to the wrong method of education. Hence the third proposition follows: *If you wish to educate a child who has gone wrong, then you must, above all, keep your attention fixed on the intersection of two charmed circles.*

A new demand, however, is thereby established. It becomes a question not only of adopting fresh educational methods, but also of watching what the child makes of them. Or, expressing it as a proposition, *Let yourself be guided in your pedagogic interventions especially by the observations you have made on the results of your former interventions.* From this follows the need for greater elasticity in the methods adopted, and above all the need for taking strict account of the *inner* effect that had been intended. Since we are concerned chiefly with keeping in view the *effects on the apperception itself* there must result, as a matter of course, a powerful impulse to study the question of educational methods. The question will no longer be one of mere external alteration—of the adoption of one educational method in place of another. The blockade established by the child himself must be pierced, and the child given back again to *the community*. Many persons have understood by this merely an education for collective existence. Adler, on the contrary, wishes it to be understood, not merely in a biological or sociological sense, but from a transcendental point of view as the reflection of a cosmic alliance. For that reason he lays the greatest stress on belief in the equal potential worth of all men, despite their empirical inequality. In his own fashion he expressed the same thought as is inherent in religion. This defends us against a world that only takes account of the empirical difference between man and man, the equality of all in the sight of God that follows from their being made in His image. The equal potential worth of all men was for Adler the presupposition of human society; and for him the goal on this earth was evolution. It is only the person who interests himself in the increasingly spiritual conception of society, who takes his part in the progress of the human race and helps to further it, that deserves to belong to a race struggling to pass from darkness into light.

This man who gave to the earth what belongs to the earth, who proclaimed that co-operation in the advance of humanity was the true meaning of life on earth; this man who also gave to the transcendent what belongs to the transcendent within us—our existence as the image of the godhead—found his first great recognition in America. The evangelical University of Springfield conferred on him an honorary doctorate, Columbia University made him a professor, and Long Island put a clinic at his disposal.

Alfred Adler loved Austria, his fatherland, although, in the same manner in which it has treated so many of its best sons, it failed to appreciate him. Our love followed him across the ocean, and it accompanies him to where he is now—the unwearied friend of man and seeker after God. God, to whom our Master has now departed, will not look on him as an alien; for he saw a brother in every man and wakened the sense of brotherhood in so many persons who were wandering in the hell of their self-created loneliness. We remember the day when Adler addressed us from this very place. He spoke about foreigners, and we did not know to what continent they belonged, but all at once we felt that in the image of their souls we recognized our own, and we quietly turned our faces away, fearing lest our neighbour should guess our secret thoughts from our expression. At that moment we examined our consciences and we recognized the pitiful limitations of our love. For those hours that gave us a clearer vision and, as a result, made us more human, we wish to thank him. We thank him, too, for the words spoken in passing and yet so sure in their aim, when he looked at us and saw that we did not know where to turn in life, but were ashamed to ask counsel from him. Above all, however, we wish to thank him on behalf of those whom he loved best—the children. The tears he dried when he taught us to train them more wisely we send forth to him into eternity; they will bear witness for him!

If the words of Cain resound through the centuries—Am I my brother's keeper?—then Adler's life-work took the form of a great affirmative answer. Everyone of us is a brother, and if anyone refuses to become a brother, his own soul calls out to Heaven against him.

Our Master fell in the fight against Cain. All the bludgeons in the world that are lifted in fratricide can never quench the answer which is the voice of God in all of us—the answer that Adler was never weary of repeating, until his heart broke on the street in Aberdeen. And that heart we shall never forget.

The track of his steps on earth
Shall not in aeons be lost.

APPENDIX III

T he writer inserts this final programme of Adler's working life, partly as of historic interest, since he died upon its threshold; and partly in order to show how far and wide the appeal of his common-sense psychology had already swept.

Had Adler been able to carry out this great programme (no heavier in its undertakings than was normal to his powers), with its differently balanced contacts and opportunities, much might have been done in England to solve the greatest problem of our age—how to develop a co-operative human being upon social lines, rather than an ego-centric human being upon anti-social ones—a being fit for the mechanical secrets he has learned to control by having learned the more vital control of his own spirit.

THE ALFRED ADLER LECTURE AND
VACATION COURSE 1937 COMMITTEE

President:
Rt. Hon. The Earl of Lytton, K.G., G.C.S.I., G.C.I.E.

Chairman: Mrs. Basil Hoare

Vice-Chairman: Sir Alfred Beit, Bart, M.P.

Hon. Treasurer, Guarantee Fund: Commander O. Locker-Lampson, D.S.O., M.P.

Hon. Treasurer, Training Fund: Ian L. Fleming, Esq.

Hon. Auditors: Messrs. Price, Waterhouse & Co.

PROGRAMME OF LECTURES AND COURSES ARRANGED FOR ALFRED ADLER, M.D., LL.D., PROFESSOR OF MEDICAL PSYCHOLOGY, LONG ISLAND COLLEGE OF MEDICINE, FOUNDER OF INDIVIDUAL PSYCHOLOGY, WHO WILL ARRIVE IN ENGLAND ON FRIDAY, 21ST MAY

APPENDIX III

24th May–28th May. Course of Five Lectures on Psycho-Pathology at the University of Aberdeen.

1st June. Public Lecture at Rowntree's, York.

2nd June. Address to Diocesan Clergy at York. Chairman: His Grace the Lord Archbishop of York.

3rd June. Public Lecture at Municipal Training College, Hull.

4th–9th June. Lectures at MANCHESTER (including course of Three Lectures to Educationalists; Lecture to Clergy; Public Lecture at College of Technology, 7.30 p.m., Monday, 7th June. Chairman: W. J. S. Reid, M.D., B.Sc., M.A., M.R.C.P.; and Lecture at Manchester Royal Infirmary, 4.30 p.m., Tuesday, 8th June. Chairman: The Vice-Chancellor of the University). For particulars apply:

Joint Hon. Secretaries

Miss Schofield, 51 Kings Road, Sedgley Park, Prestwich, Manchester,

or

Rev. E. B. Greening, B.A., 10 Hereford Street, Sale, Manchester.

10th June–16th June. Lectures in LONDON for various societies.

17th June. Public Lecture: Queen's Hall, London, 8.15 p.m. Subject: 'Social Interest: a Challenge to Mankind.'

19th June–3rd July. Lecture Course (non-resident) at EDINBURGH. Professor Adler will deliver Twelve Lectures followed by Questions and Discussions.
Dr. Alexandra Adler will also lecture.
For particulars apply: Mrs. Page, Secretary-Organizer, 22 Alva Street, Edinburgh.

6th July–17th July. Vacation Course (resident and non-resident) at University Hall, LIVERPOOL, under the auspices of Home & School Council. Professor Adler and Dr. Alexandra Adler will each deliver Fourteen Lectures.
For particulars apply: Council of Social Service, 14 Castle Street, Liverpool, 2.

17th July–31st July. Vacation Course (resident and non-resident) at EXETER, under the auspices of the University College of the South-West. Professor Adler and Dr. Alexandra Adler will each deliver Fourteen Lectures.
For particulars apply: Academic Secretary, University College, Exeter.

286

APPENDIX III

2nd August. Lecture: City of London Vacation Course in Education.

4th August. Professor Adler sails for New York on the S.S. *Queen Mary*.

15th August. Commencement of Vacation Course at Berkeley, California, U.S.A.

Further particulars from Hon. Secretary, 46 Lexham Gardens, London, W.8.

APPENDIX IV

Alfred Adler, M.D., LL.D.

Career

Took Medical Degree, Vienna University, in 1895. Studied also Psychology and Philosophy. Worked in Vienna General Hospital and Polyclinic 1895–7. Practised in Vienna as General Practitioner and Nerve Specialist 1897–1927.

In 1912, realizing need of preventing neurosis and delinquency in childhood, commenced educating teachers for the purpose and gradually organized, with collaborators, Child-Guidance Centres in thirty schools in Vienna.

In 1914 Founded *Journal of Individual Psychology* (see publications). 1914–18 Attached to Austrian Army in Vienna and Cracow.

1924. Appointed *Docent* of the Pedagogical Institute of the City of Vienna.

1927. Appointed lecturer Columbia University, New York City. Subsequently at Medical Centre, New York City.

1928. Appointed Clinical Director of the Mariahilfer Ambulatorium, Vienna.

1932. Appointed Visiting Professor of Medical Psychology, Long Island College of Medicine, New York.

1935. Founded *Journal of Individual Psychology* in U.S.A. (see publications).

Founder of the Science of Individual Psychology.

Publications

1907 *Studien über Minderwertigkeit von Organen und ihre seelische Kompensation.* Vienna. 2nd edition München.

1912 *Ueber den nervösen Charakter.* München. 4th edition.

1914 Founded Journal *Internationale Zeitschrift für Individualpsychologie.* Zilahi, Vienna VI.

1918 *Praxis und Theorie der Individualpsychologie.* München. 4th edition. London 1927.

APPENDIX IV

1919 *Problem der Homosexualität.* Leipzig. 2nd edition.

1919 *Die andere Seite.* Vienna.

1921 *Menschenkenntnis.* Leipzig. 5th edition. New York, 1928. London, Geo. Allen & Unwin.

1928 *Technik der Individualpsychologie.* Vol. I. *Die Kunst eine Krankengeschichte zu lesen.* München.

1929 *Individualpsychologie in der Schule.* Leipzig.

1929 *The Science of Living.* New York. London, Geo. Allen & Unwin.

1929 *Problems of Neurosis.* Kegan Paul, London.

1929 *Technik der Individualpsychologie.* Vol. II. *Die Seele des schwererziehbaren Schulkindes.* München.

1930 *Education of Children.* New York. London, Geo. Allen & Unwin.

1930 *The Pattern of Life.* New York.

1931 *What Life should mean to You.* Boston, Little, Brown. London, Geo. Allen & Unwin.

1932 *Der Sinn des Lebens.* Vienna. 2nd edition.

1933 *Religion und Individualpsychologie* (with Ernst Jahn). Vienna.

1935 Founded *International Journal of Individual Psychology.* (Quarterly.) Menser, 230 North Michigan Avenue, Chicago, Ill., U.S.A.

1936 *Social Interest: A Challenge to Mankind.* London and New York.

Lectures

Lectured at Universities of Berlin, Munich, Zürich, Paris, London, Oxford, Cambridge, Amsterdam, Leyden, Utrecht, Zagreb, Prague, Copenhagen, Stockholm, New York, Harvard, Detroit, San Francisco, Los Angeles, Chicago, Des Moines, Philadelphia, McGill, Hamilton, as also before various Scientific Societies in Europe and U.S.A.

Index

Aberdeen, University of, 251, 252, 254 seqq.; Caledonia Hotel at, 255, 262; City Child Guidance Society of, 257; Adler's death at, 257, 261-3; Lord Provost of, 262; King's College Chapel of, 262; Springbank cemetery at, 263
Accident analysis, 105-6
Adler, Alexandra (Ali) (later, Doctor), 86-94 *passim*, 224, 240, 261-2, 263, 265; lectures of, 265-7; Harvard and Boston accident analysis made by, 105-6
ADLER, Alfred: (*a*) *progressive survey of life of*:
birth of, 26; parents of, 26, 27, 28, 29, 30, 31; brothers and sisters of, 25, 27, 28, 29, 30, 31, 32; Jewish descent of, 26; early character of, 26 seqq.; childhood influences on, 25-34; early consciousness of 'organic inferiority', 32; decision to become doctor made by, 32-4; early pastimes of, 16, 27, 31, 37; boyhood and youth of, 35-40; youth and romance of, 41-50; marriage of, 45; as a student (Furtmüller's account), 51-2; in early practice as psychologist, 52-6; religion and, 13, 15, 22, 26, 55-6, 198; café life and political opinions of, 58-67, and Freudian circle, 68-78; Individual Psychology developed by, 80 seqq.; psychiatry as overriding interest of, after 1910, 79; children of, 86-94; patients of, 95-102, 105; 'organ jargon' discussed by, 103-8; and Nowotny, 108, 171; first book of, after leaving Freud's circle, 109; and Vienna University's reception of *Dozentur* thesis, 109-13; *Nervous Character* of, discussed, 109-14; *Understanding Human Nature* of, discussed, 112-16; and 1914 war, 117-19; post-war concept of Gemeinschaftsgefühl (Social Interest) of, 120-6; Child Guidance Clinics of,

127-33, 148; as humorist, 134 seqq.; friendships of, after war, 141 seqq.; with Glöckel, Spiel and Birnbaum, 148-55; main contributions of, summarized, 156-8; the 'pedants' and, 169 seqq.; *Journal* of, 175-9; at early post-war European conferences, 180-3; in his country home, 184-7; on criminals, 188-93; Individual Psychology of, expanding influence of, 194 seqq.; life of, in America, 202-20; Long Island appointment of, 221-8; in Holland and England, 229-40; personal impression of, 241-50; last days of, 251-60; death of, 261 seqq.; Lydia Sicher's Memorial Address for, 270-7; Professor Ferdinand Birnbaum's Memorial Address 278-84; career and works of, 288 seqq.

ADLER (*b*) *principal themes, alphabetically arranged*; *for life outline see earlier entry*:
and 'aggressive drive', 75, 82; with Allers, 169-71; and 'aristocracy', 125-6; and 'attitude' basis of personality failures, 130; and 'bagatellizing' of griefs, 53; and Berdyaev link, 22; and burglars, 189-93; character of, analysed, 13-14, 16, *and see* Birnbaum, Furtmüller, Sicher; cinema-going by, 223, 259; common-sense basis favoured by, 14, 194, 235; concrete fact respected by, 14, 61; on 'courage of the soul', 140; and the creative life, 63, 102, 200; discretion of, 95; on 'domination through weakness', 158; and Dostoevski, 189; and dream theory, 162-3, 204; eldest brother and, 27-8, 31; and the English language, 202-3, 215; and evolution, 122; and 'Family Constellation', 156, 159-61; French colleagues' acceptance of, 252; friends of, 16, 64-7, 200, 216, relationship with daughters, 220; Furt-

291

INDEX

Clouston, Dr., 266
Cocaine, Freud's discovery concerning, 70, 73
Cocoanut Grove fire, 105-6
Columbia, University of, 202, 205, 206, 210, 221; College of Physicians and Surgeons of, 205, 206
Communism, 62, 63, 123, 199; and Adler's break with colleagues, 169; and intellectual liberty, 199
Community Church, New York, 202
Conway Hall, 246
Cooper, Valerie, 231
Corgarff village (Aberdeenshire), 256
Coward, Noel, as Adler disciple, 95-6
Cracow, 118
Craigievar Castle, 256-7
Criminality, 188-93, 206, 247
Crookshank, Dr. 233, 234
Curie, Madame, on 'proprietorship' of radium, 15
Cushendunn, Lady, 247, 248
Czechoslovakia, *Journal of Individual Psychology* in, 175
Czernin Platz, lectures for teachers at, 129
Czerningasse, Adler's home in, 52, 79

Dalton School, New York, 208
Dartington Hall, Adler's visit to, 246
Davidson, Professor Stanley, 255
Davis, Charles, 12, 206, 214, 221, 246, 263
Davis, Frin, 246, 262
Dawson of Penn, Lord, 237
Deane, Bishop, 262
Dearborn, 206
Dearmer, Canon Percy, 249-50
Death, Adler's views on, 32-3, 200, 264
Death wish, the, 99; as 'neurotic retreat', 26
Delinquency, 157, 188, 200, 238, 247; in children, 188-9; and neurosis, 157 seqq.
Demonstration lectures, Adler's, 153
Dennis, Nigel Forbes, 224, 233
Depression, 99, 100
Der Sinn des Lebens, 21, 289
Detroit, 205, 210
Dey, Dr. and Mrs., *also* Miss, 203, 214
Diabetes, Adler's views concerning, 73

Dialectics, and the revelation of personality, 198
Dickens, Charles, character depiction by, 195
Dictatorships, 205, 220, 249, 265, 268
Dilthey's *Lebensformen*, 83
Dollfüss régime, 152, 181, 186, 225
Dominikanerbastei, Vienna, 52, 79, 86, 143, 204, 225
Dostoevski's *Crime and Punishment*, 189, 195, 231
Dover, Adler at, 250
Downey, Archbishop, 21, 246
Dream theories, 157, 162, 204
Dukes, Dr. Cuthbert, 233
Dungavel, Adler at, 252
Düsseldorf, Individual Psychology Conference at, 182
Dutch Red Cross, post-war work of in Austria, 142

'Eclectic' psychology, defects of, 14, 194-5, 217-18
Economics, and the egocentric aim, 205, 233-4
Edinburgh, 251; crematorium at, 263; Summer School at, 265
Edward VIII, 207
Egbert, Dr. James, 221
Einstein, 80, 84
Eisengasse, 47
Elizabeth of Austria, Adler mentions, 40
England, 95, 194, 226, 228, 229, 233, 234, 235, 236, 237, 239, 245, 246, 247, 248-50, 251-2, 254 seqq.
Erasmus, quoted, 163
Essex Hall, London, 248
Evans, Mr., 250
Evolution, co-operation and, 122
Exeter, University College of the South-West, 251, 265, 267
Experience, Adler on, 217

'Family Constellation' theory, 156, 159-61, 229
Fascism, 203, 232
Findlay, Professor A. Fyfe, 262
Fintray House, Aberdeenshire, 255, 263
Flaubert's *Madame Bovary*, 195
Fliess, 68, 82
Foreign missions, post-war work of, 142, 148

294

INDEX

Frankel, V., 64-5, 134, 170
Frank, Professor, 82
Franklin, Benjamin, and 'expressed convictions', 102
'Free association', Adler's views on, 256
'Free Psychoanalysts', The, 80
'Free School' ideas, Adler's reservations concerning, 246
Froeschel and Schrecker, opposition of to 'Social Interest' concept, 121
Freud: Adler's beliefs opposed to, 61, 68 seqq., 74, 75-8, Adler's defence of, against medical circles, 69-70; in America, 203; *Aphasia* thesis of, 109; beliefs of, not shared by Adler, 72, 74, 75-6, 162 seqq., 204; 'castration complex', theory of, 163; censorship suggestion by, 75, 76; *Civilization and its Discontents*, 78; description of background of, 70-1; *Dream Analysis*, 52, 75, 76, 109; *Ego and the Id*, 82; Frank, on 'shock' theories of, 81-2; *History of Psychoanalysis*, 77; 'Œdipus complex', theory of, 75-6, 110; as 'picker-out of parts', 72-3; and phallic symbolism in dream interpretation, 162, 204; and plagiarists, 174-5; 'sex mythology' of, 75, 76, 110, 162, 165, 204; *Das Unbehagen in der Kultur*, as symptom of anti-social bias, 149; mention of his 'Studien über Hysterie' (*Mechanismus*), [with Breuer], 81, 83; on 'woman's resentment', 165; as writer rather than speaker, 71; *Zunkunft einer Illusion*, 73; Groddeck and 234-5; Mac-Murray on, 239; general allusions to, 78, 81, 82, 127, 150, 171, 172, 175, 176, 178, 198, 256; *see also* Hilferding, Dr.
Freudian groups, doctrines, 12, 42-3, 52, 68, 69 seqq., 109, 110, 123, 127-8, 175, 176, 217, 222; and Adler's memorial service, 267
Friends' House, Euston Square, 240
Frohknecht, Frau, 230
Furtmüller, Professor, 51 52, 69, 71, 73, 111, 126; in England, 17; death of, 17

Gänsehäufel, Adler's recreations and, 37

'Ganzheit' (wholeness), 83
'Gegenspieler' device, 110
Geiringer, Grüners and 'Eggshell' lecture, 83
Gemeinde Wien, Adler's educational revolution in, 63, 155
Gemeinschaftsgefühl, see Social Interest
Germany: Austria occupied by, 11, 12, 58, 60, 68, 91, 147, 192-3; Hitler and totalitarianism in, 54, 63, *see also* Dictatorships; Adler's lectures in, 73, 83, *see also* Berlin, etc.; *International Journal of Psychology* in, 175, 178; colleagues from, 180-3; and Groddeck, 234; represented at Adler's funeral, 263
Ghosts, Adler on, 55
Glands, psychic factors and, 105
Glöckel, Professor, 63, 128, 149, 153; role of, in Individual Psychology, 149
Gower Street Club of Individual Psychology, 13, 231-4, 252; Adler removes name from, 232; Groddeck and, 234
Grey, Sir Edward, 116
Grinzing, 36, 226
Groddeck, 234-5; *Das Buch vom Es*, 234-5; on 'sore throat' factors, 104
Grüner brothers, see Geiringer

Hamilton, Duchess of, 252
Hapsburgs: and Vienna, 35; and Left Wing, 61; Stead's prophecies concerning, 116
Harvard, Alexandra Adler at, 94, 105-6, 265; Adler lectures at, 202
Health of Tailors pamphlet (Adler), 61, 279
Heidegger, and science-religion 'bridge', 198
Hemming, James, 21
Herz, Frau, 149
Herzegovina, 116
Hilferding, Dr., on Freud's jealousy of Adler, 76
Hitler, 54, 180, 243, 268; in childhood, 192; and Mussolini, 225
Hofmannsthal, 74
Holland, 175, 229, 250; Mevrouw Frohknecht's work in, 229-30; lectures in, 250, 252, 261; represented at Adler's funeral, 263

295

INDEX

Holub, Dr. Arthur, 103, 104
Home and School Council: and Cambridge lecture, 247; and Liverpool lecture, 246
Homosexuality, 166
House of Commons, Adler lunches at, 249
Human beings, classification of, 157, 167
Hungary, and Adler's background, 25

Illness, psychic factors in, see 'Organ Jargon'
Individual Psychology, 12, 13, 14, 15, 20, 21, 22, 23, 31-2, 51-2, 56, 62, 63, 70, 71, 83, 84, 111, 114, 120-4, 128, 144-7, 148 seqq., 168, 171, 176, 180-3, 199, 210-13, 216-18, 221-2, 225, 226, 229 seqq., 243, 252, 254, 256, 263; Ansbacher's works on, 68, 156, 168, 195; Birnbaum's and Spiel's work in, 152-5; Conferences of, 180-3; dissociation of from politics, 62; Glöckel's role in, 149; *International Journal of Individual Psychology*, 175-9, 215, 225; Long Island College of Medicine and, 113, 212; Medical Society of, 13, 233, 238; new London group of, 265; nature of, 194, seqq.; quarterly of (Chicago), 212; Rühle - Gerstel's book on, 180-1; twelve chief tenets of, 114-16, 122; Viennese school of, Plewa and, 12
Inferiority feeling, 19-20, 32, 157-9; *see also* Family Constellation
Intelligence tests, 165; Adler's reliance on, see Adler (*b*) Pedagogics

'J' (burglar-philanthropist), 192-3
Jackson, Mr. (Liverpool Social Service Association), 266
Jaundice, psychic factors in, 105
Jauregg, Wagner-, 109
Jews: Adler's protest against isolation of, 26-7; in Vienna, 26; culture of, in Austrian life, 35; in Germany, 180, 182, 243-4
Joachim (violinist), 25
Johnson, Dr., on café life, 60
Jones, Ernest, 68, 172
Jugoslavia, 175
Jung, 82, 195, 253; and Freud, 75; and

the 'Œdipus Complex', 75; and Steckel, 42

Kaiser Franz-Josef Ambulatorium, 12, 145, 148, 218, 255, 268
Kant, E., 198
Kierkegaard, S. A., 198
Kitzbühel, 241-3
Knight, Professor Rex, 255, 257
Kokoschka, O., portrait of Adler by, 28
Kransz, Professor G. E., 84
Kraus, Karl, 74
Kroner, devaluation of, 141-3
Kronfeld (with Künkel), 150
Künkel, 150

Lawrence, D. H., and 'Œdipus Complex', 110
Left-Wing politics, 62, 63, 180; *see* Socialism, Communism
L'Ermite, Dr., 252
Lesbianism, 166
Linton, the Rev. J., 256, 263, 268
Liverpool, 246; University Hall at, 251, 265; Adler's summer school at, 266; Social Service Association of, 266
Locarno summer school at, 11; Educational Conference at, 242
Locke, John, 'positivism' of, 83
Lomax, Dr., 106-7
London, Adler in, 231, 245, 252; alluded to, 232, 246, 261, 267
Long Island College of Medicine, 12, 113, 212, 221, 222, 253, 261, 268
Louisiana University, 210
Love and marriage, Adler on responsibilities of, 44-5
Löwy, Ida, at Child Guidance Clinics, 132-3, 146-7, 228
Ludwig, Emil, 195
Lytton, Earl of, 248

MacAndrews, Miss 142
MacEwen, Désirée, 267
Macmillan's Theatre, Columbia University, 206
MacMurray, Professor John, 239
Mairet, Philip, 13, 203, 231, 232; *Problems in Neurosis*, 112, 211-12
Manchester, Adler's lectures in, 251
Margesson, Lady Isabel, 247, 248
Marxism, 74, 181, 232

INDEX

Psychiatry—*cont*,
chologist, 197-8; Adler's methods in, summarized, 95 seqq.; Adler's principal thoughts affecting progress in, 156 seqq.; Adler's war duties in, 118-19; American schools of, Adler and, 210-13; Adler's war with pedants in, 169 seqq.; English schools of, 233-7; Freudian and moral safeguards, Adler's view of, 256; laymen and, 146; sex aberrations as interpreted by, 166; *see also* Freud; 'unmasking' technique in, 53-4, 74 seqq.

Psychic manifestations, and physical trends, Adler's acknowledged debt to, 31-3

Psychoanalysis, Adler and Stekel unmask, 74-5; Freud's early circles and, 69-74; Individual Psychology compared with, by practitioners, 123-4; interpretation of dreams and, 204 (and *see* Freud); Neuer and, 74-5; Spiel renounces, 150-1; teleological principle and, 15, 80, 81, 82; Zilahi and, 176-9; 'Free Analysts', 80, 83

Psycho-Analytical Journal, The, 19, 74, 76, 76

Psychology: Adler's, and (alignment) of progressive and retrograde elements, 264-5; Adler's American difficulties in, 214, 217-18; Adler's early dissatisfaction with progress made in, 42; Adler elects to make career in, 30 seqq.; Adler's 'Existence', 198; Adler's and Freud's contrasted, 68 seqq.; Adler's main contributions to, 156 seqq., 212; general practitioners and, 196, 197, 198, 235; Groddeck's 234-5; Individual, *see* Individual Psychology and *passim*; Sir W. Brown on Adler's, 247; the 'possessive', 20, 98; Viennese school of, 194-5; Stern and Adler in, 72

Psychosis and neurosis compared, 97

Race question, in Germany, 180-2
Radium, 'proprietorship' of, 15
Red Cross work in post-war Austria, 142
Redfern, Dr., 234
Religion, Adler and, 21, 33, 55-6, 102, 122, 198, 246-7; Freud and, 56; science and, 180

Responsibility and freedom, 13, 15, 196, 198-9; and Totalitarianism, 199
Rheinhardt, Dr. Aurelia, 253
Ricquet, Père, 252
Ronge, Dr. Peter, 264
Rossetti, D. G., 61
Roth, Mrs. (secretary to Adler), 246, 262
Royal Medical Society, the, 237
Rühle–Gerstel, Alice and Otto, 180-1
Rushford, Dr., 265
Russia, 45-8, 116, 117, 142-3

Sacher, Anna, 39
Salle Laennec address, Paris, 252
Salmannsdorf, Adler's country home, 184, 191-2, 224; selling of, 225
Saul, 196
Scandinavian writers, character depiction by, 195
Schnitzler, Dr., 74
Schönbrunn, Palace of, 22
Schöner's restaurant, Vienna, 39-40
Schrecker, Paul, 121
Schreiner, Olive, 106
Schubert, 36, 263
Schuschnigg government, 128, 152, 225
Schwarz, Dr., 170, 171; L. scoliosis, Adler on, 104
Scotland, Adler's lectures in, 255 seqq.; Raissa Adler in, 261
Seidler, Fräulein Regina, 128
Seif, Dr. Leonard, 12, 132, 162, 180, 212-13, 233, 243, 244
Sempill, Lady, 255, 256
Serajevo crisis, Adler's apprehensions at, 117
Serbia, 117
Sex, Adler's attitude towards, 20, 43, 44, 254; and juvenile shocks, 81-2; and woman's false sense of inferiority, 164; and dream analysis, *see* Freud; and 'organ jargon', 105
Shakespeare, quoted, 45, 81; and character, 195
Shellshock study, Adler's, 172
Sicher, Professor Harry, 11, 145
Sicher, Dr. Lydia, 11, 12, 144-5, 192, 193, 268; Adler Memorial Address given by, 270 seqq.
Simpson, Dr. Greta, 12, 203
Slade, Miss Lilian, 231

298

INDEX

Smuts, General, 83; Life of (S. G. Millin) cited, 83; *Holism and Evolution*, by, with reference to Adler's thought, 83

Social Democrats (Austrian), 51, 62, 63, 128, 143, 181

'Social Feeling' and idea of perfection, 32

'Social Interest' (*Gemeinschaftsgefuhl*), 62, 82, 120-6, 146, 166, 182, 188-9, 199; Law of, 157, 168, 257

Social Interest: a Challenge to Mankind, 149, 166, 168, 256, 268

Social Research, New School for (New York), 202, 205

Socialism, 61, 62, 74; project for pan-European, 232

Society of Teachers, the London, Adler addresses, 248

Socrates, simplification and, 235

Sophie (Adler's cook), 48, 87, 112, 184

Spanish Riding School, Vienna, 39

Spanish 'romantics', character depiction by, 195

Sperber, Manés, 170, 171, 173, 174

Sperber, Herr (lawyer), 16

Spiel, Oskar, 150-5, 182

Spiritualism, Adler's mistrust of, 55

Spranger, and 'Ganzheit' theory, 83

Squires, Dr. H. C., 233

Stalin-Trotsky parallel (Freud-Adler), Neuer's, 82-3

Stallybrass, Dr. 266

Stanley, Oliver, 248, 267

Stationers' Hall address, 252

Statistics in case documentation, Adler's attitude to, 211

Stead, William, on Hapsburgs, 116

Stekel, 42, 74, 82

Stendhal, character and, 195

Stephansdom, Vienna, 59, 79, 184

Stern, William, 71, 72

Sternberg, Heinz, 228, 261-3; *see also* Adler, Nelly

Strachey, John, 232

Strachey, Lytton, 195

Talbot, Anne, 249

Teachers' Conference, Michigan, 206; vacation courses for, Adler addresses, 248, 251, 267

Telegraf (Vienna), 175

Teleological principle, the, 15, 19, 20, 81-2

Telepathy, Adler on, 55

Temple, William (Archbishop of York) 250, 251, 257

Thackeray, character depiction by, 195

'The Art of Living' (lecture), 206

'The Eggshell' (lecture, Neuer), 83

The Health of Tailors (pamphlet, Adler), 61

The Nervous Character, The Neurotic Constitution, see Nervous Character, The

Theology, 195-6, 198; *see also* Religion

Theosophy, Adler's views on, 55, 267

Thorean quoted, 163

'Three Life Tasks', Adler's 15, 157, 167

Tilney, Dr., 210, 211

Timofejewna, Raissa, *see* Adler, Raissa

Torrington Square Society, The, 232, 245, 246

Trotsky parallel, 82

Tuberculosis, psychic factors in, 107-8

Turgenev, character depicted by, 195

Twenty Million Michigan Children's Fund, 205-6

Understanding Human Nature (*Menschenkenntniss*), (Adler), 57, 112, 268

University College (now University of), Exeter, *see* Exeter

Utrecht group (Adler students), 230

Vaihinger (*Philosophy of As If*), 72

Vanity, neurosis as, 15

Vassar College, U.S.A., 231

Verein opposition to Adler, Zilahi and, 175-9

Vienna, principal allusions to, 11, 12, 15, 16, 25-52, 68, 74, 79, 80, 86, 93, 116, 117, 120, 122, 123, 128 seqq., 175-9, 183, 184-6, 193, 209, 217, 218, 222, 224-8, 231, 234, 241, 244, 245, 253, 255, 261, 267, 268, 269; Anna Sacher and 'society' in, 39; the University of, 45, 56, 59, 64, 69, 79, 80, 93, 109, 113, 114, 144, 211, 215; the Adlers' first home in, 48; social life in, 48; café and intellectual life in, 58 seqq., 74, 120, 169 seqq.; education in, 63; novels and poetry characteristic of, 74;

299